THE

AUSTRO-MARXISTS

1890-1918

THE

AUSTRO-MARXISTS

1890-1918

A Psychobiographical Study

MARK E. BLUM

THE UNIVERSITY PRESS OF KENTUCKY

Copyright © 1985 by The University Press of Kentucky

Scholarly publisher for the Commonwealth,
serving Bellarmine College, Berea College, Centre
College of Kentucky, Eastern Kentucky University,
The Filson Club, Georgetown College, Kentucky
Historical Society, Kentucky State University,
Morehead State University, Murray State University,
Northern Kentucky University, Transylvania University,
University of Kentucky, University of Louisville,
and Western Kentucky University.

Editorial and Sales Offices: Lexington, Kentucky 40506-0024

Library of Congress Cataloging in Publication Data

Blum, Mark E.
  The Austro-Marxists, 1890–1918.

  Includes index.
  1. Communists—Austria—Biography. 2. Communism and
intellectuals—Austria—History. I. Title.
HX254.5.B45 1985   335.4′092′2 [B]   84-13036
ISBN 0-8131-1515-9

To Adam and Becky

Contents

Acknowledgments

Ottokar Odlozilik, a historian whose seminar on historical consciousness provided the seminal ground for the psychobiographical approach, is remembered for his wisdom and generosity. Susan Bockius Payne, whose understanding supported me from the earliest conception to the finished work, has my gratitude, as do Paul Pezzotta and Patricia Wilhoyte, whose thoughtful comments helped me shape the final version.

My research was aided by Otto Bauer, the librarian of the Buttinger Library. The Instituut voor Sociale Geschiedenis in Amsterdam made available original documents from the Karl Kautsky Archive. David Hart, an analytical psychologist, was a standard for me in the humanistic treatment of personality from several psychological perspectives.

My thanks go also to the Academic Publications Committee of the University of Louisville, who supported the final manuscript, and to Sharon Mills who spent so many hours supervising the typing and editing of its many drafts.

Introduction

The Austro-Marxists, Karl Renner, Otto Bauer, Max Adler, and Friedrich Adler, were the second generation of the Austrian Social Democratic party, founded in 1889 by Victor Adler (Friedrich's father) and other German-Austrian Social Democrats in an attempt to bring together the various nationalities of the Austrian Empire.[1] As a member of the Second International, the party was recognized as an orthodox organization of Marxist thought, one of the vanguard bodies in the proletarian struggle toward socialism. The Social Democratic political vision relied on Karl Marx for both intellectual and political reason. Intellectually, he brought the potential of a comprehensive system of social criticism to the effort to restructure society through his study of economics, political economy, sociology, history, and philosophy. The breadth of his thought demanded an interdisciplinary or multidisciplinary approach among the Marxist intelligentsia to secure the facts to prove his cultural principles, and exerted a gentle pressure for cohesiveness among them. Politically, Marxism was the dominant ideology in the Second International, and because Marxist ideas provided the basis for social planning in its member parties, a Social Democrat was wedded to ideas and values considered orthodox.[2] Any deviation from the fundamental structure of orthodox thought was made at the risk of expulsion from the party, or at least strong public censure by party members. One of the first appearances of the Austro-Marxists in the arena of Marxist ideological controversy was Max Adler's attack on the German Social Democrat Edvard Bernstein, as well as his own Austrian party fathers, for their questioning of the Marxist concept of class warfare.

The Austro-Marxists felt both the stimulation of Marxist interdisciplinary ideation and the pressure to conform to the orthodox concepts of Marxism more than had their party fathers, who relied on them to provide the ideas that could forge the new socialist world. The founders of the Austrian Social Democratic party were not theoreticians, though ideas were central to their values and vision of society. They were, rather, astute political organizers, whose energies were consumed in the creation of a coherent political party with a membership worthy of a national party.[3] They bequeathed the herculean task of interpreting everyday reality in a Marxist mode to their progeny (*Nachwuchs*).

Devoting a lifetime to this task, the Austro-Marxists furthered thinking in every realm of individual and social life, from theories of knowledge and personal identity to interpretations and constructs of political, legal, and social reality. The breadth of their vision was prompted not only by the ambitious character of Marxism; additionally, the intellectual ferment of the Austrian Empire in the decades before World War I demanded that anyone who dared to present views of life and society have a familiarity with the most significant thought in every domain of knowledge. The intellectuals who developed new ideas and established movements of thought in the natural sciences, humanities, and social sciences in the quarter century before World War I were legion in Vienna. The competition to excel intellectually was felt by Viennese youth even while they were secondary students, and every youth who aspired to high culture had not only to become an encyclopedist in a particular subject but to contribute new syntheses of existing ideas, if not original thought.[4]

The stimulation and constraint placed on the Austro-Marxists by the orthodoxies and norms of Marxism, Austrian Social Democracy, and the Austrian intelligentsia created a pressure to bring ideas to public attention before they were fully developed. Undeveloped ideas were liable to withering criticism or stultifying adulation; contemporaries of the Austro-Marxists, such as Sigmund Freud and Franz Kafka, and later Ludwig Wittgenstein, chose relative seclusion and noncommunication for long periods of their lives so their ideas could mature. The Viennese painter Gustav Klimt was said to have lost his creative spirit when he had to face the public clamor that surrounded his work, so vocal and incessant was public discussion of a creative person's vision.[5] A political personality, however, does not have the luxury of withdrawal from the public. The Austro-Marxists found immediate status and prominence in the political-intellectual world by publishing in the socialist organs of their day, but the easy access and waiting readership interfered with the thoroughness, clarity, and logic of each man's ideation. Thought for them became increasingly eclectic over their careers and less and less based on facts. There was a positive side to their reaction to the public readiness for their work: they understood the need to be current and literate in discussion and were aware of their roles as social educators. They took care to offer cogent reviews of contemporary social thinkers who were close to or in conflict with their thought, and they presented their ideas with a historical depth that enabled a reader to comprehend the background and continuity of social problems.

The problems the Austro-Marxists addressed still exist in culture: ethnicity and integration, the integrity of the individual within a cohesive or noncohesive community, the means and methods of achieving equity within the social-economic order, and the many epistemological, axiological, and social scientific issues associated with improving the quality of life. Their consideration of these problems was seminal. Even today the directions of their thought are promising, but their thought was never fully developed either in words or actions. Instead, they used ideas prematurely as vehicles for social mobility, helping them gain recognition and security in their environment, distorting the thought into a metaphorical expression that served many purposes. A study of the individual Austro-Marxist in his milieu will enable us to see the difficulties that have always faced an individual who strives to improve his culture from a theoretical perspective. The mixing of personal needs with public actions, an almost inescapable consequence of public life, creates a strain on scientific inquiry and expression. Facts are selected and shaped to serve personal preference, and preference is a condition of both conscious and unconscious needs. The result is a politics of metaphor which is clear to neither the agent nor his audience and in which what is stated is incongruent with what is done, for how can one possibly act congruently with a metaphor? Can a political thinker ever formulate unambiguous solutions so that both he and his constituents can implement an idea and evaluate its consequences? Probably not, but there is a continuum of conscious responsibility in statement and act which may distinguish a politics of semantic and behavioral integrity from a politics of metaphor. Normally, the literal meaning of ideas guides a society in the establishment of norms for everyday reality and in the maintenance of social institutions. Even when the literal meaning is diluted or strengthened by poetic allusion, or deformed by the language evasions that Sigmund Freud saw so well both in medical practice and on the streets of Vienna, the life of the body politic is governed by the implicit semantic definiteness upon which the less definite statement arose. Society is an achievement of common understanding among people. Semantic definiteness is a necessity in order to achieve the division of labor and the duration of activities that enable a people's survival and creation of a mutually satisfactory pattern of life.

Society can continue to exist, and in a healthy, even improved manner, within a politics of metaphor, if that metaphor of word and action is used judiciously. A conscious application of the politics of metaphor can create images for oneself and others that bring new insight into the implications of a particular condition and into the possible approach for solving a problem. One is anchored by the literal meaning that is the basis of any metaphorical expression, and one may keep an eye on literal reality while entertaining the figurative possibility. Colin Murray Turbayne, in *The Myth of Metaphor*, a work fundamental to my understanding and use of the term in the study of the Austro-Marxists, explores how a thinker juxtaposes formerly diverse literal meanings to create a suggestive image or assertion, the metaphor, to help himself and others begin to dwell upon something that calls for a fresh understanding. One knows that the metaphor is not a reality; rather, each literal semantic thread borrowed to create the image may help one use the image of the metaphor as an intersection that exposes new avenues for research.[6] But the thinker and his audience may forget that what he has used for insight is not real and begin to hold that "man is a wolf" or that "the economy is out of control." This second use of metaphor, an abuse, is seductive to both the thinker and the audience, for it evokes the emotion of the thing's possible significance, while convincing those who entertain it that they have defined what they still must study empirically and logically. A third use of metaphor, a more pronounced abuse, is when one begins to formulate laws based on the image, so that "man is a wolf" or "the economy is out of control" becomes the basis of a series of deductive principles and thus a quasi-science or politics of metaphor that is sterile.[7]

When a society furthers a politics or science that relies on principles that cannot be demonstrated for they are grounded upon metaphor, not concept, its reasoning may be called flight from reality. The flight can be from unacceptable social facts or from instinctual life that is too demanding for realization. The practitioners of metaphor who become enchanted by the seeming validity of their insight, as well as the audience who accepts their premises, know in the depths of their consciousness that these so-called objective statements are bearers of multiple meaning which are artfully constructed to hide the painful reality from their sight, just as a neurotic creates symptoms to hide from himself and gain an advantage in the environment that health could not achieve.[8] The flight from objective facts of the environment is often easier to recognize in society than a flight from instinct.[9] The stereotyping of members from other socioeconomic classes and the institutional attempts to deny the presence of people and conditions that cannot be faced leave imprints that are more readily recognizable than the symbolic distortions of the instinctual realm. This study of the Austro-Marxists will reflect upon forms of defense against both the realities of instinct and the environment but will highlight patterns of thought and action that are called "denial."[10] Denial enables its practitioner to ignore selectively the facts of a particular external situation while accommodating reality in other areas; with the cooperation of associates, one can practice denial in certain areas and respond to reality in most other dimensions of one's life. When a broadly shared cultural pattern distorts instinctual or external reality, ideas that relate to that reality will be truncated so as to probe no more deeply than understanding can comfortably sustain. In such a society ideas that touch upon painful areas will be seen to serve limited functions, and the failure to present an adequate grounding of thought in factual demonstration, or to act in correspondence with the ostensible literal meaning of one's words, will be tacitly accepted. Every society is prone to some avoidance of reality given its inherited social and economic structures.[11]

The meaning systems of denial which the Austro-Marxists shared with other members of their political party belied the social democratic principles inherent to the Marxist perspective. Instead of a democratic structuring of their own political party, with two-way communication and democratic participation facilitated among all members, the Austrian Social Democratic leadership emulated the political structure of the non-democratic Habsburg dynastic state. Instead of establishing the community of work as the social basis for equality and equity within the party as a model of their future aspirations, they created an elite group of oligarchs based upon level of education and personal favor. Instead of a cultural program for Austria that respected the rights of every citizen based solely upon his dignity as an individual, they promulgated one's rights as a member of a nation; therefore, rather than supporting the rights of every national within Austria, they promoted a chauvinistic nationalism that insisted that among the nine nationalities of Austria, only the German culture had civilized value. The Austro-Marxists and their fellow party members had other ideas that can be construed as evidence of denial. Their hesitation to assert socialist principles when in positions of power or to support workers in assertive action against the government reflected a temporizing character that was often justified by metaphorical "theory." Their inability to make timely decisions and their passivity in the midst of social crisis can be seen as symptoms of their inability to assimilate social facts into their publicly stated mission.

These obvious disjunctions between the Marxist principles of their inherited vision and the words and acts that frustrated the development of a truly social democratic party (and, when they assumed political power after World War I, frustrated the development of a social democratic state) were normative patterns that had their origin in the middle-class milieu of German Austria. These normative behaviors protected a way of life in a state that favored Germans, but at the price of full political and social control over one's life, even as a German. These norms are well drawn in the cultural histories of Austria by Carl Schorske, William M. Johnston, and Allan Janik and Stephen Toulmin. A study of these norms of denial as they appeared in the political personalities of the Austro-Marxists may be called a microsociology of the men, in the sense used by Johnston in *The Austrian Mind*. Johnston states that a microsociology of thinkers examines how certain ideas and attitudes were formed in them by their social milieu as they grew from childhood into adulthood. It is a "micro" sociological study in that it shows the group norms as they appear in an individual's thought and action; a "macro" study would consider the formal and informal social institutions that formed the individual patterns. The presence of shared social patterns of idea, attitude, and behavior in an individual is governed by that person's intellect and emotional maturity; a person can change himself to correct inherited norms, even when they are strongly reinforced by his society. Johnston calls certain thinkers *engagé intellectuals* when they seek to change the norms of their milieu.[12] Any change in the norms of a culture requires an equivalent change in oneself before one can change others. It may be impossible to change totally an inherited normative pattern, but one may modify one's ideas and actions if they seem clearly harmful or grossly belie one's more idealistic notions. The process of such a change is not easy, and it involves a consciousness of self that men such as Sigmund Freud won very painfully. Freud's gift to the culture is a study of how the human mind creates defenses against social and personal facts that it cannot accept and how one can modify those defensive structures of thought and behavior, enabling more accurate thought and more congruent action and as a consequence a life free of mental illnesses.

I will use Freud's concept of ego defense, with its several modes of deformation of idea and action,[13] to make clear how the norms of thought and behavior of the Austro-Marxist political personalities were formed and how they were used to protect the individual egos of the men in their public lives. Identification of the social norms influencing the individuals will be the microsociological aspect of the study, while the formation and use of these norms will be viewed from a psychodynamic perspective, with the help of Freud's psychology and that of Carl Gustav Jung and Alfred Adler, who accepted and employed Freud's concept of ego defense while bringing broader explanatory causes to individual motivation than Freud's etiology.

The Austro-Marxist politics of metaphor contains a shared cultural level and a personal level that reflects individual family experience, as well as the unique depths of individual character. The personal level cannot be seen in a political personality as clearly as can the cultural level. The biological and psychic inheritance that formed personalities apart from the cultural conditioning of public life may be inferred in the thought and actions of the political personality but are not as prominent in their appearance as are cultural norms. Nevertheless, the psychobiographer can see characteristic expressions and actions over the life of a thinker that cannot be fully explained as cultural norms and may be associated with family or personal origins. Such personal signs within the thought and behavior of a political personality are not an indication of mental imbalance, as Peter Gay's study of the relationship between ideational style and personal temperament in noted historians demonstrates.[14] Although the neurotic political personality leaves signs of the personal levels of causation in all his public actions, a highly personal style should not be considered a sign of abnormality. The Austro-Marxists displayed distinct temperaments that influenced their political lives; if we are to understand the men fully, we must recognize that their psychobiological inheritance influenced their life choices in a manner that can be distinguished from their defensive personal or cultural motives. Jung's conception of psychological types, wherein an inherent temperament inclines one toward a particular mode of response to experience, may help us to see a healthier side of the men's decisions.[15]

The Austro-Marxists were physically and mentally capable individuals; the ego defense they displayed is an inevitable individual and group phenomenon in a culture, and one must consider a range of defensiveness when deciding whether such defenses are unhealthy yet normal or extreme enough to produce a neurosis or psychosis.[16] The culture of Austria, particularly among the German-Austrian intelligentsia, had norms that must be classified as unhealthy and creating preconditions for individual neurosis. Nevertheless, this same cultural community had beneficial norms, especially its dedication to the arts and the sciences and its demand on individuals for breadth of knowledge and participation in discussion. On the whole, Austrian culture must be seen as normal, having produced men and women whose contributions in the arts and sciences still nourish civilization.

Otto Bauer and Friedrich Adler were extremely neurotic at various times in their lives, and their personal problems dominate even the cultural forms of ego defensiveness in their writings and actions during these periods; however, both men contributed to their culture, stimulating others with their thought and action. In studying the ideas of the Austro-Marxists, I will dissect the sound kernel of thought which continues to nourish from the weakness in denotative clarity, the metaphorical intrusion, and the incomplete ideation and political act, which typified the dross of a cultural attempt to avoid encountering seemingly insoluble so-

Table 1. Cultural Dominance

Nationalities	Number of Universities	Number of High Schools
Germans	5	180
Czechs	1	83
Poles	2	35
Ruthenians	0	3
Slovenians	0	0
Serbo-Croats	0	6
Italians	0	8
Romanians	0	0

Source: Jaszi, *Dissolution of the Habsburg Monarchy*, p. 278.

cial realities. The value of the seminal ideas will be considered as they responded to Austrian political and social conditions, as well as in their continuing value for political and social analysis. The distortions in ideas will be demonstrated as syndromes of political activity that must be recognized in any society if one is to understand the reasons for the disjunctions between word and deed which cripple responsible social action.

The cultural inheritance of the Austro-Marxists, especially the norms of the German-Austrian intelligentsia and the Austrian Social Democratic party, must be examined if we are to appreciate the appearance of these norms in the words and actions of the men.

Austria was ruled by Emperor Franz Joseph of the Habsburg family from 1848 until 1916. Like his predecessors, he supported the hegemony of German culture in the multinational state. The Austrian Empire consisted of seventeen "crown lands,"[17] which were populated by nine nationalities. Cultural dominance (Table 1) and government power (Table 2) were in the hands of the German nationality, although it comprised only 35.6 percent of the Austrian population, according to the 1900 census.[18]

Vienna, the capital of the Austrian Empire, was a cosmopolitan city with ethnic diversity, but its majority population was German. The German intelligentsia centered in Vienna; the weight of their cultural influence far exceeded their numbers, partly because German was the dominant cultural language and the language of the government.

The intelligentsia of Austria made up only about 1 percent of the population. Perhaps the foremost common characteristic of the intelligentsia was reverence for the written word, the dominant means of communication and self-assertion in the Vienna of the Habsburg Monarchy. As Stefan Zweig emphasized in his book of reflective judgment upon the

Table 2. Government Power

Nationalities	Distribution among 1,000 Austrians	Distribution among 1,000 Officials
Germans	357	479 (+122)
Czechs	232	232
Poles	165	125 (−40)
Ruthenians	132	29 (−103)
Slovenians	46	32 (−14)
Serbo-Croats	27	12 (−15)
Italians	28	35 (+7)
Romanians	9	4 (−5)

Source: Jaszi, *Dissolution of the Habsburg Monarchy*, p. 278.

two decades before 1914, "The word still had power. It had not yet been done to death by the organization of lies, by 'propaganda,' and people still considered the written word, they looked to it." The gift of language and the preoccupation with that gift came early to the youth of Vienna. Zweig, recalling his intellectual awakening at the age of sixteen, comments: "We [secondary school intellectuals] were masters of all the tricks, the extravagances, the venturesomeness of the language, we possessed the technique of every verse form, and in countless attempts had tested every style from Pindaric pathos to the simple diction of the folksong. Each day we showed each other our work, mutually pointed out the slightest discrepancies, and discussed every metric detail."[19]

One gained identity with his fellows through the written word, and thus the competition to be read led the intellectual to attempt very early the development of a *Weltanschauung*. If he had an organized set of opinions concerning life, the young intellectual might be recognized by his contemporaries and even followed by disciples of his thought. Dangers in the demand for an articulate world view early in one's life were the eclecticism that confused experience with the parroting of adopted ideas and the chance that dependency on one's mediated view of the world could restrict one's vision of life's immediate possibilities. Hermann Bahr, the dean of the pre-1914 Viennese intelligentsia, bemoaned the universal literacy of the time, with its tendency not only to prodigy but to prodigious glibness: "There are no bad books anymore. Every educated person looks around him carefully, has thoughts about what he sees, and knows how to render what he has seen or experienced in a proper literary style, indeed, often in a masterful fashion."[20]

The number of newspapers and journals published in Vienna between 1890 and 1914 gives meaning to the words of Zweig and Bahr. The city's population in 1890 was approximately one million. That year 863 different newspapers and periodicals were published, 622 of them in the German language. By 1914, the population of Vienna had increased to approximately two million people, and the volume of publications had increased accordingly: there were 1,535 newspapers and periodicals, of which 1,475 were in the German language.[21]

The ideas offered by this vast literary production seem to have been as abundant as their vehicles, for periodicals tended to be read only by those who adopted their notions, and their life spans approximated the duration of their ideological popularity.[22] No matter what side of a polemic one might be on, however, or what philosophy of existence one might advocate, all expressions were born of the same conceptual heritage—a century of German philosophical idealism. The written word had a cultural history that inevitably placed it in a universe with identifiable limitations. The problematics of the literary German mind traveled within the boundaries instilled by a systematic education that was known by the expression *Bildung*.

Bildung has, as its root, a combination of "image" (*bild*) and "to form or constitute" (*bilden*). Thus *Bildung* proved to be a pattern of courses from elementary to graduate school (the university) in which very specific images of reality were developed in the mind of the individual.[23] The world of the individual who passed through this *Bildung* tended to depend forever upon the patriarchal images and the few men who had fathered them.[24]

Karl Renner, writing a tribute to one of the founders of Austrian Social Democracy manifested the importance of the German cultural tradition to the Social Democratic intelligentsia: "For Pernerstorfer the task of socialism existed above all in making the advanced culture and civilization created by the German intellectual heroes accessible to the people. For him, socialism was the inheritance of Goethe and Schiller, Kant and Fichte, Beethoven and Wagner, an inheritance which at the time was monopolized by a small elite whose sacred and national duty lay in making this knowledge available to the masses."[25]

But Pernerstorfer and Victor Adler, founders of Austrian Social Democracy, assumed the role of a new elite. They considered themselves vanguards of a new social order that would be the culmination of the German inheritance. Moreover, all of Austria, Germans and non-Germans alike, would inherit the fruit of their labors.

The Austrian Social Democratic party was born of a newspaper. The editorial opinions of *Die Gleichheit*, under the guidance of Victor Adler from 1886 to 1889, established the program Austrian socialists adopted at Hainfeld in 1889, when they gathered to found a unified political party

Table 3. Occupations of the Viennese Membership of the Austrian Social Democratic Party in 1914

Occupation	Party Members (number)	Membership (percent)
Intellectuals	259	0.6
White-collar workers	2,285	5.3
Independent (businessmen, factory owners, etc.)	2,027	4.7
Proletariat	37,988	88.1
Others	173	0.4
Unknown	387	0.9
Total	47,119	100.0

Source: Robert Danneberg, "Ein Blick ins Innere der Wiener Arbeiterkewegung," *Der Kampf* 7 (June 1914): 396.

to carry on the "class struggle" in Austria.[26] But *Die Gleichheit* was only one of many newspapers that represented views of socialism. The other socialistic papers remained in operation after Hainfeld and conducted a literary war with the newly formed Austrian Social Democratic party, which was controlled by Victor Adler and the policies expressed through *Die Gleichheit*.[27] From 1889 until 1892 the editorial board of *Die Gleichheit* (the name was changed in June 1889 to *Arbeiter-Zeitung*) made all decisions about the actions of the new party.[28] Adler's editorials were the marching orders for all those who considered themselves Austrian Social Democrats, the yearly meeting of Austrian Social Democracy (the Parteitag) being merely a rubber stamp for the daily policy made by the newspaper.[29]

The Austrian Social Democratic intellectual of Vienna, when included within the sphere of decision making by Victor Adler, became an oligarch.[30] The number of intelligentsia in the party was small (see Table 3), but because Victor Adler had organized the party structure like that of an army (see Figure 1), their decisions created and controlled all party policy at all levels.[31]

The party chain of command, as the figure shows, emanated from the Executive Committee, a body permanently located in Vienna that ranged from twelve to twenty members over the period 1892 to 1918. All daily political action was controlled by the Executive Committee, which thereby effectively determined the interpretation of the party program. The Executive Committee was elected at the annual or biannual meeting of the representatives from the various nations of Austria (*Gesamtpartei-*

The Hierarchical Organization of the Austrian Social Democratic Party
(German Austrian Social Democracy, after 1911)

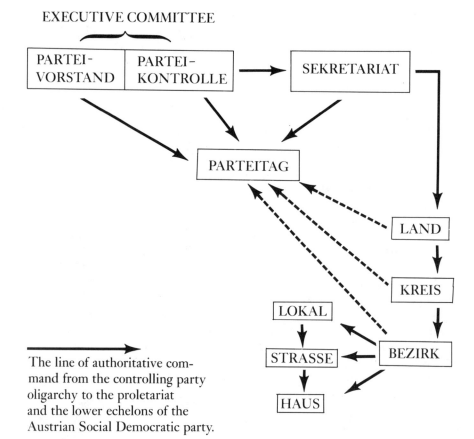

EXECUTIVE COMMITTEE

| PARTEI-VORSTAND | PARTEI-KONTROLLE |

SEKRETARIAT

PARTEITAG

LAND

KREIS

LOKAL

STRASSE

BEZIRK

HAUS

The line of authoritative command from the controlling party oligarchy to the proletariat and the lower echelons of the Austrian Social Democratic party.

The line of communication from the proletariat and the lower echelons of the Austrian Social Democratic party to the controlling party oligarchy.

Source: Parteitag, 1913. See also Clifton Gene Follis, "The Austrian Social Democratic Party, June 1914–November 1918" (Ph.D. dissertation, Stanford Univ., 1961), p. 16. Follis does not depict the line of authoritative command emanating from the party oligarchy.

tag), but this election, which was purportedly to permit the masses to pick their own leaders and choose their own policy, was only nominally democratic. Of the approximately 300 party members who were entitled to attend the party conference, only about 170 were elected delegates, and all came from the higher levels of the organization (two for each *Bezirk*, *Kreis*, and *Land*). The remaining 130 places at the party conference were assigned on an oligarchic basis. The Haus, Strasse, and Lokal, the grass-roots level of membership, had no direct access to participation in party policy. The entire Executive Committee, Secretariat, and the club of Social Democratic representatives in Parliament were automatically entitled to attend, as were the heads of all trade unions. The party conference was, then, an assembly of disciplined career Social Democrats, all of whom were highly placed. The highest among the real leaders of the party were consequently able to persuade the conference to adopt their policies with monotonous regularity, especially since the proceedings were always conducted by the members of the Executive Committee.[32]

Theoretically, a party member might take issue with the leaders at any time, but conflict might occur only within the walls of the party, not in public. All physical manifestations of belief contemplated by a party member had to be approved by party headquarters. The Austro-German Social Democrats of Vienna, the leaders of the party between 1889 and 1934, could justify their military chain of command by reminding their critics of the class warfare in which they were engaged. As Victor Adler told the anarchistically inclined radicals of the party: "Yet a word to these comrades who fear 'centralization'. . . . A party that would bring about Social Democracy must be structured in a manner that is well ordered and in its turn capable of ordering. The organized party structure of our opponents is the chief factor of their power; if we wish to be victorious, we must not condemn ourselves to impotency with a childish fear of 'party tyranny.'"[33]

An Austrian Social Democratic state that resembled Austria was gradually developed; it was necessary to obey the party's legal, executive, and administrative institutions if one were to remain a citizen. The Austro-Marxists were inevitably molded by this state within a state. A steady diet of polemics, once removed from any possibility of political actualization, poorly prepared them for the world of action outside their small arena.

The intellectual's alienated position in Austria, particularly aggravated by the universal views engendered by his education, was not overcome within the workers' party. Rather, Austrian Social Democracy provided him with an audience that ineluctably fed his ego while maintaining his isolation from the working class. Franz Blei reflected that in the early days of Austrian Social Democracy, Victor Adler was called "the Doctor," reflecting the inclination by most workers to pay a class respect to the "educated." He remarked that this embarassed the Austrian Socialist intellectuals, but seemed an inescapable role in the interaction.[34]

The Austro-Marxists, on the other hand, achieved the power and position they enjoyed in the Austrian Social Democratic hierarchy because of their insensitivity to the dilemma indicated by Blei. For them, being a vanguard of the proletariat was not an embarrassment, nor did it appear to be a metaphor. They had reified their positions as beacons to the masses sufficiently in their understanding and their everyday actions so that they could be used by the metaphor with an equanimity that enabled them to justify actions in the name of the proletariat that assured their leadership positions in the party.

The Austro-Marxist sense of leadership and mission was expressed in the first Austrian Social Democratic platform at Hainfeld in 1889, which they inherited: "The Austrian Social Democratic party, working for the whole people [*Das Volk*] without distinction of nation, race, or sex, strives to free the people from intellectual atrophy . . . to organize the proletariat politically, and to fill them with a consciousness of their position and their task, to make them ready physically and mentally for battle and to maintain this readiness."[35]

The habits of their intellectual background inevitably transformed revolutionary ideals into thought tailored to the regularity of their lives as Austrian citizens of the middle class. As a young student, Max Adler, in distinguishing between the "true proletariat" and the "student proletariat" (as unemployed bourgeois students often chose to depict themselves) drew a picture unwittingly of himself and his future Austro-Marxist associates as well as of virtually every other Austrian Social Democratic intellectual: "The chief characteristic of the proletariat . . . is their constancy and dependency (as a class subjected by capital). This is not the condition, however, of the student proletariat, whose goal, rather, is to work themselves out of their difficulties into a good bourgeois position. . . . Thus, the greatest betrayal of youthful ideals is to be found with students. This feeling of belonging to the bourgeois class, if only reflected in the hope of eventually bettering one's position, separates the intellectual proletariat from the industrial proletariat."[36]

The Austro-Marxists were chosen as leaders by their cultural fathers and their peers because of their weaknesses as well as strengths. They were able to articulate the issues of everyday life and monumental history in terms of Marxist thought, clarifying and giving direction to events according to an inherited paradigm. They were also chosen as leaders because they typified certain blindness and incongruencies in their thought and action. In external politics, their thought stopped safely within the parameters that preserved existing norms of policy and action. In political practice within the party, they maintained the norms that denied participatory democracy to the rank-and-file members. Contemporary research in group dynamics confirms that leaders will express the expectational norms of their group if they are to be esteemed as leaders.[37] To break the circular pattern of such behavior, the Austro-Marxists would have to experience the support of a democratic state and democratic norms of social interaction. As Immanuel Kant perceptively saw of his fellow Germans in 1793, one had to practice democracy in order to be adept at it: "We cannot ripen to this freedom if we are not first of all placed therein (we must be free in order to be able to make purposive use of our powers in freedom). The first attempts will indeed be crude and usually will be attended by a more painful and more dangerous state than that in which we are still under the orders and also the care of others; yet we can never ripen with respect to reason except through our own efforts (which we can make only when we are free)."[38]

When World War I ended, the Austro-Marxists had their opportunity for democratic socialism, and, as Kant had predicted, their first attempts were less than successful because of their inexperience in the practice of freedom, either toward others or within themselves.

I

1890-1914

We all know that our actual life is more or less a deformation of our potential life . . . the task is for one to test his actual life within his given situation against what his life could be. As a biographer, this allows us to test the degree of integrity the actual life has.

—*José Ortega y Gasset*

1

The Austro-Marxist Idea

The Austro-Marxists did not represent a "school of thought."[1] They were separate thinkers who shared membership in the Social Democratic party but were a generation younger than its founders, lived in or were closely associated with life in Vienna in the quarter century before World War I, and contributed significant theoretical and practical analyses of the many social issues that concerned the party.[2] Although each man adhered to such Marxist concepts as the dialectic in history, class conflict, and the alienation of the worker from the value of his labor, each based his thinking on different philosophical positions, and so treated these concepts in different ways.

Even when the Austro-Marxists seemed to share common ideas, as when Otto Bauer used Karl Renner's notion of "personality" as a basis for national identity, Bauer's transformation of the concept created a distance between the men. Renner was essentially a man of "common sense" for whom materialism was self-evident. He preferred John Stuart Mill to Hegel, so although he saw the importance of ideas in influencing history, he approached social reality as a reformist within a stable world; he did not see the world as a place of dialectical change based upon laws of social transformation. Bauer, on the other hand, saw in every living thing and social institution a competitive striving for survival; his thought was close to Social Darwinism, and he preferred Marxism, perhaps because of the class struggle and the human values associated with it. Bauer believed that the dialectic in history was a law that had its own reality in the material world and was not dependent upon the translation of this reality in human consciousness; the numbers that made up each social class, and their relative strength within the social fabric, determined the movement of history. His quantitative view of how classes transformed history, though never clearly drawn, indirectly reflected his understanding of biological competition and natural selection.

Max Adler was a neo-Kantian, who brought his analysis of human consciousness to every historical event or social issue. Among the Austro-Marxists, he came perhaps the nearest to Marx's Hegelian notion of a dialectic movement of events based upon human motivation and thought, guided by social structures created by certain orientations of human idea and value. Renner's study of legal norms in various periods of Western culture could have helped Adler for it demonstrated the interaction between social conditions, laws based upon these conditions, and human values, as well as the change in these relationships over time. Renner, however, saw these interactions and changes from a Lockean viewpoint, in which a gradual emendation and accretion of ideas could transform society, not as the result of a radical altering of consciousness and social structures to correspond more truly to the social being of individuals, as Max Adler's amalgam of Kant and Marx implied.

Otto Bauer was attracted to the radical implications of Adler's neo-Kantian Marxism as a young man but rejected it as a "metaphysical" diversion, favoring a natural law of the environment over one of the mind. Friedrich Adler shared Max Adler's certainty that an interaction of human consciousness and the material world created a dynamic, which was the foundation for individual and group movement in history. Friedrich Adler, however, studied the mind as an adherent of the physicist-epistemologist Ernst Mach, who denied that the Kantian a priori categories of consciousness existed and for whom absolute laws in thinking, science, or social planning were anathema. Mach's relativism was based on his view that because material being created and conditioned consciousness, every new historical ordering of environment and society required new measures and values to enable the human society to correspond and to cope with what existed. The relativism had radical implications, for society could be transformed every generation if the changes met reality. The material determinism of Mach's view was also attractive to Friedrich Adler because it enabled dialectical materialism to find justification in the natural sciences. Neither Renner, Bauer, nor Max Adler could accept the denial of enduring measures or laws of human and societal development.

There was a second major reason why the Austro-Marxists did not represent a school of thought besides their diverse orientations to Marx, nature, and culture. An authentic school of thought shares a body of clearly defined concepts, which it applies as interpretive and explanatory mechanisms in treating the realities with which it deals. A school of thought is a body of ideas that can be a medium and a guide for later thinkers and remains valid over time. The ideas of the Austro-Marxists, with a few exceptions such as Renner's study of legal norms, were time-bound because they stopped short of the thorough, empirical grounding that would have clarified their operational definition and allowed their testing in experience to demonstrate their validity and reliability. Nevertheless, the ideas of the Austro-Marxists stimulated even when they failed to solve; and although the pressures of these men's milieu and personality needs curtailed the clarification necessary to make their ideas survive over generations, they still can be applied to present problems.

Intellectuals in contemporary Europe have looked to the Austro-Marxists for insight into theoretical and practical questions of integrating socialism and democracy. Young socialists and Eurocommunists such as Detlev Albers, Josef Hindels, and Lucio Radice, are attracted especially to Otto Bauer's thought.[3] Among the ideas considered relevant for contemporary concerns are Bauer's post–World War I views that social revolution should be stimulated among the working classes in all countries and that workers should be aided in cooperation across national boundaries, whether the nations are communist, socialist, or capitalist.[4] We will see that this notion was rooted in Bauer's prewar view of the fundamental, evolutionary nature of the class struggle. Only a socialist who experienced the multinational issues of Austria before World War I could appreciate the need for a broader base of cooperation than nation and could perhaps intuit an avenue of solution. Other contemporaries have turned to Max Adler as a source for the critical study of consciousness that may shed light upon the forms social institutions assume or might assume given the nature of social intelligence.[5] The Eurocommunists and social democrats of modern Europe have found a rich source among the Austro-Marxists for approaching the problems of unifying the European community in a social democratic polity, but much original thinking is necessary to complete the Austro-Marxist perspectives.

The appearance of unity among the Austro-Marxists, noted by historians such as Raimund Loew, was created by their common concerns, which bridged philosophical differences, enabling them to cooperate in practical projects for common ends. They were members of a political party that had an articulated mission of social change—the creation of a socialized, democratic state. As such, they considered themselves intellectual leaders with the common responsibility to be "vanguards of the proletariat," educating the masses in the scientific criticism that would enable them to accept the Marxist view and prepare them to participate in the tasks of social change. The Austro-Marxists collaborated in developing educational programs for workers and students, though a close look at the curriculum and pedagogy shows that their personal differences carried into all these activities. The necessity to win political power in Austria led to cooperation among the Austro-Marxists within the tactical decisions of everyday Austrian Social Democratic policy, including their support of socialist participation in the Austrian parliament. The radical philosophy of Max Adler and the integral role of class struggle in the thinking of Otto Bauer strained their cooperation with the bourgeois political parties, but the weight of the pacifistic, civilized norms of Viennese culture dominated the thinking of both men; they joined their fellows in the maintenance of a unified political program that was much more evolutionary than revolutionary, reflecting, as Vincent J. Knapp has indicated, more a Lassallean democratic socialism than a Marxist socialism. Before World War I the Austro-Marxists were prone to follow the lead of Victor Adler and the other party fathers in matters of practical policy; after the war some of the more radical implications of Marxist social theory were promoted by Max Adler and Otto Bauer, even though the prewar norms of compromise and vacillation still accompanied these trends.[6] On the nationality question the Austro-Marxists joined the majority thinking in their party, which favored the hegemony of German culture within a multinational Austria, in short, the system that had existed for centuries. There was a sound economic reason for continuation of a state that included territories in which other nationalities were the majority of the population; the truncated German Austria after World War I demonstrated their wisdom in seeking to maintain a larger, more economically varied territory. In 1897 the Austrian Social Democratic party had created a federal structure for its organization in an effort to appease the separatist aspirations of other Austrian nationals within the party. Its state policy was similar but did not emanate from a sense of equality; rather, it was a compromise all the German-Austrians agreed upon in order to preserve the state as it was.

Every period of culture inherits a particular set of problems and a momentum in social behavior from its antecedents. This inheritance affects what individuals in that society come to consider as valid purposes, as well as how they choose to pursue those purposes. Although the Austro-Marxist inheritance contained many biases and cultural weaknesses, it included a respect for science and the historical breadth and depth of European humanism. The Austro-Marxists wished to modify society, but even more vital for them was the completion of a scientific basis to serve that change. Their interest in the historical development of ideas and in epistemology reflects the value their culture placed on mental experience and thought; conversely, it indicates the lack of reinforcement the culture gave to change in the material facts of the environment. The Austro-Marxists, and Austrian Social Democrats, ascribed to Karl Marx's eleventh thesis on Ludwig Feuerbach, that "the philosophers have only *interpreted* the world, in various ways; the point, however, is to change it";[7] yet they realized that scientific study of the problems of life in society in many dimensions was needed to prepare a ground for thorough, effective action. Their treatment of ideas as entities to be studied, rather than too quickly applied, did not reduce them to ineffectual social agents.

Karl Marx, whose thought grew in a time and place when western European culture reinforced material change in social, economic, and political conditions, never completed an adequate epistemology to support his ideas of praxis, dialectical materialism, or alienation; his writings on the role of consciousness and language in cultural activity are more suggestive than demonstrative. Moreover, he did not develop evidential studies that clearly demonstrated his general theory of dialectical development of social-cultural institutions in history, although his work on capital was a model for such studies. One man cannot transform society by himself. Marx's seminal ideas awaited the work of social theorists such as the Austro-Marxists, who could bring facts to light through investigations of law, politics, industries, art, education, and so forth, which validated and amplified the constructs Marx had bequeathed to his *Nachwuchs*.

The full development of an idea in its meanings and applications requires generations. An idea provides the what, why, how, where, and when of what it comprehends; it provides the direction of the evidence that will substantiate it and suggests methods to pursue its validation in culture. One generation may work at articulating the broad or environmental implications of an idea; a second generation may devote its thought to methods of proof; a third generation may dedicate itself to applying the idea as a change agent in culture.[8] The Austro-Marxists were an ideal generation to complete the establishment of proofs for Marxist thought. They had inherited a stable if oppressive society; their conative and cognitive education proceeded by reasoned steps. They were not Marxist revisionists, for unlike Bernstein they did not see Marx's ideas as inadequate for modern society but rather as needing full development. The problems of their generation were dictated by the comprehensive scientific and social paradigms of their forebears, which carved out a universe of meaning that awaited detailed proofs and social implementation.

The strongest element of the Austro-Marxist set of ideas was its connection to past thought. Their writings always had a relational explicitness that linked their ideas to cultural predecessors. Max Adler's study of pioneers in socialist thought, *Wegweiser. Studien zur Geistesgeschichte des Sozialismus* (1914), remains a readable and informative source of intellectual history. Relational thought has positive and negative implications in the development and transmission of effective ideas, and the Austro-Marxists exemplified both. When one stresses relational thought, he can have a healthy counterpoint with the past or present thinker, developing another's thought in the light of his own ideas and thus broadening the context of argument. He can use the other's evidence and argument to legitimize his own. Such a habit of mind breeds an evolutionary attitude toward one's social environment; because the main idea one treats has existed over time, the world in which the idea was engendered is respected. The negative elements of relational thinking enter with this respect for past thought. When a thinker adheres to the principal definitions and implications of a past thinker, he may consider himself part of a family, for the secure meaning provided by an accepted thinker in a past generation, particularly if he has created a school of followers, can be comforting. The genealogy of fellow thinkers allows the same easy access and support in idea that a family tradition secures. The Austro-Marxists tended to devote an inordinate amount of energy to what Nietzsche condemned as *Epigonentum*, a historicity of thought that subtly negated the creation of new ideas. Evolution often requires a revolutionary short-term action, as Freud demonstrated in his relation to medical psychiatry. Leon Trotsky avoided the Austro-Marxists while he lived in Vienna before World War I because he sensed that their awe in the face of their cultural fathers would rule them out as revolutionaries.[9] Nevertheless, relational thought provides one's contemporaries, as well as intellectual historians, with a coherent network of ideas and sources with which to assimilate a statement. The Austrian-German intellectual, as a rule, promoted cultural evolution through the care he took in providing a well-annotated guide for all those interested in continuing study or practice in the ideas and institutions he celebrated. Max Adler's *Wegweiser*, Karl Renner's *Staat und Nation* (1899), Otto Bauer's *Die Nationalitaetenfrage und die Sozialdemokratie* (1907), and Friedrich Adler's *Ernst Machs Ueberwindung des mechanischen Materialismus* (1918), each a major work of the author, are excellent histories of ideas.

The Austro-Marxists were not untouched by the intellectual current of "subjectivity," which Europe cultivated between 1890 and World War I. The subjective value of human thought and the human personality was reaffirmed against the materialism of the nineteenth century. Austrian-German intellectuals were leaders in this return to selfhood. The art of expressionism, the physics of relativity, the psychodynamics of the unconscious, and literature, drama, and poetry emphasizing individual existential responsibility surrounded the young Austro-Marxists. Max Adler and Friedrich Adler were particularly susceptible to these influences, perhaps because of an inherent psychological disposition which Carl Gustav Jung describes as the "introverted thinking type."[10] For the introverted thinker, the subjective aspects of experience are seen to condition how one perceives and shapes external reality. The two Adlers balanced their sensitivity to the role of individual consciousness with an awareness of the interdependence of individuals, thus avoiding a subjective attitude that would have ignored the social being of the individual. Their care in probing the manner in which the individual mind responds to reality ensured that they would escape the one-sided social view that failed to investigate how and why individual decisions in social interaction are made. Max Adler furthered the thought of Immanuel Kant and Friedrich Adler augmented the ideas of Ernst Mach in their common view that the history of culture was one of progress in the social ordering of society based upon an increasing awareness of human interdependence. Both Kantian and Machian philosophies were significant reinforcements to the return to subjectivity for socialists in particular because their focus on identifying the laws or processes of consciousness, and thereby the socializing principles of the human mind, stressed a dimension of selfhood that was the same for everyone. With this knowledge, the human community might more quickly discover and adequately implement forms of social interaction that allowed for the full development of human potential.

Karl Renner and Otto Bauer were also positively influenced by their age's reinforcement of individuality and the subjective realm of human experience, although their natural inclination was not in that direction. Renner and Bauer may be described as the "extroverted thinking type."[11] The extroverted thinker finds meaning in events rather than ideas, or if he is sensitive to epistemology and psychology, he will choose a philosophy that subordinates consciousness to external influences. Jung points out that if an extroverted thinker represses the truths of subjectivity, his thought will begin to reflect these omissions in a negative manner; the logical development of his constructions will be invaded by personalized aspersions to other thinkers and petty references to his own person. Similarly, when the introvert neglects the objective breadth of reality, his thought will suffer the intrusion of this aspect of existence in the use of mundane, overgeneralized examples of human interaction and public life. Renner and Bauer did recognize the individual and subjective in their treatment of issues of nationality and ethnicity, just as the two Adlers compensated their emphasis on consciousness with a view of social reality. Austro-Marxist ideas that remain seminal are so because of this balance. Renner was more adept than Bauer at blending individual and autobiographical example with his writings. Bauer experienced recurrent personality problems, which stemmed from his earliest years and obstructed his introspection and his ability to see the individuality of others. The value of Renner and Bauer for their time, and for ours, may be traced to their extroverted inclination. Extroversion in a politically active individual, if tempered with theoretical distance, can enable intelligent concentration on day-to-day events, the very stuff of social reality from which the introvert withdraws. Both Renner and Bauer combined an intense involvement in the activities of their culture with an ability to analyze and synthesize political events according to ingenious structures of idea; and even when these formulations are incomplete or distorted by cultural biases or personal problems, they provide a platform for reflection upon the issues involved.

The issues that Renner and Bauer inclined toward involved their political and social environment: nationality and ethnicity, the structure of government, the conduct of politics, economic development, and foreign policy. Although Max Adler and Friedrich Adler occasionally addressed these issues, they did so only in moments of social crisis, and then they did not treat the issue with a timely, tactical strategy but with a philosophical principle that was held to be valid at any time. Renner and Bauer could be theoretical about nationality, Parliament, the Danube economy, and Balkan diplomacy, but their strength was in writings that made choices and suggested strategies, using theory analytically rather than as a deductive construct. The nationality question was central to Renner and Bauer because of its omnipresence in the politics of of the Austrian multinational state and the special problems the concepts of nationality and ethnicity raised for a Marxist. If national boundaries and ethnic enclaves were merely a consequence of certain stages of economic development, then perhaps such cultural distinctions should disappear. Renner argued for preservation of ethnic integrity, and he sought to create an idea of the multinational state that could be justified in the light of Marx's caution against past concepts of order such as the hierarchical state or territorial nationality. He conceived the notion of a national "personality" that transcended territorial boundaries and would be integral to the identity of an individual even in a socialist state. He borrowed the concept from the Carolingian legal code, ingeniously shaping ancient law to fit modern needs. Renner's deliberations included sociological theory as well as legal history; he explored the questions of nationality and ethnicity extensively enough to leave a body of literature that can help us think through these concepts as they increase in importance for our culture.

Otto Bauer saw ethnic integrity as only a moment in the social-economic movement of history; for an individual to adhere to an ethnic heritage that had no roots in the reality of the social-economic present was an error of consciousness that prevented him from making history. Ethnic groups such as the German nation were justified by the conditions of the time; they were culture-makers. Most Slavic nationalities within the Austrian state were seen as representing outdated heritages; they would be closer to historical truth if they were assimilated to the German nationality. Bauer based his arguments on the dialectical materialism of Marx. Yet despite Bauer's bias toward German culture, the questions he raised about the substance of ethnicity and nationality are significant. He introduced the classic debate between cultural anthropology and biology over the fundamental cause of individual and group character.[12] As a Marxist, Bauer strongly supports the role of culture in creating what he terms a "community of character"; he recognized biological causes in character but was less skillful in using inherited traits in his arguments. He used a variation of Renner's personality principle of nationality to justify the ability of an individual to change nationalities on the basis of intelligent decision, no matter what territory he might live in or what heritage might encompass him. This dimension of his discussion reflects Bauer's struggle to deal with a highly painful family background and his Jewish heritage, which his father's generation had largely rejected.

Finally, in introducing the Austro-Marxist ideas, we must touch upon the relation of the thinkers to new social scientific research methods and forms of evidence developed at the turn of the century. The mid-nineteenth-century thinkers such as Marx and Darwin had formulated comprehensive theories that promised to explain the causes and connections of all phenomena in their respective areas of study, but their substantiation of these grand schemes had hardly begun. Researchers in the generations that followed devised new strategies for the collection of evidence in behalf of these guiding theories, seeking proofs within the environments of natural and social life. The research methods of the social sciences in the nineteenth century stressed documentary evidence—statistics, demographics, and thoughtful and thorough discussions of what could and should be, as well as of what was. The natural sciences had introduced field observation, but it was informal, and even more so in the infant social sciences. The new forms of research in the social sciences intensified field work, developing four areas of seeking evidence that would be used to validate ideas: study of cultural artifacts, inferring human intention and meaning; study of direct communication, that is, verbal and nonverbal expression; study of the mind's operation and structure and their implications to social life; and observation of human behavior. The Austro-Marxists used some of these forms of evidence and avoided some. Consideration of their research methods in the light of what was being done around them helps us to understand their strengths as thinkers and can provide us with further knowledge about the reasons for their failure to develop certain directions of thought.

Detailed content studies of cultural artifacts to elicit the lines of thought that shaped them were made in fields that ranged from law, literature, and the fine arts to psychiatry at the turn of the century. Contributors to this sphere among the German contemporaries of the Austro-Marxists included the sociologist Georg Simmel, the anthropologist Franz Boas, the psychiatrists Sigmund Freud and Carl Gustav Jung, who contributed to all four areas of new research, and the neo-Kantian social philosopher Rudolf Stammler, whose critical review of legal codes opened up a new approach to cultural interpretation. Karl Renner's study of law was similar to that of Stammler in that it related the semantics of the legal expression to a broader cultural intention. The careful study of an artifact, turning it around in one's mind's eye until all its possible meanings and implications were discovered, was a particular strength of the Austro-Marxists. It may have reflected the inheritance of a cultural style of Austrian humanism. The Austrian humanist was like Monet at his lily pond; he spent the greater part of a lifetime rendering interpretations of the same subject with a constant attitude and idea. Max Adler did with intellectual biographies of social thinkers what Renner did with laws; for Adler, a thinker and a body of thought were both artifacts to be probed for obvious and hidden implications. As with Renner, his study was not simply traditional criticism; it expanded into what may be termed phenomenological study, for it constructed inferential worlds of meaning beyond, yet based upon, the artifact's obvious qualities and intentions. Friedrich Adler reserved these investigations to the history of scientific method, and we see flashes of it in some of his Marxist writings. Otto Bauer is the only Austro-Marxist who lacked the patience for these thorough reviews of cultural artifacts, a consequence of the tension placed upon his thought by his emotional problems.

The second area of social evidence, direct communications, was new to cultural study. Psychiatry had opened the way through Freud in the 1890s, and soon sociologists such as Max Weber included firsthand reports on cultural activity as vital evidence in interpreting cultural meaning.[13] Formal interviews or even informal recording of the statements of others were never significant to Austro-Marxist thought. Nor did they pursue the study of human behavior. There are several reasons for their neglect of these areas, one lying in the nature of the Marxist paradigm, another in the norms of the Austrian culture, and another in their inherent style of thought. The Marxist paradigm sought cultural explanation in social conditions; words and behavior were related to more general causes; no words or behavior were unique to a person, rather they were common styles of classes of persons. Institutional patterns of behavior seen at a distance were sufficient to expose class traits; language was a vehicle of class ideas, thus the printed word was adequate to capture the semantic evidence. The norms of Austrian culture legislated against the direct observation of normal fellow citizens or interviewing them to seek evidence to support hypotheses. Although these methods had been introduced by Max Weber to the German culture in the first decade of the twentieth century, they were used sparingly in social scientific research before World War I. When used, they were applied in industry to workers but not to middle- or upper-class citizens. Literate Europeans used the arguments of social science to justify a social-economic philosophy and to ascribe right or wrong to social practices. Weber's effort to bring what he called "ethical neutrality" and objectivity to society through these new methods that judged an individual's language and behavior from a "value-free" distance was seen as a violation of the literate person's disclosure of values.[14]

The Austro-Marxists used language and acts to justify their rightness and listened to others in order to blame or to educate them, as was the norm with other politically aware citizens of Austria. The temperaments of the Austro-Marxists and their style of thought also prevented adoption of these new methods. Max Adler and Friedrich Adler chose to study inanimate artifacts rather than undertake intense scientific work involving contact with living persons, a preference reflecting their introverted nature. Karl Renner and Otto Bauer thrived on interaction, but it was competitive in Bauer's case and genial for Renner; neither man wished to study contact with another person but preferred as an extravert to be nourished by the direct emotional and intellectual meaning of the social exchange.

Study of the mind's operation and structure in order to gather evidence that could support a clearer understanding and implementation of social intelligence was the most important means of investigation for both Max Adler and Friedrich Adler. Their interest in the laws of consciousness was significantly different in its major aim than the new direction of depth psychology pursued by Freud, Alfred Adler, and Jung, or even the similar epistemological motive of the phenomenological school begun by Edmund Husserl.[15] These investigators of the mind neglected the theme of socializing consciousness in their studies, conceiving social reality as a negative concept arrived at by the addition of individual realities. Both Max Adler and Friedrich Adler could have made profound contributions to the psychology and epistemology of political values and social change, but neither developed these promising theoretical directions because of a hesitation to become an original contributor to culture, a tragic aberration in each man that has denied posterity important thought. The theoretical ground for their study was completed sufficiently to provide a basis for further investigation. Max Adler's works on Kant and Marx are still prolegomenas for future thinking about the nature of social intelligence, and

Friedrich Adler's biography of Ernst Mach is a history of science that demonstrates how the processes of consciousness may be located in the mind's artifacts, that is, in the study of scientific theory and its construction. Actual study of the mind in its operative modes and discovery of its laws requires observation of the mind's activity in relation to the creation of human artifacts.

Max Adler's studies of other thinkers might have been the source of the analysis needed to dissect the nature of social intelligence. In one brilliant passage in which he analyzed Goethe's Faust in the midst of reflection, Adler demonstrated a path of phenomenological criticism that may yet be developed.[16] But Adler did not follow his own insight. There were many social philosophers whose use of artifacts in the study of laws of consciousness could have reinforced him, such as Georg Simmel, for whom he had a guarded admiration, and especially the neo-Kantians, who sought evidence of social intelligence in ethics, law, and pedagogy.[17] His use of other thinkers is largely appreciative and critical but not productive in the sense of developing a philosophically refined outline of social consciousness. His irrational self-limitation was rooted in his hesitation to become a cultural father with a mature body of work; he remained what Jung has called a *puer aeternus*, an eternal youth. This study will elucidate how he diverted his thought, perhaps how to continue it to its promised fruition, but most certainly, how the psychological defenses of the personality can turn the careful construction of a complex idea into a metaphor that dissipates thought.

Friedrich Adler likewise refused to become a productive cultural father. He constantly undercut his own accomplishment by subsuming his intellect and vision to that of both his personal and his cultural father. He lived uncannily in the model of the tragic figure of Oedipus, a life script that channeled his independence and intellectual promise into a circular strife of inherited problems. The German-Austrian intelligentsia who overcame this inheritance did so only because they identified the problems clearly and lived through them with their intellect and action relatively uncompromised, neither giving in to the norms prematurely nor distorting them. Men such as Freud, Franz Kafka, Robert Musil, Wittgenstein, and Husserl dealt with the historicity that swallowed new insight and perpetuated a laziness of thought that overlooked incongruent action by offering new forms of self-observation and cultural criticism. Their thought helps us in modern culture individually arrive at the facts of our immediate life. The Austro-Marxists might have helped us arrive at the collective facts of our social life with an equivalent insight if they, too, had adequately confronted the negative aspects of their inheritance.

2

Karl Renner's Search for a Home

Karl Renner's tribute to Marx in 1908 on the twenty-fifth anniversary of his death can be seen as the credo of Renner's life:

The worker who wished to understand his relation to Marx must, as I do, think back to his father, his grandfather, and his ancestors as far back as they go—then he will encounter men who were not industrial workers or proletarians, rather fathers of families [*Hausvaeter*] . . . who lived in their own homes and exercised an iron rule over their children and domestics. One never spoke to one's father and mother in the familiar "thou," for one's parents were authorities [*Obrigkeiten*] who were the highest authorities next to God and the emperor. . . . And the despairing words "I do not know why I was born" were seldom heard and considered wanton. Nothing appeared more taken for granted than "where one came from and where he was going." "We have come from our fathers . . . we will become fathers ourselves, and then return to our fathers from whence we came." . . . And on this path of life man enjoyed much happiness and suffered much pain, but he lived his own life among men of value—he was indeed a person. But then a magical upheaval came to the world and threw our ancestors and grandfathers from their homes into the street. A person on the street—it makes no sense! How can a man play his part of father of a family in the rubble of the street? Is that a home? . . . A man who lives in the street, where does he come from? Where is he going? No one knows, least of all himself . . . and if he dies in the street, how does he then find his way to his father's home and his father's grave for his burial. . . . Thousands have asked themselves from the graves of the streets: "For what purpose am I in the world?" And found no answer. *Those workers, however, who have conceived the whence and whither of this capitalistic world according to Marx, win back their world again.*"[1]

Eventually, Karl Renner was to take Karl Marx as his grandfather, Victor Adler as his father, the Austrian Social Democratic party as his ancestral home. As he wrote to Victor Adler in 1909: "As far as my knowledge of myself goes, I know: I do not belong among those who must outdo the next man; I have no incentive to compete. . . . My so-called 'ego' wants nothing. Rather, as far as socialism concerns me, I would like to use the proud words of the Nazarene: 'In my father's house there are many rooms.' There are so many spiritual areas [*Bezirke*] opened to us by it, so many still not built."[2]

Once within the patriarchal domain of socialism, Renner found a peace his life had lacked; he transferred mental and emotional bonds to his family developed in his childhood to the party fathers of Austrian Social Democracy. *Transference* is the concept used in psychoanalysis to explain how and why emotional and mental conflicts that were experienced and unresolved in childhood are lived out with the analyst. Transference, however, is not limited to a psychoanalyst's office; it can occur in any human situation that provides the individual with a person or persons and an environment that are conducive to reenacting parts of the past that cry out for understanding and resolution.[3] By transferring past conflicts to a new situation, one can recapture the emotional depth of childhood and overcome psychic obstructions to growth by reentering, and conquering, the conflict situation in the new environment.[4] Unless one realizes that he is inappropriately treating the present environment with past emotional values and relations, however, he will approach the demands of the present inadequately and use people and events metaphorically, as representatives for a past psychic struggle. Renner never fully recognized his inappropriate associations of a personal past in his relationship to the Austrian Social Democratic party, and as a result, he treated the party structure as a home to be enjoyed and used for many primary needs other than those of representing the working class in a social struggle. "Otto Bauer once said about Renner that just as there are occasional drinkers, so also there are occasional theoreticians and occasional politicians, and the typical example of this was Karl Renner. . . . In later years, when the demanding cares of his life were conquered, Renner loved ease, comfort, sociability, relaxation, and amusement. Those qualities often led, indeed, to idleness."[5]

His transference of deep personal needs to the Austrian Social Democratic party enabled Renner to be a productive party member, but at the relaxed pace of what his idea of a proper family life should be. His instinctual needs and value imperatives became concentrated within the party and its Marxist mission. For Renner, his association with Austrian Social Democracy was a primary bond, rather than the secondary relationship that most individuals have to their employment or broader social commitments. The primary relationship to a group is usually reserved for one's personal family; it is an association of total emotional and psychic commitment. In a secondary relationship there are clearly defined emotional and mental limits to one's investment of energy. A work group can become primary, especially for political revolutionaries or individuals who derive a deep satisfaction from their employment and link significant personal and social values to that activity. When the emotional and mental commitment usually reserved for one's immediate family is given to a larger cultural organization, it is termed *sublimation*—the transfer of instincts such as aggression, sexuality, nourishment, or other instincts into the service of cultural practices that will benefit the entire society. Service for the society demands that one love what one does and sacrifice for it, but still one cannot live his full interpersonal life within its locus. Sublimation can be a solution for an individual whose personality requires total dedication to public values, or it can be an escape from the balance and completeness of a variegated interpersonal existence.[6] When one seeks to realize his entire instinctual life within a sublimated role of cultural service, his behavior will show characteristics of transference.

Renner and the other Austro-Marxists sublimated instincts in behalf of social democracy; however, each man in some degree brought emotional and mental needs that were beyond the ability of a large, secondary organization of individuals to solve. Perhaps the structure of the party and the ambitious nature of its mission encouraged that sublimation, for the goal of Austrian political parties in the last decades of the nineteenth century was a new existence that only the party could bring to society.[7] The process of civilization demands sublimation of instinct in behalf of the whole society, but the society often creates institutions that either demand too much or too little sacrifice of instinctual energy; a healthy society is one that establishes sublimated activities that still permit an individual freedom to realize personal needs in private channels.[8] Karl Renner and the other Austro-Marxists each brought a special set of problems to Austrian Social Democracy, which were to distort the Social Democratic mission as each man imposed his design on its political life. Renner's transference had largely to do with the loss of his childhood home and the search for a father who could guarantee security. He wrote: "A child that is born to a family of winegrowers experiences the gradual dissolution of his family's economic security as a result of their many children, agricultural depression and inflation of land prices, and then experiences the final shock of the auctioning of his family home [*Vaterhaus*] and is driven into the proletariat, into the place away from home [*Fremde*] with his brothers and sisters."[9]

The socioeconomic overtones in this autobiographical statement from the 1940s demonstrate the continuity of his identification with Marxist conceptions of reality over his lifetime. Renner's political, legal, socioeconomic manner of describing himself and his setting was fixed in his youth. In 1890, he described himself in these lyrical lines:

> Through incurred debts
> House, Court, and Field were auctioned off
> The young ones were driven into the world
> And the old ones into the poorhouse.
>
> For a goodbye said the father:
> "God will help you further in life."
> And so when I was twelve years of age
> I nourished myself and was my own guide.[10]

The roots of Renner's sensitive appreciation of the reality of public institutions in the life of individuals did not come in 1890 or even in 1882, when he was dispossessed; it came in the initial development of his ego, when he first knew the world and his relationship to it. This process, during which a person distinguishes between his own thoughts and person and the objects and individuals beyond himself, is called introjection.[11] The child's ego has its own characteristic patterns of perception and its own sense of the significance of things in its world. The degree to which external or internal realities are important to the child, called introversion and extraversion, is constituted within the process of introjection. Thus introjection is central to the development of early character, giving distinct emphasis to the child's individual and social experiences.[12] Often, the child will identify with persons or objects of the environment so strongly that they are introjected as part of his ego, either as an association that becomes integral in all his dealings with the world or as an element of his own identity. These close identifications with others are fundamental to the forms that his future relationships will take.[13] Renner's introjection of certain family realities, mainly those that hinged on insecurity and loss, became the source of his inclination to structure his identity and to direct his life choices within the constructs of the public world.

Karl Renner was born as a twin on December 14, 1870, in Unter-Tannowitz, a German cultural pocket in southern Moravia. Sixteen children preceded the twins. His insecurity began with his place within the family: "The eternally similar course of the every day, the normal, makes the brain sleepy and the heart sluggish. The conditions of my birth . . . were not the usual and may awaken wonder in the present generation: I was the youngest child of my mother, and never sure if I was the seventeenth or eighteenth child."[14]

Armbands of different colors, red and blue, were placed on Renner and his brother Anton so they could be distinguished at the baptism. Karl, the youngest, wore the red armband. Immediately after the baptism the armbands fell off. Renner's statement implies that he was unsure if he indeed was Karl, for the identity of the twins was based on the judgment of one of his sisters. Because his twin died shortly afterward, the doubt was reinforced by the sense of loss that must have developed as he grew more conscious of his origins.[15] Renner ends the story of his birth and baptism by reflecting: "No one could know what deep meaning the red network of fabric [*Masche*] would win for my entire life."[16] He obviously means the symbolic red of socialism. At the deep emotional level, which reinforces more rational choices, the congruence of socialism's red and the primal proof of his identity may have had some significance in his choice of a political home, but more concrete reasons for his being a socialist stem from his family development, youthful experience, and values. These reasons are incorporated in Renner's choice of the word *Masche* as a synonym for the small ribbon (*Bändchen*) he introduces into the story. *Masche* can also mean a link of mail (in ancient armor), a net used to catch fish, or an expression of understanding (untangling the threads). Austrian Social Democracy provided all three alternative meanings for him: it was a defense against the uncaring, ordinary world of which he speaks when he introduces the conditions of his birth; it embraced the missionary character of early Catholicism, the socialists being "fishers of men"; and the social science which was its basis helped Renner to understand the fate of his family.

His membership in a large family contributed to his receptiveness to a close-knit party structure in which a "family" of decision makers controlled Austrian Social Democracy. His early experience as a member of an interdependent whole in which each person helped to fulfill the needs of the group, predisposed him to similar associations as he matured. But his ego development was not simply one of ease and joy with such associations, for in many ways his family organization introduced problems into his life. He was one among many, and no one had time to give him special attention. In this large family that struggled to keep the homestead together socially and economically, the interdependence was one of constant movement and change that seemed to have no clear purpose. His mother had to work even if she was sick or on the day of childbirth. Pursuit of a living took his father away for weeks at a time. His parents did not seem to enjoy their activity. The economic imperative of his lower-middle-class position and the threatening institutions to his family security were felt but not yet seen. He felt them in the anxiety of his parents, in the clumsy, frightened pace of his father that earned him the public ridicule of the townspeople, who nicknamed him *Schlunkermatz* (Matt Renner, who runs around like a ship without a rudder, caught in a storm).

Certainty was gained by linking himself to the invisible but omnipresent public world that he felt in his parents' emotions and actions. That is the world of which he speaks in his tribute to Karl Marx in 1908, when he voices his childhood pain: "A person on the street—it makes no sense! How can a man play his part of father of a family in the rubble of the street? Is that a home? . . . A man who lives in the street, where does he come from? Where is he going? No one knows, least of all himself."[18] Perhaps if he could grasp the world that so disoriented his parents, gain knowledge of it and power in it, he might bring happiness and security to himself and his family. In his youngest years, however, there was an intuitive yearning toward the force and authority of that world that might appease his emotional hunger and answer the silent questions of purpose and order that his developing ego required. In his autobiography he speaks of the sources of order and authority that he found in that world beyond his parents:

A child from religious parents, himself filled with a deep religiosity and wholly enmeshed in the myths and legends of the Catholic church, experienced during his years of study at the *Gymnasium* (into which he had gained admittance only through inexpressible hardships), the world of the classical age. This experience freed his thought and led him to the school of modern science and philosophy. It enabled him to learn at the university the science of state and society, and thereby, through his own study and acquired knowledge of socialist thought to come to the teachings of Karl Marx.[19]

The first organizing source of the public world was the Catholic church, not in its organizational hierarchy but in its stories that illustrated the meaning of everyday experience and gave hope for miraculous solutions to impossible situations. Renner was to become a constant teller of stories; his writings from the autobiographical to the most technical theory reflected the devices of story. He identified with these early stories, making himself a hero with a sense of place and purpose that the inattention of his family denied him, and appropriated the art of storytelling so that he could inform others, thus becoming a powerful person not only in story but in reality. In the early years of ego development, he discovered a form of power and personal identity by identifying with the aggressor, a behavioral ploy which psychoanalysts say enables a child to gain autonomy in the presence of threatening people or situations.[20] The aggressor was the invisible authority that controlled the emotions and attention of his parents; the authority of the church was appeasing in its stories that gave significance and order, but it was also threatening because it had answers whereas his parents had none. Another source of his propensity for storytelling, also associated with the behavior of identifying with the aggressor, was his imitation of his father, whose limited contact with Karl was as an educator and storyteller. Freud tells us that in the Oedipus complex between father and son, the son wins power with the weapons of his father; for at three years of age, when the son begins to express his genital autonomy, that is, his integrity and separateness from others, he has only the model of his father as a male.[21] He seizes his father's sword, as it were. His father told stories that were often self-demeaning or were nonsense tales (*schnuerrige Geschichte*). Karl describes his father as a knowledgeable man (*kenntnisreicher*) who lacked seriousness.[22] Karl's stories were the opposite—serious discussions that nevertheless functioned as stories.

Karl Renner's stories were implicit in his structuring of a factual account of events. Through the use of an artful juxtaposition of facts and hyperbole, everything that he said took on a multiple meaning, so that the simplest statement seemed to suggest several realms of experience. An obvious example is his rationale for writing his autobiography; by juxtaposing his individual person to World War II, with a dash of hyperbole, he suggests that by understanding his life we may also understand the causes and development of the struggle between fascism and democracy: "Events of special importance in the course of the past five years have given me courage to publish the memoirs of my youth, and present to the public the evolution of a single individual. My extraordinary career in extraordinary times, under extraordinary civic conditions, gives a vivid picture of the origin of these conditions in which we live and work today."[23]

A less obvious example may be seen in the sentence with which he introduces his birth, a story construction that harbors a deep insight into his view of the public world and how one may effect change in it. By describing ordinary reality as "the eternally similar course of the every day, the normal, [which] makes the brain sleepy and the heart sluggish" before the report of his birth, whose conditions were "not the usual and may awaken wonder in the present generation," he creates in the reader the expectation of something that has more than ordinary meaning. For Renner and for the analytic listener, the articulations of his life in these lines affirm the unique time and space of the *Maerchen* or fairy tale. "Once upon a time" (*Es war einmal*) occurs to us as we see that the day of his birth is at first related to all days that occur eternally, days that are common and deadening and in need of the extraordinary. His birth is also given a special meaning that occurs in fairy tales, that of mistaken identity, that of the youngest son, and that of twins separated from birth—universal themes in folklore.

The public world for Renner was always this twofold space—one was mundane, monotonous, and unchanging, and the other was a miraculous appearance within the ordinary world of a person or event that altered the former. But the unchanging world was never changed too much, and the force of the change was a passive miracle, the force of traditional elements making an almost predicted appearance. Renner approached political life with this view: the changes needed in society were to be ordinary outcomes, and the force of the change was to be the customary methods. The miraculous quality of the custom was in its heroic implementation by a protagonist who exemplified the qualities of a German burgher. His contemporaries were often aware of this quality in the presentation of his arguments. Oskar Helmer, an Austrian Social Democratic associate, commented on this trait in his recollection of introducing the young political aspirant Renner to the critical appraisal of a Social Democratic nominating committee in the provinces: "All opposition to Renner was dissipated as soon as he himself spoke, creating a picture of his own personality. It sounded like a fairy tale. Indeed, the good fairies had given humanity, courage, and truth to the child in the cradle of the poor farmer's family. But close by loomed the dark specter of misery."[24] Story, then, was used as a way of linking his identity to the power of tradition, the conventional plot, the customary hero; his identity became magnified in his own eyes, and he met each situation in life accompanied by the charm and confidence his connection to traditional outcomes gave him. The social changes which Austrian Social Democrats expected of his leadership were to be obstructed by his half-conscious identification with tradition. History could not change culture too much because it harbored stories that had fixed patterns, and thus his handling of events remained metaphorical because he dealt not only with objective situations but with the elements of story that undergirded them.

The second major source of authority that helped to organize Renner's world was education. His love of learning and the security that he derived from it began in his home. Although neither of his parents had time to oversee the children's schoolwork, their verbal encouragement gave him direction. "My father owned a thick book, a topography of Moravia," he writes. "As soon as I learned to read, this book became my favorite reading matter. Before I had set foot out of my immediate neighborhood, I knew the name and location of most of the cities and monasteries of our homeland. The surrounding world where I grew up had in this manner become an integral part of my mind." Renner's absorption with topography, his ability to locate himself in geometric space, reflects his hunger for a public world that could provide him with the security his childhood world lacked. By knowing the names of the towns and their distances from one another, he could know where his father was during his long journeys and accompany him in imagination. That knowledge of location gave him a sense of control over his life and the habit of linking issues and events to an abstract geography. We see in an account of his father's business an indication that the obtrusiveness of his topographical thinking functions in a metaphorical manner:

My father took over the wine trade from my grandfather and was required to travel by horse and wagon to Silesia, thus remained away from home for long periods. This situation did not alter, even when the railroad extended itself to northern Moravia. The distance Vienna-Bruenn, which by Brannewitz (two and one-half hours of travel away) approached our location, was already opened; the distance Bruenn-Olmuetz had been finished in 1851; in 1854 the railroad was extended further northward; in 1868 there were on the soil of old Austria 4,533 kilometers of track, in 1875 10,336 kilometers of track, and by 1890 20,000 kilometers had been built. In spite of that my father's business was transformed in 1870 from a transport business to that of a wine merchant.[25]

Renner's reflections upon persons and issues in the world often reflected this quality of abstraction as if he wished to affirm his ability to measure the thing and define its place and thereby demonstrate control of the physical reality. To some degree, all learning served that function for Renner; as a youth it was a definite compensation for an uncertain environment:

On the day after I knew of the loss of our family home, I lay in bed with a light fever. But youth! . . . On the second day I took my school bag and went [to the *Gymnasium*]. . . . I went to my desk and sat down. Professor Zelenka came in and began to describe, in a wonderful voice, the double-sexed life of the algae, this wonder of the pond-ooze, this harbinger of the highest development of organic life. I was immediately his prisoner. And Professor Kornitzer came and lectured on Livius, enchanting me with ancient Rome with its stories of heroes. *And over the gaping chasm of my thought* spread the magic of a thousand years of science and art—the healing cover of forgetting.[26]

The third source of authority and order Renner discovered in his search for an explanation of his life was the science of society. He was to arrive at this science slowly over the course of his education, but the scientific attitude began as early as his loss of his family home. He was forced to compare his situation in the world with that of others his age. Comparison is the root of all knowledge. When he spent summers at the home of his maternal uncle, Leopold Habiger, in northern Moravia, he would attempt to compare the life situation and cause of the Habigers with those of his parents. The Habiger household became the prototype of the ordered state in Renner's eyes: "What deliberation, what constancy, what decisiveness in comparison to the conditions of my place of origin." Using metaphors that suggest its social significance and profound importance in his life, Renner praised the Habiger household and environs: "Impressive was the fact that the whole property of the Habigers was laid out in a single, undivided piece that extended from either end of the main house, which itself was built four-cornered, in the four directions of the compass . . . my place of origin (on the other hand) had streets where the houses were stuck together and the neighbors continually saw and heard one another, whereas in the case of my father's house the building itself could be divided in the middle into two families."[27]

Renner called the inside of the Habiger house "another world" and detailed the layout and furnishings of each room. The house had been built in 1648; the Habiger family was among the first waves of German settlers in Moravia after the German victory over the Czechs at White Mountain. The house and family seemed to be a living symbol of German culture in the Austrian state. The atmosphere of the family, as depicted by Renner, seemed to be an archetype of *Ur-Germanentum*: "One did not refer to Herr Habiger as father; everyone, even his wife and daughter, call him 'farmer' [*Bauer*]. 'Farmer' designated in the wholly patriarchal sense 'father' and 'master of the house.' He had an authority over all the inhabitants of the house that was quite unknown in my homeland. His wife was called 'woman' [*Frau*] and behaved as one who is much lower in status. The domestic servants formed a regular hierarchy."[28]

Renner's transference of the paternal role to Herr Habiger began after his first summer there, just before his physical separation from his immediate family's house in Unter-Tannowitz. Renner contrasts his feelings upon preparing to leave the Habiger household with those at his return to Unter-Tannowitz:

Never in my life had I been able to carry on my studies in such a secure state of mind, in such leisure and in such a state of physical well-being. . . . Physically, I had grown so that the clothes I had come in were too small. My uncle allowed me to have a suit made with the village tailor—its cost and pattern were in no way expensive, but at least it was big enough. My uncle took me in his wagon to the train at Zwittau, bought me a ticket, pressed two Gulden in my hand, and put me on the coach. And so I returned, not without a certain melancholy and not without apprehension for my immediate future, to Unter-Tannowitz. With a feeling of dread I entered the house of my father. There I found no one [*niemand*] home except my mother and father, my eldest brother Matthias and my sister

Anna. Mother and father were depressed with their grief and misery. Matthias was sick and thin as a skeleton, Anna . . . obviously tortured by a secret burden. Hour by hour my anxiety grew.[29]

The world of his parents, and what it represented, was to be a constant presence in Karl Renner's life, for it was the bedrock insecurity of reality. To deny that reality was to deny the source of family love, as difficult as living that love was, because of social-economic pressure. Renner's lifelong involvement in social issues was to correct the pain he knew as a victim. The world of Uncle Habiger often tempted Renner to leave the distressing realities of society for a private security. When he was older, he almost entered the Habsburg administrative system because of the social and economic certainty it would provide. Uncle Habiger was a force that did leave a permanent imprint, however, upon Renner's thought and actions. The Habiger household formed an integral part of Renner's superego, those rules and images that constitute the invisible voice of authority in what should exist in behavior, what is right.[30] He experienced the Habiger household in the years immediately before and during puberty, a time of the formation of this element of the ego, in what may be called a second phase of introjection.[31] The child psychologist Jean Piaget refers to these years as those of formal reasoning, when the youth begins to form values and ideas that relate him to all mankind.[32] The conservative values and lifestyle Uncle Habiger represented promised decisiveness, order, continuity, freedom from loss, a secure state of mind. Although socialism promised alleviation of his parent's situation, the way socialism would order the lives of its citizens took on the look of the Habiger reality when conceived by Renner. The traditional German character of Uncle Habiger's mores reinforced Renner's earlier ego trait of relying upon custom and the stories of the public culture to determine meaning.

Whenever he left the "healing cover of forgetting" that the Habiger household or his schooling provided, he faced the insecure reality of a state where inequities and lack of opportunity reigned: "As I left the closing ceremonies, after taking my leave of my teachers, with the *Matura* certificate in my hands, I didn't think of the conditions under which I had entered secondary school, or the troubles, suffering, and humiliations of my young years and still less on the triumph I had won and surely had earned—a sudden emptiness filled my soul, an infinite anxiety [*ewige Bangigkeit*], almost a torturing anguish [*qualende Angst*]. I should leave a surrounding [*Lebenskreis*] that had filled me so completely and had so satisfied me and saw before the void [*das voellige Nichts*]."[33]

Renner had also known fear and emptiness upon the loss of his inherited faith in Catholicism. His soul-searching at that time revealed the well of abstraction from whose waters Renner would always find nourishment. Renner turned to the symbolic treasures provided by his *Bildung* to find some other universal paternal cloak for his nakedness:

I read Lessing's *Nathan the Wise* and the tale of the three rings thrilled me. . . . It was true without doubt that each of the rings was equal in value to the other. But the ring is only a symbol—the same truth can appear in many, different symbols—but what is it in itself, what is the truth? And what is it in the story of Lessing that cloaks itself in the symbol of the spiritual and wise father? In the full moon of an Easter night, following my loss of religious faith, I wandered alone up the holy mountain . . . seated myself on a stone in front of the church and brooded. . . . "The time has arrived, when a new religion must come into the world, a religion which by means of science can bridge the gap between the Jewish, Arabic, and Indian heroes' tales and unite the three rings into one. Probably somewhere the founder is already born."[34]

In truth, the founder in Renner was already born, having emerged from the pond-ooze of the *Gymnasium* equipped with the intellectual tools that would soon create a unified personal world within Austrian Social Democracy. But upon his graduation from the *Gymnasium*, the most obvious medium to fill the personal vacuum was the state. And so Karl Renner turned to the haven of the Austrian military service. He enrolled as a one-year enlisted man (*Einjaehrig-Freiwilliger*), deciding to fulfill his obligation to the state before entering a university, where he would again have to face the world as an orphan struggling alone for his existence. Renner, moreover, felt that now he was a young adult and that he must come into contact with the state and gain knowledge of it. In the summer before he entered the military, he prepared himself for this direct encounter with the adult world in the same manner that he had once employed in defending himself against the voids of his childhood world of Moravia. He translated the approaching world of the state and its obligations into a palpable abstraction: "To become acquainted with the state seemed the most important thing at this time. So in the second half of my vacation I began to visit the office of the mayor of Kunzendorf, and often walked to Maehrisch-Truebau to stare at the outside of the district commissioner's office, the tax office, and the district law court."[35]

As Renner matured and moved into the world, his fascination for topographical abstraction was at times replaced by seeing the presence of the state in its artifacts. The invisible whole was in the part. His relation to custom was similar. Practicing the customary act made one a protected member of the institutional whole. He seldom neglected custom, and his participation gave him peace of mind. Thus he relates that on his graduation from the *Gymnasium*, "we remained sitting together for a long time even though the atmosphere had long since dissipated, and drank a great deal more beer, which was our duty, because the custom so demanded." Likewise, he became a member of the Austrian military, "the custom of my homeland demanded that the recruit give himself 'a good day' on the evening before his enlistment. I allowed this to happen." [36]

In September 1889 Karl Renner left for Vienna to serve in the main supply depot of the army. He was to spend his next fifty years in Vienna, where the customs of this German city rounded out his identity—the customs of the "good old Viennese families, whose classical literature and music, liberal mode of thought, social graces, and a *moderate* national consciousness sought to keep alive the old traditions." [37]

His post appealed to him; it was suited to the conceptual talents he had developed through his adolescence. Only now instead of the topography of Moravia, the entire Austrian state became his passion. And instead of the geometry lessons of the *Gymnasium*, a new spatial presence absorbed his attention. The supply depot was Renner's introduction to mass economy and mass organization. His one year of duty was to introduce him to his future state:

Gradually, my partial knowledge [of the supply depot] became a knowledge of the whole organization, and this became my sole interest: The machinery of supply for a garrison in peace and an army in the field is an economic activity that in its magnitude and through its organizational interplay of wheels and spokes is quite impressive. . . . So it was that in the supply depot I first became inclined to political thought; basically this is not so astonishing, and it will always be the case. For the military service is the most exclusive and at the same time the most serious requisition the state makes on the citizen, and must awaken in those who are capable of thinking at all, political thought. In this service, one not only deals with the various forms in which life can be molded, but also one has the duty to die for the state. Only the thoughtless and superficial nature can serve his time without concerning himself critically with the state. [38]

At the end of his year in the military, Renner decided to attend the University of Vienna, in the faculty of law, and carry on his study of the state. Characteristically, Renner found in the idea of his future study a vehicle that would serve to embrace all life: "One had to study political economy and law in order to understand the state in its individuality— that was what one needed in order to accomplish something in the world. My decision strengthened not to study philosophy, rather law. *Only thereby could one grasp and form living essences.*" [39]

The legal and organizational antecedents of the Austrian state and of Western culture in general were to provide a synthesis of all the previous moments of Renner's self-definition. Through them he would acquire a context of identity and a lexicon for self-assertion that would be a permanent crust over the former abyss of self-doubt. An example is the historical treasure of canon law: "I attended lectures on canon law given by Gross. The subject was strange to me for some time, I couldn't get at its inmost essence, until I recognized in it the organizational art of a world power: I learned to admire their art of adapting to the thousandfold changing forms of state from the Roman Empire to the laws of family of the early Middle Ages, to feudalism, and up to the state of the present day."[40]

His seminar in constitutional law with Eugen Phillipovich, one of the leading academic socialists of his day,[41] introduced Renner to the ideas that would be the beads of his Marxist rosary for the remainder of his life under the Habsburgs—the problematic of nationality contra state as formulated by his "liberal" predecessors in constitutional theory (see Chapter 2). The eventual theoretical formulation of Renner in the area of nationality and state that Oscar Jaszi has termed a "brilliant solution" to the problems that plagued the Austrian state proves on closer study of its historical antecedents to be more a work of "biblical annotation" in the spirit of his fathers than a creation of something new.[42]

It is consistent with Renner's character that the first socialist writer to impress him was Ferdinand Lassalle rather than Karl Marx. Lassalle sought a symbiosis of state authority and German socialist ideas, a union of Bismarck and *Kultur* for the masses.[43] Renner described the joy of his discovery of Lassalle in his first years at the university:

Here was a goal, a purpose in life, a task which intoxicated me immediately. Wasn't I too from the depths of the people; hadn't I sought too in the dark the way to science? And here sounded the call above, from the heights of the collective *Bildung* of the time, a call that would raise me to its heights so that I never again would go under. Science and the people, science and the worker! . . . Even the most callous reader, who through disappointment in his early development has become a skeptic, will appreciate the intellectual and moral force such a goal might have on a young man whose intellectual development had taken the course that mine had.[44]

Lassalle dealt in areas of conceptualization that were much more sympathetic to Renner than the epistemological and psychological implications of Hegelian Marxism—the brand of Marxism that Renner heard from his University of Vienna contemporary, Max Adler. Renner met Max Adler in 1893 and formed with him part of the small nucleus of students interested in socialism, who called themselves the Free Association of Socialist Students (Freie Vereinigung Sozialistischer Studenten). The group existed in a quasi-political relation to the Austrian Social Democratic party under the immediate sponsorship of Engelbert Pernerstorfer.

They met at a local coffee house called zum heiligen Leopold in Leopold-stadt, a district of Vienna; it was there that Renner was first introduced to the socialist world through a *Gymnasium* student of the Sperlgymna-sium in Leopoldstadt whom he had been tutoring. Renner was to partic-ipate with his new comrades in a "systematic study of Karl Marx's *Das Kapital*, the belles lettres of socialism, and the famous journal of Kautsky and Mehring, *Die Neue Zeit*."[45] But the philosophical-revolutionary per-spective of Max Adler and the other Jewish intellectuals who made up this group was at odds with Karl Renner's respect for the concrete consti-tutional value of the traditional forms of state. For Renner, the state was not in the Hegelian sense an idea that constantly found a new embodi-ment; rather, it was a set of institutions whose basic elements were eternal building blocks. In this respect he stood close to the English constitutional thought of Burke, and indeed, Renner admired English constitutional ideas throughout his life.[46] Renner counterposed the ideas of John Stuart Mill to the Hegelian dialectics nourished by his Austro-Marxist fellows. Writing in his autobiography as though the Austro-Marxist contributions of Max Adler and Friedrich Adler had never existed, Renner states: "I find it deplorable that the socialism of Karl Marx, whose whole teaching is a powerful *induction* from the facts of economic life . . . even today is still interpreted in the abstract-destructive (*sic*) sense of Hegel, and that no one has yet translated Marx into the John Stuart Mill style of the *con-crete inductive* method.[47]

Although most of the major questions of existence were gradually allayed by the university *Bildung* and the promise of Austrian Social De-mocracy, Renner still experienced the anxieties of his adolescence when faced with solitary day-to-day existence in Vienna. In 1891, when he first entered the university, he spent much time walking the streets of Vienna: "As often as I passed a house, whether it be a palace or a cottage, I had the desire to see how the people inside lived. All during my life that has been a burning curiosity with me."[48]

The public world provided Renner with the tools and rationale for life. The uncertainty but warmth of loved ones still provided the neces-sary emotion. Renner saw his internal needs reflected in the homes that he passed, and in that year he formed a lasting relation with Luise Stoisis, a young woman whose family resembled the Habigers: "There was an intimacy of family feeling that [my wife's family] shared with the people of the land [*Voelklein*] at that time . . . a singularly deep emotional life and a devotion to the ancient customs [*uralten Sitten*]. Passionate feelings united the sexes and a bountiful blessing of children was the rule. The parents even enjoyed a great respect with their adult children."[49]

Luise was to provide an emotional depth as well as a family that satisfied Renner's longing for a stable household. Adolf Schaerf, an Austrian Social Democratic contemporary of Renner, wrote that he would have been lost without the constant support Luise provided him. Schaerf described Luise as a classic German *Frau* in the mode of Frau Habiger, who practiced submission (*Hingabe*), the spirit of sacrifice (*Opfermut*), and the willingness to be neglected (*Hintanstellung*) while Renner pursued his career.[50] Without this emotional support and private domain, Renner would have brought more energy but even more problems to the family of Austrian Society Democracy. Renner's relaxed acceptance of Otto Bauer's assumption of party leadership in the early 1920s reflects emotional balance or perhaps the lassitude of which Bauer accused him.[51] An emotional solution made at the expense of others can never be healthy, however, and the way Renner organized his family was reflected in his politics: the activity of others had to be within his policy. Immanuel Kant's warning about the debilitating effect of "self-incurred" tutelage must be the regulative idea in considering the health of Karl Renner's family solution to emotional balance.[52]

Renner did not marry Luise at first in a recognized ceremony because by 1891 he had already formed socialist ideas and was repelled by the thought of establishing a bourgeois marriage. He may also have been hesitant to commit himself to a family because of the memory of his parents' failure to realize a stable household for their children. Not all aspects of the bourgeois life were abhorrent to Renner, however, for he accepted the security of state employment throughout the 1890s. While a tutor in the early 1890s he articulated that hesitation that would keep him from joining the bourgeois with a formal commitment: "Would I be able to be a divided man, externally an accommodating teacher without the privilege of his own opinion and internally a burning brand of revolutionary ideas, who must stand apparently in a society of people in complete contradiction to the ideas I would live?"[53]

This seed of dissonance which was nourished by his anger and pain of childhood deprivation, sublimated to the cause of all who had and did suffer in a similar manner, kept him moving toward the commitment to Austrian Social Democracy. His respect for authority and order and his fear of economic hardship, especially when he became a father, however, kept him linked to the bourgeois world: "For the time being I would have to win for myself a secure economic position in society from which I then could be effective [for the interests of the proletariat]."[54]

Thus, while currying his Marxist contacts in the university and in the recently established Austrian Social Democratic party, Renner continued to make a place for himself in Austria. For instance, he sought to become an officer in the reserves—a position ordinarily held only by bourgeois of some means.

His zeal for a secure position in the bourgeois from which he might be effective also led to a post in the Library of Parliament, where he worked from December 1895 until 1906, when he ran successfully for a seat as a member of Parliament under the sponsorship of the Austrian Social Democratic party. Renner was proud of his position as civil servant in the Library of Parliament. His book of memoirs, *An der Wende Zweier Zeiten* (At the turning point of two epochs), ends at the moment he accepts the job. The title, in part, implies the end of youth and the beginning of manhood as he leaves the university world behind and finds his role in the state.[55] The acceptance of the post at the parliamentary library necessitated several changes in Renner's life, among them the impossibility of overt political action as long as he was employed, because "I must serve all political parties equally. Nevertheless, I decided to apply for the job immediately."[56]

Renner also was required to make a legal marriage out of his hitherto common law relationship with Luise, a demand he seemed to fulfill with relief. He completes the account of the end of his youth with his interview with Baron Gautsch, the minister of the interior, who with tongue in cheek regarding Renner's "moral" oversight, congratulated him on his entrance to state service: "His proud, noble [*hoheitsvoll*] appearance impressed me greatly, and he bestowed a few words to me with a smile: 'Your appointment has caused a few difficulties! I expect that you will justify the trust of your sponsors.' With this momentous act my youth was ended, and this wish 'from the mouth of authority' [*aus hohem Munde*] led me over to manhood." He added a last comment on this moment of truth: "Who would be satisfied with me in the future, Phillipovich [a career in law], Pernerstorfer [a career in Austrian Social Democracy] or Gautsch [a career in the service of the Austrian state]? The future would decide."[57]

The phrasing of Renner's question, written many years after the event, shows the place of traditional story in ordering his universe. His division of the choices into three recalls Lessing's story of the three rings, which Renner had pondered on the night he lost faith in Catholicism. But for Renner, the extrovert, there was no fourth realm beyond law, the state, or social evolution. Neither one nor the others but all three would prevail in a compromise whose fulcrum was in Renner's freedom to shape his public and private life as he willed. Austrian Social Democracy was the viable vehicle for the amalgam, a Social Democracy that was legal, conservative, yet productive of change. Renner as an extrovert knew how to use the elements of his environment for his purposes. His abilities of adaptation had been consciously cultivated since his youthful years as a tutor for the wealthy: "Surely, nothing is so useful for the physical and intellectual development of a young man as the frequent change of environment and the conditions of his fortune. It not only enriches his experience, *it heightens his ability of adaptation* and powers of resistance, it strengthens his self-confidence so that even in the most trying of circumstances it will not leave him."[58]

His adaptation was often close to simple accommodation, but slowly using the materials of society, he sought a social reality that he could believe in and that expressed the complexity of his person. He found himself able to adapt to all three modes of thought and action, which in the Austrian state was not so difficult as Renner would have it seem, disregarding even his talents of accommodation. During his service at the parliamentary library, Renner moved up on the civil servant's ladder from the tenth to the eighth level and to the eventual salary of 3,600 Kronen a year, which provided a more than comfortable bourgeois existence. He also published ten books and articles under various pseudonyms, dealing with topics of the state and society. The pseudonyms were a polite official evasion, for the milieus of Gautsch, Philippovich, and Pernerstorfer all knew and admired his publication. Of the reception of his *Der Kampf der osterreichischer Nationen um den Staat* (*The Struggle of the Austrian Nations over the State*), published in 1902, Renner wrote:

This book brought me into contact with the highest levels of the bureaucracy (Koerber, Bilinski, Baernreiter, Franz Klein) and the highest military authorities like Schoenaich, Auffenberg and others. . . .

It brought me into contact with the leading men of all the Austrian nations, as Kramar and Masaryk, Vajda and Hlinka, etc., and also well-known foreign writers as the Englishman Seton-Watson and the Frenchman Louis Bisenmann, who had written many valuable books on Austria. This work of constitutional law caused Professor Bernatzik to suggest that I use it as an inaugural theme [*Habilitierung*] that might gain me admission to the law faculty of the university.[59]

In spite of the favor of these various other interests—such as academia or the Austrian bureaucracy in which he had such a good beginning—Renner chose in 1906 to embrace a career within Austrian Social Democracy. Why? The answer must be sought in a correlation of Renner's background and personality with the archetypal personality projected by the Austrial Social Democratic patriarchs and the institutional pattern developed by the Austrian Social Democratic party. Renner had discussed his possible future in the party with Victor Adler as early as 1894 and had since that time proven himself to have the qualities Adler desired in a party oligarch. Renner's doctoral degree in law, which he acquired in 1896 shortly after his employment in the parliamentary library, his meritorious service at the library, and the many scholarly works that he produced before 1906 were the proofs of a responsible maturity. Moreover, men such as Adler and Pernerstorfer served as spiritual mentors who gave a meaningful goal to his own development;[60] and the structure of Austrian Social Democracy, a party in its first flower (yet with a truly Austrian stem), would allow Renner to explore the many rooms of his father's house, some of which still needed an interior designer.

Thus Renner was nominated in 1906 to represent the Austrian Social Democratic party as a delegate from Neunkirchen in elections for the Austrian Parliament. He was successful and represented Nuenkirchen through two parliamentary elections, holding this office until the end of World War I. Renner also served as a member of the Lower Austrian *Landtag* as a Social Democrat from 1908 through World War I. As an active member in the educational offices of the Austrian Social Democratic party, Renner contributed as an editor and journalist, teacher and speaker. He was one of the editors of *Der Kampf* from 1907 until 1919, wrote regularly for the *Arbeiter-Zeitung*, and participated in the various Austrian Social Democratic *Bildung* associations in Vienna.[61] In all these functions Renner brought to the workers, bourgeoisie, and intellectuals of Austria the echo of his own life theme: Return to the well of your fathers. Recognize by means of *Bildung* provided by your German *Kultur* the potential of the Austrian state with its vanguard the Austrian Social Democratic party to achieve a progressively higher civilization. Then your dispossessions will be at an end.

Of revolution, Renner spoke not at all. The conquest of the state, the proletarian revolution, was to him a process of legal osmosis. Renner was to tell Friedrich Adler in 1937 when asked to join the underground resistance movement against the Nazis: "Illegality is unavoidable, it is necessary, even though it has little value now. It cannot, however, be perpetrated by people who have aged in forty years of legality. If I am not capable of a certain kind of action, then I remove myself from it."[62]

It seems odd at first glance that Renner chose the ideas of Karl Marx as a framework within which to develop his language of adaptation, his language of national resurrection—Marx, who exposed the temporal egotism of legality and the state, who rejected the metaphors of nationality as a limited consciousness of man's true relation to society. Had another mode of thought been predominant in Austrian Social Democracy at the time of Renner's contact with it, he probably would not have been an Austro-Marxist.[63] But as we examine his Austro-Marxist creations, we will discover that Marx proved flexible enough for the world of Karl Renner; Marx, after all, was a German and a product of the same *Bildung*.

3

Renner and the
Interpretation of the State

The themes of Karl Renner's theoretical writings were directed toward the public world that sustained his identity. His attachment to society and its norms recalls Freud's term for individuals who have a firm belief in their indissoluble bond with the external world: "Out of this world, we cannot fall."[1] As he matured in Vienna, he became a doctor of law, a civil servant, a member of Parliament, and a participant in the oligarchy of the Austrian Social Democratic party. His writings dwell on the negative shadow of the public institutions that nourished him, as well as on the positive changes that might be made through them. Three themes pervade: (1) the relation of the individual Austrian citizen, especially the German, to his nationality and the subsequent relation of nationality to the Cisleithanian state; (2) man's alienation from the physical possession of property as reflected by the evolution of the legal concept of property; and (3) a historical and legal rationalization of the Austrian Social Democratic political program, especially its support of parliamentarianism as a method of realizing a democratic union of nationalities within the Cisleithanian state.

Renner's *Staat und Nation* introduced his labyrinthine theories and in the classic tradition of first works also reflects the author's personal genesis. In *Staat und Nation* Renner uses legal language to formulate a constitutional change in the status of the Austrian nationalities but interweaves theoretical and often contradictory sociological and psychological appreciations of nationality. Renner's reputation as a political theorist was made on the basis of his legal pronouncements; thus this analysis will begin with a survey of these major ideas.

Of state and nation, the primary essence for Renner was the nation, qua nationality; the state was merely a legal expression, in territorial terms, of certain interest groups that exercised their will and possession over property. Renner emphasized that nationality must not be confused with territorial boundaries, although this was the western European nations' concept of nationality.[2] Such a perspective limited nationality to arbitrary boundaries of historical chance. Rather than a nationality derived from territory, Renner proposed a nationality that was supraterritorial, derived solely from a corporation of individuals who shared the same language and customs. Territory and state should be subordinated to this more basic reality. Thus the Cisleithanian state, a historic creation of power, must realign its structure to accommodate the nationalities that formed its flesh and blood.

In the period under consideration, the Cisleithanian state embraced its nationalities within seventeen constitutional subdivisions known as the crown lands, territorial entities inherited by the Habsburg rulers from the holdings of the feudal aristocracy assimilated in the evolution of their state. Each of the crown lands had a legislature (*Landtag*) that was empowered to draft laws pertinent to the inhabitants of its own territory but not to interpret or administer these laws because the judicial and executive function resided with the emperor and the centralized bureaucracy of the state.[3] Thus the crown lands had no real autonomy in the sense of being self-administering units, such as federalist structure might provide (as in the United States or even the counties of England). This system was particularly impractical for the Habsburg Empire because several nationalities made up the population of each crown land, and in this era of growing national consciousness, each sought to articulate its identity through the most immediate source of state power—its legislature. In Bohemia, for example, there was a bitter rivalry between the Germans and Czechs, and although the Germans were in the minority, they had enough power to stalemate the legislature for more than sixty years.[4] Moreover, because the nationalities were dependent on the legislature for funds for their cultural needs such as schools and churches, many of the minority nationalities had no chance for satisfaction of their demands within a crown land dominated by another nationality—thus the Slav nationals in German areas such as Lower Austria had little hope for maintaining their cultural desires.

Renner felt that the nationalities, the Germans in particular, were misguided in attempting to control the *Landtag* of the crown lands as a means of realizing their national demands. Such a policy limited national aspirations to the historical chance of territory, and even if successful, they still were subject to the whims of the Habsburgs. Renner was also critical of the nationalist groups such as the Pan-Germans, who sought a union with Germany as an escape from the frustrating crown land system.[5] Renner rejected such a union as the goal of the Germans in Austria because it was too limited: "If the German-Austrians were democratic instead of chauvinistic the mission of the German nation [*Deutschtum*] would not end at Bodenbach, rather at the Bosphorus. Since they have not grasped this, they wish to fly home to the lap of mother Germany, *a position of desertion* [*ein fahnenfleuchtiger Post*]!"[6]

Renner's democratic means of realizing German cultural growth within the Cisleithanian state was in the context of his proposals for all nationalities. He would first create between the crown lands and the local communities new territorial units called districts (*Kreisen*), which he referred to as *Mittelstelle*.[7] The districts would be created according to economic, trade, and financial considerations and would be the new seat of territorial legislative, judicial, and executive government. The district would be more autonomous than the crown land had been, with an initiative responsibility in all phases of local government that made its relation to the central bureaucracy of the state that of a limited federalism. By rendering the historical crown land empty as a constitutional form with any effective force, Renner hoped to neutralize its tendency to seduce the nationalities of its territory into a parochial identification with its territorial boundaries. The aspirations of nationality would then be free for Renner's next theoretical stroke—the establishment of "national corporations" on the model of the Catholic church (whose organization had fascinated Renner when he was in the university).[8] Although the nationalities might be scattered over the various districts (*Kreisen*) that made up the new governmental structure of the Cisleithanian state, they would form a higher unity, a solid body that transcended the physical limitation of their particular district. Thus the individual member of a nationality in Austria would have a dual allegiance, subject to the law of the community, district, and central state authority and also as a member of his national corporation subject to its laws.

Renner called this dual allegiance the "personality principle." It was so named, ostensibly, because the legal identity of the individual in the state would be derived from his "organic" relation to his "cultural and language community." Such a focus for the inhabitants of the state was juxtaposed by Renner to the "territorial principle," in which the individual's legal basis in the state was framed by the authority of the central state power either with no necessary cognizance of individual nationality or with a cognizance of a nationality defined by the chance of territory rather than the more primary reality of language and culture. The personality principle was a legal term that had its origin in the Carolingian Empire. There it had acquired a meaning that suited the metaphorical needs of Renner's feelings of nationality and his hunger for law that would meet all the requirements of his abstract world: "In the Carolingian Empire, a judge who decided the legal disposition of the individual would ask, '*Quo jure vivis?*' According to what law do you live? Then the party gave his declaration of nationality. Then the judge knew according to what law the party must be sentenced. This served as the so-called personality principle. Under this principle the Carolingian Empire governed ten nations with different languages and different laws."[9]

The subjective nature of his choice of language, in particular legal borrowings such as the personality principle, raises questions. What was "personality"? In particular, what was Renner's "personality"? This question always intrigued Renner, as attested by his continuous production of autobiographical poetry and prose. Of relevance in this regard is a letter Renner wrote to Victor Adler in 1901, in which he politely admonished Adler for not allowing publication of his poem praising Adler as a personality:

Naturally, I am quite crushed. You are a true Cato and—pardon me—harmful to the cause, in that you desire to keep your person in the background. With us . . . all is unfortunately personality—but why should the party allow this advantage to escape them, since they have the favor to have one such personality (and the misfortune, to have only one such personality). . . . My opinion is: A party that represents a new world should not appeal only to the head, but also to the heart, above all to the imagination. We are too abstract. Tell me can a man sing better of abstract freedom and equality or the concrete. . . .

Only that is poetry which *actually comes to presence*; what is beautiful to us can only appear in persons, individually or in the mass.[10]

Renner's lyrical appeal is to the absent father, personified by Victor Adler, to whose appreciative eye he wanted to demonstrate his gifts. All the many dimensions of Renner could be integrated with party activity but would come to presence only within the primary atmosphere of a family setting. Austrian Social Democracy was never a complete family for Renner. In a metaphorical sense the personality principle expressed his relation to Victor Adler and his Austro-Marxist cohorts: he was a nation to himself, using Social Democratic activity to integrate the needs of his background and present into an effective person respected by those around him. Objectively, he could do so because he and the others shared the same broad social values and aims and his mores were of the same normative inheritance as those of most other German-Austrians. A second metaphorical use of the personality principle was in the desire Renner and others within Austrian Social Democracy shared to keep the German culture distinct and powerful in the public life of Austria. The personality principle theoretically allowed every nation to preserve a separate national character, but the unspoken assumption was that the Germans would neither suffer mixture with the other national characters because of Austrian laws furthering integration nor lose their dominance in Austria's established public language. These metaphorical threads weakened the concept as a viable idea to achieve equity for all nations in Austria.

When the concept was examined by his contemporaries, it was seen that no individual really lived or believed in practices that were distinct from the territorial activities in which he or she engaged. Renner, when pressed, could not name purely German cultural activities that were distinct from cultural activities pursued by all Austrians given the socioeconomic realities of the culture. Critics attacked especially Renner's theory of national corporations—the primary organic unity wherein the individual took his identity and thence his constitutional identification as personality. Renner's theory of national corporations was termed "a solution outside of space" and a "Platonic realm theory."[11] Renner's critics could not conceive how or where the national corporations would exist. They saw only a single Habsburg taxpayer who owned or rented a house on a certain street, who was protected by the police of the state and the state's fire company, who voted in the elections that placed delegates in the district legislature or the state Parliament, who worked in some capacity of the state economy, and so on. Where was the national corporation located and what did it do? To whom and for what did the citizen owe national allegiance? Renner answered some of these objections with a series of articles that explained more fully the physical organization of the national corporation. In his article "Die innere Gebietspolitik mit besonderen Ruecksicht auf Oesterreich" (The Politics of internal areas with particular regard to Austria), Renner stated that "when we speak of a state, a city, or a street, we always mean a piece of ground" (*ein Stueck Erdboden*). He then proceeded to his favorite task—the topographical study of the Cisleithanian state and a geometric division of the lands according to his theory. Perhaps hoping to silence the critics who called his schemes Platonic, Renner added another detail to the notion of the national corporation— within the districts (*Kreisen*) separate lands would be set aside, in the manner of national parks, for the national corporations. In these special areas the culture of the separate nationalities would thrive. These lands would include about one-fourth of the Cisleithanian state and be free of any authority other than that of the nationality.

One can see shining like a dark star within the addenda Renner published in the months after *Staat und Nation* the question he never answered: what is national culture in the modern state? Nowhere in Renner's writings do we find what activities would take place in these separate national lands. Picnics? Tribal rituals? Culture and state, divided in Renner's conception, were entities that were supposedly synonymous for a Marxist, at least in the pages of Marx's classical theory. For the orthodox Marxist culture was essentially an empty concept that embraced all the patterns of daily existence for the individual of the modern state—the economic, political, social—everything that was immediately experienced in one's environment. Renner's separation of culture from state, his positing of a dual allegiance in the day-to-day life of the Austrian citizen, is a metaphorical key to his own dualism of mind in this period before his entrance to Parliament and successful career in the Austrian Social Democratic party. During these first years as a theoretician, Renner still grappled with the ghosts of his past—the ambient never-never land of the national corporation, a future home where all dreams might be realized— and the objective presence of the state that had not yet become a true home.

Renner shifted his position to the state in his writings after 1907, concentrating his plans of national autonomy more within the state's objective framework, and dropped forever his notion of the separate national lands. This change, no doubt, was both a result of his subconscious recognition that the state was an effective means of satisfying his needs and the embarrassing realization that his earlier position contradicted Marxist principles. He wrote in 1908: "The pure personality principle as I earlier described [i.e., the creation of national lands] is impossible to achieve within a bourgeois society; it would be possible only in a socialist order, where there were no private owners of property. Thus, in the present economic condition of our society we must turn to more realizable measures within the context of the state in order to protect nationalities."[13]

These "more realizable measures" dealt with the areas of language and *Bildung*. Renner joined the other Austrians who were interested in promoting national rights in the most prominent arena of nationality conflicts—the questions of one official state language versus the requirement of two or more languages for every state official and of guaranteeing the national minorities of a crown land their own schools. These themes (language and its conceptual products) were the nearest Renner ever came to dealing specifically with national culture. His stance on these issues, despite Marxist circumlocutions, was the same as that of every German nationalist. In the matter of an official state language, he supported the exclusive use of German and supported his conviction with his inimitable logic: "First, the German language is spoken by 70 million people and opens all doors to those who seek the treasures of intellect [*Gesitesschaetzen*] created by these 70 million; the other languages are far below the level [of the German language] and thus offer nothing equivalent. Second, unless German is supported as the state language, the number of German intellectuals who are capable of making accessible the great treasures of the French and English languages will be lessened, thus diminishing contacts with the distant West." And there were other reasons: "Besides, there are many concerns of state that must be conducted in one language such as foreign defense and internal police security; one cannot catch a fleeing bank robber if one must first send the telegrams to a bureau to be translated."[14]

His position on schools for minority nationalities was practically tailored to the distribution of Germans throughout the realm. Thus he agreed with other Marxist theoreticians that two languages should be used in every state school in areas of mixed national population (the language of the predominant nationality and of the second most numerous one).[15] But he stated that in areas where one nationality was overwhelming, there was no point teaching the second language, adding, "If the Germans of Lower Austria eat bread made by Slovaks . . . this does not mean that they should speak their language." Following this passage in his article on the problem of schools for minority nationalities comes a curious exercise in subjective dialectic that is a hallmark of Renner's expressionistic forays into objective evaluation:

One ordinarily conceives the question of language laws as the *right to be permitted to speak*. That is senseless *without the right to be understood*. He who speaks to his fellow citizen will also be understood. The minority claims the right to be allowed to speak—the majority can equally claim the right to be understood, whether they speak as a group or individually. . . . I admit: the farmer who hires a Czech menial [*Knecht*] hopes to be able to communicate with him in matters of domestic and economic activity. The same man [the German farmer] may say, however, as mayor in the city hall: "I don't understand you." It is another matter, though, in a court of law: the public has a right to understand; it would be excluded if the trial was not conducted in its language.[16]

The majority in Renner's arguments is almost taken for granted to be German. And the other nationalities hardly assume flattering positions in his metaphors: they appear as menials, criminals, and the culturally deprived. Renner's arguments are hard to follow, for they are constantly invaded by figures of speech that swallow up the major theme. In a characteristic aside when speaking of the necessity of legal protection for the "new" national, that is, someone who has adopted the cloak of German culture, Renner states: "A German-speaking Negro who lives in Vienna will hardly be recognized as a fellow national by other Germans. This man, however, must obey the law of the state within the language of that state. Every authority will speak to him in German, and expect an answer in German! The school laws will compel him to send his children to a German school. The state must consider him a German. The lawyers make such fine points of law more precise by the addition of a 'Quasi.' Thus we can name the Negro 'quasi-German.'[17]

It was in the second aspect of *Staat und Nation* that Renner dealt with the will-o'-the wisp of nationality that haunted his writings. Renner dared to grapple with the conceptual chimera of what comprises nationality where he had not dared in the more specific question of what was national culture because the former question required concrete artifacts. Renner was strengthened in his courage by the German heritage of theory in this philosophic domain of conjecture. He opens *Staat und Nation* with the problematic: "How can nationality as a sum of individuals, on the one hand, and as an ethical-psychological quality of single individuals, on the other hand, be adequately comprehended?"[18] In answering the question of nationality as a sum of individuals, he turned first to one of the German mentors of his university *Bildung* for a formulation of the possible solutions—Ludwig Gumplowicz and his exhaustive study of national character written in 1875, *Rasse und Staat*.[19] Gumplowicz admits in the introduction to his study that there is no precise way to determine the meaning of race (*Volksstaemme*) qua nation (*Volk*). He states that in 1874 at the Saint Petersburg International Statistics Congress three possibilities were reviewed toward a legal definition of nationality: through ethnological characteristics; through the "mother tongue"; or through the language used in social discourse (*Umgangssprache*).[20] The congress decided on the latter mode of calculation. Gumplowicz (and so Renner) was satisfied with this solution; in some respects it presented a certain promise for an Austrian-German, particularly for it allowed that one could assume a new nationality by the assimilation of its language. This was later to be a programmatic hope of most Austrian-German Social Democrats, especially the German-Jewish ones, as a solution to the nationality conflicts of the empire (see Chapter 5). But Gumplowicz (and so Renner) felt that this solution was in other ways superficial—some distinction should be made in the language of discourse that allowed an evaluation of the nationality itself. In other words, a normative basis must be established to determine whether a group of people speaking one language should be entitled to a *true* nationality (*Volk*). Gumplowicz then opens the door to a principle of national discrimination that Renner and the other Austro-German nationalists readily followed:

Even though one may speak of nationality as an entity defined merely by language, nonetheless the fact remains that in the area of nationality one must draw the distinction between *active* nationality and *passive* nationality. Only the educated [*gebildete*] classes can possess a consciousness of a communal national culture, whose expression they find in the learned [*gebildete*], the written language of their nation. The uneducated masses do not possess this consciousness, they are completely incapable of a true feeling of nationality, they have only a sense of common origin or religious affiliation: The higher true national feeling, which presupposes a certain grade of culture, is to the uneducated mass always and everywhere foreign. . . . This distinction explains the various manifestations of public life among nations, for example, that the aspirations and efforts of national endeavor occur only among the educated middle classes, and that the common mass only follow in their wake. Eoetvoes was quite correct in his observation: "We see that no matter how great the efforts are of those who stand at the head of national movements in the name of the people [*Das Volk*], to the people themselves the concept of the people remains strange."[21]

Those of the German cultural community, especially its leading intelligentsia, were raised by this conception to the status of an active nationality. Moreover, they were of a nation that through its heightened consciousness and philosophical *Bildung* had created the idea of *Volk*. What better mandate could there be for their assumption of cultural leadership in the question of other, more passive nationalities? Thus on the strength of Gumplowicz's distinction Renner approached with the confidence of a German scientist the problematic of national etiology in the individual and as a sum of individuals. But here his eclectic dependence on the German cultural fathers made his arguments contradictory. Renner first considered the theme of national origins in the philosophic-idealistic tradition of Wilhelm von Humboldt, Johann Herder, and Johann Fichte. Nationality was not an acquired entity; rather, it was rooted in the thought and feelings of a community, and these were expressions of that people's literature and language. The mystery of nationhood lay hidden in this inheritance. The external accidents of environment did not affect nationality, for nationality was not a product of physical geography: "National differences arise only from the commanding thought and feeling motives of a people. There is no necessary relationship between national consciousness and a definite territory." Yet only two pages later Renner seemed to reflect on his adherence to a political party that advocated materialism, and he restated the idea of national etiology: "Thoughts and feelings, the community of which gives rise to nation, are not generated without a cause. They are the reflexes of external happenings, especially human interaction. In nearly all connections at the present time these are controlled by the state and legally defined. National feelings are primarily influenced by the organization of the state. The more independent the state from national desire, the more endangered national life, the more stifled its development."[22]

Renner's search for a logic of the nationality that was so real to him thus involved him in a host of mutually exclusive principles and resulted in an obvious injustice to the actual state of national consciousness among non-German peoples in the Cisleithanian state. If a nationality were viewed as an inheritance of a traditional language and literature, a product of a community's deepest thoughts and feelings, then the notion of assimilating other peoples to the German nationality was hardly feasible. If, on the other hand, nationality was a creation of territorial conditions, especially the state, as Renner's second etiology affirms, then how might Renner explain the growth of national consciousness in a state whose constitutional structure he considered hostile to national aspirations? Renner had ventured into the trick currents that hid an insoluble contradiction— the linguistic nationalism of the German liberal philosophers of pre-1848 Germany, which found its expression in the philosophic sociology of Gumplowicz, and the antinationalistic materialism of Marx, for whom nationalism was merely a certain level of consciousness and nationality a product of its fictions. There was little hope of a resolution to this enigma for Renner as long as his nationalism remained, or as long as he tried to force his nationalist feelings into the guise of Marxism.

The language of law and the state gave Renner his freedom and his home. The Marxist language of conception was an incidental obstruction worn gradually down to harmless proportion through the tools of a legal methodology, the legal metaphors of his constitutional-lawyer fathers.[23] The language of Renner's university *Bildung* served as a bridge on which the nameless longings of nationality could pass to the promised land. The vague obsessions of his past remained at the heart of his writing, antedating the eclectic phraseology Renner developed from the liberal constitutional thought confronted in his seminar with Philippovich. Yet it is this bridge of thought, not the life that crossed it, that is remembered. When we examine the ideas of Renner, we see nothing original. His suggestions for a constitutional revision had their model in the Kremsier constitution of 1848–49—an attempt to give more autonomy to the industrial nations of Austria by creating national *Kreisen* within the crown lands along ethnographic lines.[24] His insights into the territorial limitations of national expression were first put forth by Joseph Eoetvoes, with whose writings he was familiar;[25] his proposal of a dual system of administration was a variation on the plans of Adolf Fischhof;[26] and his ethnological, sociological, and psychological appreciations were a mixture of Gumplowicz, Marx, and the other olympian figures of German idealism. Moreover,

Renner was not the first of his generation to use the ideas of those mid-nineteenth-century predecessors: Otto Lang, F. R. von Herrnritt, Alfred von Offermann, and Etbin Kristan seemed to provide the stimulus and anatomy of discussion for Renner's proposals in *Staat und Nation*.[27] Renner appeared as the champion of the platform of a federal system of nationalities within the Cisleithanian state only because of his fortuitous rise to power within the Austrian Social Democratic party and his subsequent position as chancellor of German Austria. By that time his earlier problematic had been interred with the Habsburg dynasty and the specter of his frustrated longing for a home given a concrete body. Hidden forever was the strong nationalist German core of his utterances, which even before assuming respectability in legal terminology had risen to the surface on Renner's first encounter with socialist literature.

Renner's original link to the world of socialist thought was August Bebel's *Die Frau und der Sozialismus*, which he had read while in the army supply depot.[28] Bebel articulated the problem of the individual and nationality in an intuitive and emotional way that won Renner's heart. Renner later wrote a critique of this book that sheds light on the more primary levels of the problematic that became *Staat und Nation*:

While Marx writes for all peoples in all times, Bebel's *Frau* is above all specifically *ours*. It is a *German* book, a part of our struggle, our emotion, immediately a product of the evolution of German socialism at the turn of the century and the world of feeling attached to this struggle, in a way that no other book is. . . .Bebel speaks not of world economy and the state, not of economic and political matters, but . . . immediately of our social conditions, of the daily, everyday life, the relationship of man and woman, of the mystery of the German family. . . .Bebel's book lacks a clear and logical sequence: the unarticulated thought is the hallmark of the book! This blemish in the book speaks most audibly of how specifically German it is, and most obviously of how it is born from the unique emotional world of the German.[29]

It was from the "mystery of the German family" that Renner's problematic sprung, and although his language was more logical than Bebel's unarticulated cry from the womb, Renner transformed his German womb to the transpersonal hearth of the state and to politics, where the cry of nationality had a more sophisticated format.

Renner's views on the state and Parliament reflected his deep belief in the individual's organic relationship to his nationality and, to a somewhat lesser degree, his class. For Renner, an individual was never an autonomous person; rather, the individual was a unit of a greater whole, which created certain obligations: "The good citizen must understand how to obey and command, practically and theoretically, and realize that civil virtue is the authority of these two points of view. The art of ordering and obeying is, as we disciples of Social Democracy call it, our greatest virtue! Without commands and obedience there is no working together, no community of workers, no union, not even a union of friends. The art to order and obey is discipline. . . . Who would order must first learn to obey."[30]

In his second major publication, *Staat und Parliament*, published in 1901, Renner demonstrated the continuity of this authoritarian strain in his thought in a more subdued but equally fundamental manner. In that work he argued for a system of proportional representation for the Austrian Parliament that would be free of economic or territorial restrictions. The system would be similar to that of the French Republic in its support of a pluralism of diverse, nationally shared interests. But these interests for Renner were essentially limited to those of one's national identity, as well as one's class. There were no secondary interests that would coalesce shifting groups of individuals. Moreover, the nation and the class are posited as unified wills that do not brook individual variance. Renner's articulation of the individual's proper relation to his corporate interest and to the state is so antidemocratic that one senses him stumbling in his thought, almost embarrassed:

The state exists to satisfy the collective interest of the people . . .[the state] naturally wishes that one law binds everyone. Thus the state should permit this *one* law, which binds the *will of all* ergo the *general will*, to be formed as law by its millions of citizens, in order that the people [*Volk*] and the state remain and be, one. Every individual has his own interest and his own will, to be sure . . . which includes the various differences of estate, of occupation, social and social-ethnic interest. Every individual and every stratum has its interest, moreover, that runs contrary to the general interest, thus is from the beginning hostile to the state [*staatsfeindlich*]. That is obvious. For everyone is limited in his daily life a hundred-fold through the law of the general will, and he strives to remove these civil boundaries. No individual can be seen as a supporter of the state [*staatserhaltend*] and no class, only the whole [*Gesamtheit*], that is, everyone in mutual limitations of each other. If one can speak of a class that supports the state at all, then this honorable title [*Ehrentitel*] must go—as paradoxical as it sounds—to the workers, whose interest . . . almost always runs parallel to the interest of the whole.[31]

In these thoughts on the best protection of freedom for the individual, four philosophers are implicit, even though they are mutually incompatible—John Locke, Thomas Hobbes, Jean-Jacques Rousseau, and Karl Marx. The four points of view show the conflict in Karl Renner's personality in regard to the nature and objectives of Social Democracy. Locke, who represents Renner's common sense, is present in the idea of mutual limitation created by diverse interests; the Lockean concept of minimal government of "least harm" steers a middle course between interests. Lockean government is by consent of the people, however; it is not a structure toward which the people can be enemies (*staatsfeindlich*). Hobbes is evident in the notion of the state as the necessary entity to bring stability and security to a confused populace. By incorporating Hobbes, Renner reflects his need for structure and evidences the displacement of his need for a permanent German hearth in the reification of the state, which his sounder sense of Locke's minimal state seeks to modify. Renner's integration of personality as he matured was expressed indirectly by such theoretical conflicts in his writings. Rousseau, for example, is clearly present in Renner's general will statements, which modify the harshness of his idea of subjugating the individual will; Rousseau allows the individual to find the general will as an autonomous thinker, and it is always more of an existential arrival at a personal categorical imperative than a submission to group thought.[32] Finally, Marx is present in the afterthought that the corporate interest of class is closest to the general will. Renner is not convincing in this articulation of Marxist idea, using an aristocratic bestowal of "honor" (*Ehrentitel*) for his recognition of inequity. Nevertheless, the memory of his own family's pain and a genuine recognition of social injustice keep Renner from succumbing completely to the superego demands for obedience and submission to the invisible family of the state that he carried with him.

Renner's ideas for a proportional representation attracted the Austrian Fabian society, a group that modeled itself upon the evolutionary, moderate socialist ideas of the English Fabians. Renner was introduced to the Fabians by his former professor of constitutional law, Eugen Phillipovich.[33] He and the Fabians engaged in a mock election in the auditorium of the Ronacher Theater in Vienna to see if the proportional scheme of representation he had designed was feasible.[34] His contact with Phillipovich and the Fabians reflected the balanced rationality of Renner's character; but his need for the superstructure of the state, which was reinforced by the norms of German middle-class thought that agreed with the state idea, led to a Marxism in Renner that emphasized a nondemocratic interpretation of the class struggle: "To be sure, the proletariat lives its own extraparliamentary life and grows through what one might term—without its usual connotations—direct action. But it needs the free tribune, the continental control of the government, it needs above all the means to combat harmful laws and to fight for good laws, it needs Parliament."[35]

Parliament, the body of the people, is seen by Renner as an organ of the state which controls the direction of the people's energy. Perhaps, Renner concedes in another article, the common people might one day be capable of governing themselves without the guardianship of the extant bourgeois and aristocratic hierarchy of state authority, but not until they have lifted themselves above their ignorant state through the proper *Bildung*: "These people [*the Lumpenproletariat*] cannot reject the in part unasked for guardianship [*Vormundschaft*] as long as they remain inarticulate. They deserve this guardianship when and as long as they remain lunatics, and tear themselves to pieces in hate-filled battles among themselves. They need the guardianship of ministers, servants of the state, district supervisors and policemen as long as they are not rational enough to replace their struggles with a national system of laws."[36]

Renner refers in this quotation to the spontaneous demonstrations by individual nationals who took to the streets in a direct expression of their will. The law as it functioned in the bodies of the state was the proper vehicle for social change, not the arbitrary will of individuals or collectives of individuals who acted outside the law. The abstract presence of the state could be humanized through a change in its physical presence, its institutions, and its spiritual presence, the laws, but it could not be flouted. Renner's dependence upon the abstract dimensions of the state can be traced to the problems of his personal genesis. The brilliant Marxist legal analysis that he made in *Die Rechtsinstitute des Privatrechts und ihre soziale Funktion* (*The Institutions of Private Law and Their Social Functions*), published in 1904, was a sublimation of his personal alienation into an objective work that studied the expropriation, or legal alienation, of property by capitalistic laws.[37]

The expropriation of property from its creator or owner, for Renner, was not solely the result of the economic system of a society, as Marx saw it, but coequally the result of the laws of that society. As Renner states in describing the intention of *Die Rechtsinstitute des Privatrechts*: "The main theme of this enquiry is the relation between law and economics in the evolution of history, observed and examined here from the aspect of legal institutions; regarded with the eye of a jurist who, with a vision extending beyond his native field of legal rules, recognizes that everywhere the law is as much bound up with economics as economics is bound up with the law."[38] Raising the law to a status equal to that of the economic system as a cause of social conditions was a modification of Marx's thought. Marx's well-known formula that ranks the fundamental causes of social reality reads, "The sum total of the relations of production constitute the economic structure of society—the real foundations on which rise legal and political superstructures."[39] The formula is even more clearly articulated in Engels's preface to Marx's *Eighteenth Brumaire*: "The law according to which all struggle, whether in the political, religious, philosophical or any other ideological field, is in fact only the social classes whose existence and hence collisions of their economic position, their methods of production, and their manner of exchange dependent thereon."[40]

Renner saw the law as a partner of the economic state of a culture, not in the relation of the moon to the sun, or as a superstructure that gains its reality from the substructure. Both work in their own ways to condition society; Renner stated four theses to this effect: (1) Fundamental changes in society are possible without accompanying changes of the legal system; (2) it is not the law that causes economic development; (3) economic change does not change the law; and (4) development by leaps and bounds is unknown in the social substratum, which knows evolution only, not revolution.[41]

Renner recognized the significance of relations of production, that is, the social substratum, as having its own rules for the organization of individual and collective life, but he was equally insistent that the law has its own momentum untouched by the economic force of the culture. One must give special attention to the law if it is to be changed to correspond to social reality. One can be a "revolutionary" in changing the law. One can change the economic substratum only by evolutionary means. Renner thus made himself an economic Revisionist[42] and a revolutionary only in regard to the formal laws that shape the state and the relations of its citizens. When given an opportunity to revolutionize laws, however, as in his drafting of the Austrian constitution in 1918, he proved himself a conservative (see Chapter 10).

Renner's sensitivity to the law enabled him to perceive subtle distinctions in its governance of social relations. An insight indicative of his cultural-historical penetration of the language of the law is his comparison between its language in the modern state and in the ancient state:

The ancients usually spoke in direct imperatives when they recorded their norms in stone and metal, or papyrus and parchment, e.g., the code of Hammurabi, the Mosaic decalogue and the Twelve Tables of Rome. . . . we replace it by impersonal rules, as "The factory door is opened daily from 5:45 to 6:00 A.M." This assertion, which does not refer to a subjective agent, can only be justified as prophecy. . . . Where a norm takes the form of an assertive rule, the commanding and obeying individual disappears from sight; where it takes the form of an imperative order, the relation between individuals is emphasized. Ancient laws which employ the imperative are thus fascinating in their powerful expression. Modern laws prefer an obscure diction which makes it necessary to go through a process of interpretation to find out who are the persons concerned and what are their duties.[43]

Whereas in the narrow unit of patriarchal family and tribe all relations were between man and man, and all interaction was explicit and direct, in the modern state all is abstract and bloodless. Instead of the benevolent despot, there is the invisible tyrant. Renner did not wish to return to a master-slave ordering of social relations; rather, he desired a society with more interpersonal frankness and emotional directness. Karl Marx wished the same honesty in work relations:

When communist artisans associate with one another, theory, propaganda, etc., is their first end. But at the same time, as a result of this association, they acquire a new need—the need for society—and what appears as a means becomes an end. In this practical process the most splendid results are to be observed whenever French socialist workers are seen together. Such things as smoking, drinking, eating, etc., are no longer means of contact or means that bring together. Association, society, and conversation, which again has association as its end, are enough for them; the brotherhood of man is no mere phrase with them, but a fact of life, and the nobility of man shines upon them from their work-hardened bodies.[44]

Renner sought such a society, but he repressed this wish because it recalled a family past in want of such comradeship. The pain of what he did not have made him translate his need for open love and caring into the desire for imperative command, a symbolic distortion of warmth and nurturing. Marx saw the need for personal integration and self-consciousness in order for an individual to receive from life what he desired: "Assume *man* to be *man* and his relationship to the world to be a human one: then you can exchange love only for love, trust for trust, etc. If you want to enjoy art, you must be an artistically cultivated person; if you want to exercise influence over other people, you must be a person with a stimulating and encouraging effect on other people. Every one of your relations to man and to nature must be a *specific expression*, corresponding to the object of your will, of your *real individual life*."[45]

Renner was conscious of the objective lack of care and honesty in modern social relations and how through covert means the directly honest imperative became a subtle manipulation of others:

How the authority of another person ("the heteronomous will") is imposed on the wishes of an individual (his "autonomous" will) is a matter of common experience. He is coaxed or threatened, talked round or browbeaten; fraud and coercion, either physical or mental (hypnosis) play their part. There is, however, this mysterious difference: that in modern times all law is laid down, in the name of all citizens, by the state, conceived as an entity. Instead of one man's will prevailing over the will of another, the common will is regarded as imposed upon that of the individual. How this common will arises—for it is clearly not the "general will" (volonté générale)—is one of the fundamental problems of jurisprudence.[46]

He sought a higher consciousness for society, but not for himself, through a clarification of the legal norms that reinforced social dishonesty and rewarded impersonality. Legal analysis could help raise a culture lacking self-consciousness to an awareness of legal changes that could improve human relationships:

There is no legal regulation, then, of goods or of labor within bourgeois society, whereas the whole of the medieval world was obviously built on such conscious regulation. Society, the conscious organization of mankind, in the eyes of the law an entity, here denies its own consciousness. It prefers blindness to recognition of the distribution of the goods, it pretends to be deaf so that it need not listen to the complaints of the dispossessed, it abdicates as a legal entity, as the common will, in favor of the individual will. But though it feigns death, it is alive, and inanimate stones cry out where it remains silent. . . . The so-called bourgeois society, distinct from the political society of the organized state, is not conscious of itself. *It confronts the individual as a dark power of nature*, a ghostly inhuman force which does not talk in imperatives to the member of the community, which does not utter commands or threats, which does not punish afterwards in forms of laws, which requires to be divined by speculation and destroys him who does not grasp it, which achieves its object by the force of blind matter and allows this to rule over man.[47]

The emotional metaphors of this passage indicate the importance legal analysis had for Renner as a clarification of the social world and thus, indirectly, as a self-clarification. Such a dual purpose had to distort the objectivity of the legal analysis, but if we avoid the metaphorical intrusions, his legal analysis is still a significant direction for social criticism. He presents historical formulations of law and shows how they either adequately expressed the existing state of socioeconomic reality, giving it organization and regulation, or limited the development and change of social transaction: "Legal analysis confines itself to collating the totality of norms, the systematic understanding, logical exposition and practical application thereof. Legal analysis is of necessity determined by history like its arsenal of concepts, its terminology."[48]

Renner attempted to provide a broader historical framework than the average legal interpreter, yet he implicitly recognized that his own interpretations would be a product of the history he lived, growing from the concepts that surrounded him. There is a modesty in the lines quoted above that is evidence of the rational man who endured as a change agent in the Austrian culture.

By legal "norms" Renner meant the context of legal language that defined certain repeated patterns of social interaction. These norms served as a means of personal identification and self-regulation. As Renner stated, these norms once had been manifested to the member of a community in the form of direct imperative—clearly and humanely; but as society altered and technology changed the facts of personal interaction and disposal of property, these norms assumed different functions to legislators and men of property. The norms acquired new definitions; the legal conceptions took on new applications, so that the possessors of authority and the controllers of property could justify their actions. The law became a cloak for the frequent violation of what the norm originally defined. Renner cited as an example of this process the norm of sale and purchase and the mode by which its language assumed a new function for the authorities of an economically altered society:

The sale of one's patrimony was formerly illegal or at least condemned by society. The idea that property existed only to be exploited by legal transactions, only in order to be sold, was inconceivable to anybody. . . . Ownership at the period of simple commodity production was essentially and with few exceptions exercised without any intervention of other legal institutions and required no other act in the law. The soil was cultivated and its fruits consumed. In so far as property served as a system of production by artisans, the work was done directly for the customer or for a local market, generally in the form of a contract of work and labor, or of *sale and purchase*. But sale and purchase here relate to the finished article alone, there was no incessant flow of sale and purchase involving anything and everything. The sale was merely the final act of the labor process, and the exercise of ownership was as a rule the technical disposal of the object. Now, however, the exercise of this right by the act in the law becomes the specific function of the non-owner, and the owner acquires the social function of distributing goods among labor and consumers.[49]

Thus with the creation of the middleman and the advent of the capitalistic form of economy, sale and purchase as a conceptually defined pattern of actions becomes the abstract cover for the physical patterns. Again Renner's choice of illustration signified the ever-present animus and impetus of his personal growth—the "inconceivable" and exploitive sale of patrimony. Here Renner showed the first acts of dispossession in the European society and the first abstraction of terms that confused the legally unschooled mind of the common man. Renner emphasized that legally this manipulation of norm was unjustifiable and that although the change of function may be reinforced through the decisions of individual judges, it is only because they have not yet become fully conscious of the transformed social basis of the societal organization. Once a society becomes aware of the actual nature of its social character, it will redefine the norm and give it a terminology appropriate to its action, thus allowing a greater justice and legal protection for its individual members.[50] Until that time, the cloaked manipulation of the older norm must be seen as harmful to the will of the individual: "In the eyes of the law this exchange of dominant *personae* is *alienation* from the point of view of the owner and the appropriation from that of the new dominus. It is not enforced by the law, it is factual expropriation and appropriation. It is . . . a factual shifting of the dominant *personae* of property and other kindred legal institutons, not in terms of a change of ownership imposed by a court of authority."[51]

The norm as guarantor of individual rights thus was conceived by Renner as having a life cycle—a right is acquired; it is enforced against interfering third parties; it is lost.[52] On its factual death, the aware citizenry must ensure that its ghost does not haunt the further growth of its community, warping its interaction; the citizenry must frame a new norm.

Much of Renner's legal theory would pass in the eyes of the layman as a logical discussion of the evolution of Continental law, which with diligent study, makes eminent sense. Fortunately, there is an English edition of Renner's *Die Rechtsinstitute* which contains a voluminous annotation by its editor, Otto Kahn-Freund, a reader of law at the University of London. Kahn-Freund places Renner's legal formulation in its historical European context and compares its various theoretical positions with the English common law, thus showing his deviations from his fellow lawyers in Austria.

On Renner's conception of a life cycle for the individual legal norm, Kahn-Freund comments: "The metaphorical personification of 'rights' which are said to have a 'life-cycle' is germane to Continental legal thought. Owing to the existence of a highly integrated system of legal abstractions, it is capable of conceiving legal institutions—which are, in fact, merely groupings of legal norms—with the symbolic imagery taken from nature. Such language is alien to the 'remedial' method of Anglo-Saxon legal thought." Here is evidence of the role of Renner's *Bildung* in his function as a political theorist. The "organic" conception of the personality principle as a constitutional-legal solution to the nationality conflicts of Austria assumes even more the character of a conceptual tour-de-force, enforced by the peculiar matrix of Renner's Germanic legal education. Renner writes: "Wherever the community has the power of command, as it has in every society, it exercises this power by means of individuals acting as its organs." Kahn-Freund comments: "Renner assumes the validity of the doctrine [principle of organic representation] as a matter of course,—another instance of the influence of Continental legal thought on Marxist legal theory."[53]

Kahn-Freund's ignorance of Marx (who shared the symbolic tendencies of Continental legal thought) must be ignored. Kahn-Freund identifies Renner's stance toward the legal norm and its change with the positivist school of law, which was predominant in Austria in the period that Renner wrote. The positivist school considered the norms of property, contract, and so on to be "empty frames" that gave form to the existing organic order of society and denigrated the lawyer's or judge's capacity to do more than apply these frames in their strict definition to the case at hand.[54] Kahn-Freund objects to this "idealistic" conception of the law and the diminishing of individual judgment in the judge:

Positivism is a utopia. The law is neither consistent nor self-sufficient. Whatever theorists may say and whatever he himself may think and say, the judge constantly recurs to an analysis, articulate or inarticulate, or the moral, social, economic function and effect of the rules and principles he applies, and of his own decision. The task of the law maker and that of the law finder cannot be kept in water-tight compartments, and judges have always acted and will act on the celebrated principles of the Swiss Civil Code of 1912, that, in the absence of a statutory or customary norm, the judge must decide "in accordance with the rule he would lay down if he were the legislator."[55]

The European judge was far less flexible, Kahn-Freund asserts, than his English cousin because of the former's positivistic fetish of norm. The English judge showed far more initiative in adapting the legal rule to the shifting economic basis of society and thus effected many changes which on the Continent had to await the intervention of the legislature. Thus the failure of European law to adapt itself readily to the social changes of society (the failure that Renner identified in its guise as "change of function" in the norm) is labeled by Kahn-Freund as the rigidity of the European legal tradition and its "fiction of continuity of norms," not necessarily, as Renner would have it, a blindness in the legislator, judge, or layman to the existing social conditions.[56] The alienation of the individual from property was abetted by a superconsciousness of legal terminology which bound the judge to the cage of his own logical system of rules. This explanation sheds ironic light on the path that Renner sought as a way to freedom, a way he would have the masses follow—the way of a *Bildung* that would cure the illness of dispossession with the solution of its original virus.

Kahn-Freund points out one other facet of Renner's positivism that helps our understanding of Renner's political mind. Renner understood all law as a command or imperative addressed from one individual to another. As we have seen, Renner depicted the immediacy and interpersonal openness of this imperative in the ancient world. Kahn-Freund states, however, that not all European positivists saw the law as an imperative. He mentions that one of Renner's contemporaries, Hans Kelsen, saw the law as a "hypothetical judgment" rather than imperative.[57] In other words, Renner invested the language of the law with personalistic, one might say anthropomorphic characteristics, that his fellow lawyers saw as merely a system of definitions that aid the individual interpretation of the judge. For Renner, the law always spoke with the force and authority of the prophet and allowed no contradiction. Modern law might have iniquities, but the individual must abide by them because the laws were revealed truth. Only after a new norm was framed by law might the individual act in accordance with whatever needs existed in the realities of everyday life. The law stood always above the subjective imperative.

Renner's tendency to rely on the abstract language of legal definition was also the hallmark of his Marxism; his insistence that a new logical system of rules was necessary for every change in the social foundation of society acted as a conservative buffer in his stance to social action. Later, when he played a leading role in the shaping of Austrian Social Democratic policy, this dependence on the legal norm and obedience to the letter of its authority was to hamper the spontaneity of his party's response to the immediate demands of the workers.

Renner's adherence to the law of Austria and his reliance on its norms are reflected in his support of Parliament. Between 1907 and the outbreak of World War I, no major social legislation was passed by Parliament. The obstruction of conflicting national groups made it impossible to reach agreement on social issues.[58] Although Renner recognized the de facto impotence of the Austrian Parliament in its effort to resolve the conflict of nationalities, he argued over the years 1907 to 1914 that Parliament was the best organ to handle the problem. In 1909, during disputes between members of Parliament's lower house (*Volkshaus*), Renner wrote that though these struggles exist, it is better that the national conflicts come to light in the national Parliament than remain hidden in the *Landtag* or appear on the street. The need, he added, was not for additional public demonstrations over the failure of the *Volkshaus* but for the election of better representatives.[59] In 1910, the *Volkshaus* managed to arrive at a reform in its order of business, a plan in part drafted by Renner, after sitting for five nights and six days. Intoxicated by the change that promised to facilitate the communication of issues, Renner boasted of a new face of Parliament in his next article: "Never has a night session appeared so disciplined and sober . . . in this sitting there wasn't one drunken member."[60] But within the year no improvement in the parliamentary situation was apparent, and Renner's jubilation was transformed into a temporary depression that saw no immediate resolution. He still refrained from expressing disillusionment with Parliament as a mode of political solution, and in an article entitled "Politische Windstille" (Political Calm), laid the blame on history for the Austrian state of affairs. Borrowing the dialectical arguments of Otto Bauer, Renner sighed that there existed an equilibrium (*Gleichgewicht*) between the forces of the proletariat and the forces of the bourgeoisie. What might seem as a government paralyzed by national obstruction was actually a state that stood in the calm between two social storms; before any advance could be made in the condition of either nationality or proletariat, there would have to be a change in the distribution of strength on either side of these two opposed camps.[61] The irony of this theoretical aspirin that Renner employed for the parliamentary headaches lay in his failure to mention or to recognize that Bauer's abstract quantitative approach to the "strength of class" was the basis for the subsequent argument, that Parliament would be useless as an arena for the class struggle in the next stage of conflicts.[62] Although Renner promised better times, inflation began to ravage the Austrian economy, and the people again went to the streets to protest the failure of the government to take appropriate measures. Renner attacked these civil expressions in an article called "Soziale Demonstrationen," written in October 1911. He castigated the people who chose to behave like anarchists and called for a solution to their problem through "state power" and the platform of Parliament.[63] Renner never gave up hope of the parliamentary way; long after his fellow Austro-Marxists considered Parliament as a lost cause for the social revolution, Renner continued to excuse its lack of social action. The ground of his continued optimism must be seen not only in his respect for traditional legal forms but also in the spiritual fulfillment his membership in that august body permitted. Renner, who often drafted the Social Democratic faction's proposals, and thus daily engaged in the foreground of national politics, was slow to criticize this role as having little moment. After seeing a tax bill that he had drafted passed in the *Volkshaus* shortly before the outbreak of World War I, Renner was to refer to Parliament through the words of Goethe: "The good man even in the darkest straits is conscious of the proper path."[64]

4

The Party as Family for Otto Bauer

Otto Bauer was born September 5, 1881, in Vienna, the oldest child of a German Jewish family. His only sibling was his sister Ida, fourteen months younger than he. Bauer's father was a wealthy textile manufacturer, one uncle on his father's side was a prominent Viennese lawyer, and another was a well-known physician. Although spending most of his youth in Vienna, Bauer attended the upper classes of the *Gymnasium* in Reichenberg in northern Moravia, where his father had moved to open a textile factory. Thus, like Renner, Bauer experienced the cultural complications of a German minority in a territory dominated by Czechs. (Bauer's relation to the nationality question differs from Renner's in that Bauer was an assimilated German, for his grandparents on both sides were Jews from eastern Europe, so although he strongly identified with German *Kultur*, in his approach to the question of national minorities differed from that of Renner's strongly ethnic biases.) Bauer returned to Vienna after graduating from the *Gymnasium summa cum laude* and began the study of law at the university. After his graduation from law school in 1906, which coincided with the success of his first book, Bauer was able to devote himself entirely to Austrian Social Democratic activities; he was the prime example of the *Nachwuchs* sought by the Austrian Social Democratic patriarchy. The German Social Democrat Karl Kautsky compared his sudden emergence and brilliant, unflagging activity to that of the father of them all: "When I think of the young Marx, I see him as Otto Bauer."[1]

Bauer was an archetype of the Austrian political leader of his generation. He was a university graduate, his roots were solidly in the middle-class norms of Vienna, and he was fluent both in conversation and in writing. His habits of mind and behavior, reflecting the Austrian mode of cultural denial—the styles of thought and human interaction into which a citizen is schooled by his society to avoid and to distort the facts of his existence which he cannot accept—were also typical. Bauer's manner of handling facts and political problems subtly influenced others to regard him as a leader—like is attracted to like.

Bauer suffered doubly in his development as a political personality. Raised within the norms of German-Austrian culture, his political style was typical of the equivocating Austrian who sought always to avoid confrontation and achieve a compromise that left problems unresolved but the conflicting parties at their ease (*durchwursteln*). Otto Bauer's equivocation was compounded by his personal development within his family: his inability to be decisive in moments of crisis and the lack of congruence between his stated principles and political behavior were the products of a family milieu that was not conducive to normal development. His mother, Käthe Gerber Bauer, tyrannized the family with obsessive-compulsive habits and anger, generated perhaps by the infidelities of her husband Philip. Bauer's family has the dubious distinction of being preserved in history as the family of Freud's patient "Dora," the classic case of a hysterical personality.[2] Ida Bauer was Dora.

Hysteria is a defense against unbearable facts and emotions that cannot be given full recognition. The perpetual war between their parents forced Ida and Otto to comprehend actions that were incomprehensible to their young minds. In their daily life they were constantly exposed to intensified emotions and neurotic and evasive behavior—not the nurturing environment that supports normal mental and emotional growth.[3] The children sought to help their parents as mediators but gradually withdrew into pained isolation as they grew older. Undoubtedly, Otto's healthy attempts to relate to his parents and resolve their differences developed strong interpersonal abilities in him which became evident later, when he played the go-between among the warring generations in the Austrian Social Democratic party. The emotional weight of negotiating between their parents proved too heavy for the children, however, and both developed psychoneurotic defenses against the facts of their lives. Otto shared the hysterical symptomatology developed by Ida. Ida suffered more acutely from the illness, yet Otto, too, used the symptoms of the psychoneurosis as a character style.[4] Although he was not overtly incapacitated, except for short periods, and not directly embarrassed by the effects of this psychosomatic illness, the psychic and emotional symptoms of the condition warped the manner of his activity and the nature of his achievement.

The hysterical symptomatology developed by Ida and Otto was similar in many respects. Although all hysterical symptoms share common qualities, their particular combination and expression reflect an individual's compromise between the emotional and psychic facts he wishes to avoid and the daily needs of the real world in which he must function. Thus a style of living emerges that allows one to be passingly capable among others yet secure in one's defenses against those elements of self and environment that must be shut out. The psychosomatic symptoms, such as migraine headaches and catarrh, enabled Ida and Otto to be concerned with their own needs and translated their emotional pain into more tangible form.[5] The aberrant cognitive and emotional symptoms they shared included extreme unsociability, depression, and a dwelling in states of expectation, a flight from present reality.[6] Ida's and Otto's pseudo-historical organization of the facts of their lives, a form of rationalization connected to hysteria, is especially interesting to the cultural historian, as it is a customary trait of any individual or group that seeks to create a historical continuity to hide or obscure cultural facts in cannot accept.[7] Otto Bauer's pseudo-historical syntheses of his own and world affairs is a hallmark of his politics. Other cognitive habits shared by Ida and Otto in their attempts to cope with their home environment were a hyperintellectuality that resisted with emotional vigor any idea that did not suit its criteria of truth, and a propensity to see reality in a dramatic guise.[8] These mental and psychosomatic defenses that the children erected to maintain some equilibrium in their parental household remained a part of their characters and were repeated in other contexts as they matured whenever the frustrations of their world became too much to bear.

Whereas Karl Renner found in the ideas of Karl Marx the security of a lost childhood home, Otto Bauer found in Marx a metaphorical promise that might free him from his original home and lead him to a new land. Bauer's original home was a place of pain and irresolvable conflicts. Marx gave him a body of thought, and Austrian Social Democracy gave him a political home that enabled him constantly to defend himself from reality as it was, in the name of what might be.

A child normally begins to formulate the values and style of relations that govern his transactions with the world beyond his immediate family in adolescence. The development of a consciousness of the point of view of another person, which allows empathic decisions, and the sense of cooperative enterprises, in which rules can be made in common with others, are also accomplishments of the adolescent mind. It was at the inception of these critical years of mental growth that Otto Bauer wrote *Napoleon's End*, a play that reflected upon the linkage between the politics of the world and the family concerns of public figures. The emotional and psychic tensions of his own family were captured in such scenes as that of Maria Luise begging Napoleon not to wage war on her father, the Austrian emperor, for the sake of their son, who shared the blood of both families. The family conflict is repeated between Maria Luise and her father, Emperor Franz I, with whom she pleads for her husband Napoleon's welfare. Czar Alexander, who witnesses this scene between father and daughter, comments, "Whoever cannot comprehend Europe's misery, cast your eyes on this scene."[9] The young author clearly draws a relationship between family disharmony and its consequence in public actions. In a moment in childhood when the child's mind naturally opens to the complexity of human rules and relationships, Otto exhibited an intuition that might have steered him toward health and effectiveness in life. He might have stepped outside the play. The weight of his family, however, which continued to envelop him into his adult years, dimmed his insight, and he lived out in his own political life a metaphorical version of the play's tragic polarities of potential family harmony and actual public discord.

Why did Otto Bauer choose politics at such a young age as the analogue for his family situation, a model to be overcome or followed? An adolescent is naturally a political scientist for it is the time when he constructs conceptually and emotionally his place in the *polis*. Moreover, Otto Bauer was extroverted in his psychosocial development, and the events of his immediate and broader public world would serve as examples as he deliberated on the meaning of his life. The extroverted attitude opened him too vulnerable to his family's problems, however, constraining his development of a subjective, private world that might have been a buffer between him and his parents' strife. Bauer chose politics as an analogue for his family discord for two additional reasons that emanated from this adolescent exposure. He was cast by his parents as an arbitrator beyond the pale of family loyalties, a demand that created political acumen in him but distorted emotional proportion. He attempted to reject the role of arbitrator, but the essential fairness characteristic of this period of adolescent development impelled him toward that role. The second reason was his family's public involvement with others, as indicated in the relations with the K. family in his later teenage years.[10] His father seemed to expose the family members to a world outside of their private circle as a matter of course, opening the children to intimidating violations of their privacy that must have been almost unendurable and certainly made the family context into more of a league of nations than a separate society. We may infer that Otto was compelled to comprehend this style of manipulation and to emulate it in an identification with the aggressor.[11]

Drama became an integral element in Bauer's conceptualization of the world and in his manner of interaction. Whereas Renner would create an illusory picture of stability and stasis in society, a soporific that forestalled change, Bauer would create the impression of a constant conflict of issues and events, in such a dramatic guise that practical involvement in political realities was discouraged and conflict that might be resolvable was allowed to continue. The dramatic is a distortion of the flow of reality. The fictive action and closure of the dramatic perspective enabled him to manipulate the facts of world events into highly personal "histories." His personal life shaped his public perception and action; the personal appeared in the public as a distortion of the public into metaphor. With such a mental strategy Otto Bauer sought to sustain a perpetual equilibrium of forces in the Austrian state and to be a middleman between the various conflicting forces in Austrian Social Democracy, inciting and pacifying in turn, recreating to the extent of his powers the psychic and physical environment of his childhood home.

There is in each of us a seed of health whose presence announces itself in the midst of our activities, just as there is a seed of sickness that also has calling cards. Out metaphors serve to suggest paths to health, as well as serving as vehicles of escape into pathology, if illness seems to be our only way of coping. A neurosis is a compromise with an unresolved problem that allows us to perform in everyday reality. Drama for Bauer was an indicator of health as well as illness; health was using theater to recognize motive and plot, illness was assuming a role in the action. The closing thoughts of Napoleon in Bauer's play, whose title, *Napoleon's End*, stresses a reality-oriented perspective on the human dimension of history, poses the question of human fallibility, and exposes the illusion that one can remain permanently larger in human capacity than the people one will lead. Bauer has Napoleon say: "Man's fate is inconstant. The whole of Europe trembled before my power. . . . I made France into the mightiest state, I was a God to my subjects, and a second Attila to my enemies. And now?" [12]

When a child is confronted with his parents' struggle for power, he becomes in imagination, if not actuality, a political force who would control and shape the situation. If he is able to heal the situation among the warring adults, he gives himself evidence and motivation for leadership. We must infer that Bauer succeeded at times in ameliorating immediate situations; certainly, his sister looked to him for help, and in later years he took charge of his father's affairs at his father's request. [13] Ultimately, however, he failed, as any child must fail to change the choices and personalities of his parents. Thus he recognized as an adolescent with his healthy consciousness that even for Napoleon, short-term victories could not maintain a permanent state that was against the actual nature of all the powers that be. Health would have been an adult recognition of such limitations. His mistake as an adult was to trust that he could support an entire political movement with his independent judgment, an error he was led to by the impulsion of his superego, which demanded such responsibility from him. As he evidenced in each of the major crises that preceded his final flight from Austria in 1934, he was incapable of developing a viable policy or program that would withstand the realistic challenges of Austrian Social Democracy's political enemies, although he insisted on the right to make such determinations.

Bauer's belief that he could manipulate Ignaz Seipel and the Christian Social party into improving the situation of Austrian Social Democracy after the tragic July 15, 1927, debacle typified his theatrical sense of his ability to steer history.[14] Coupled with his hubris of decision was a "counter-will" that resisted the carrying out of decisions; most of his decisions involved not acting too assertively or postponing action. The "counterwill," a hysterical trait, may be said to have arisen as a reminder that just as he could not solve the politics of his childhood home, he could not single-handedly solve the politics of Austria. He had imperfectly assessed his own strength, his ability to guide others in times of stress. Interestingly, Napoleon evidenced lapses in his career that were similar to those Bauer experienced in moments of political conflict. The individual flights from Egypt and Russia are called political opportunism, but they can also be seen as dramatic choices of the hysterical personality to salvage only himself. One may infer that as great a leader as Napoleon proved himself to be militarily and diplomatically, he probably engineered his downfall with the "expectational" fatalism, the pseudo-historical rationalizations, and the intellectual intransigence that Bauer was later to use in his own political self-paralysis.[15]

There are many parallels in the adult careers of Bauer and his childhood hero Napoleon. Both men rose to the top of their respective political arenas between the ages of twenty-five and thirty. The ability of both to articulate the tensions of their society in self-evident analyses won them immediate reputations as being politically astute. Both could balance the political dissensions within their locus of power. Of course, Napoleon's military genius in planning and carrying out campaigns were talents conspicuously absent in Bauer, although Bauer had an equivalent genius in the tactical strategies that kept him a leader of the Austrian Social Democratic party for more than two decades without participating in radical social change. Bauer was able to justify suspension of public action of a socialist nature with such notions as "temporary equilibrium" of the classes.[16] Bauer was an archetypal leader for an organization of individuals

who thrived on the denial of cultural realities. In his hysterical symptomatology, he appealed to the habits of mind of his pre–World War I milieu
that would rather not square their environmental activities with their professed principles.

Thus his meteoric rise to power within Austrian Social Democracy
reflects the correspondence of diverse character traits, many abnormal,
which gave hope to the abnormal expectations of the times. Bauer's ideas
were always more provocative than clear; they were stated in a dialectical
construction that posed black-white polarities which were rarely developed beyond slogans. His discussions of political events were stimulating
but less than thorough; he embedded selected facts of a situation within
Marxist categories in a deductive manner that disallowed any counterex-
planation. The culture of his Austrian-German intellectual contemporaries thrived on didactic, challenging formulations. They burned with the
fever Robert Musil attributed to that age—a desire for the emergence of
a new order.[17] Nietzsche's vision of a culture of uncompromising intellectuals who would radically change society according to a vision that erad-
icated the pitfalls of inherited values was an ideal that enchanted even the
conservative party fathers of Austrian Social Democracy. Victor Adler
had been attracted to Nietzsche's historical writings, especially his attack
on too much historicity in one's approach to culture. Adler's son Friedrich
was named at least partly with Nietzsche in mind.[18] The elder Adler
thought highly of Otto Bauer, especially admiring his self-confidence in
party interaction and his boldness of thought, which always stopped short
of revolutionary action and thus could preserve the existing style of the
party.[19]

Bauer's thought appeared to crystallize the movement of reality,
which seemed to be changing too quickly to allow more careful definition.
His thought offered models that put societal forces in a dynamic juxtaposition and seemed to clarify the ferment of the times. Marx's dialectical
materialism offered Bauer an array of concepts and a way of opposing and
resolving them that allowed him to live in a conceptual world of change,
an escape from the unresolved problems of the present. Marx, however,
built his concepts and the dialectics of change from concrete circumstances and based his study of capital upon careful research done over
many years. Bauer used Marx metaphorically, not with a semantic definiteness that exposed the factual data that grounded his conceptual sche-
mas. Marxist thought enabled Bauer to hide from his consciousness the
concrete history of present and past "homes." For within his present relationships, and in the childhood relations upon which the presents were
built, were issues so complex that seemingly they could only be left behind by the changes of dialectical history, not resolved. In political reality

one can form new states, resolving social complexities with new legal structures, but perhaps a truth we have learned in our psychological age is that one cannot apply the same methods in resolving one's personal problems: one will recreate them again and again until they are solved.

In the airy realm of conflicting ideas and ideology, Otto Bauer burned as a Marxist meteor, a desert star that highlighted the mental theses and antitheses of his environment. The rigid polarities of Bauer's language and the generalizations that obscured the facts it claimed to represent are seen strikingly in Bauer's editorial introduction to the first issue of *Der Kampf*:

Struggle is the law of development for nature and man. From the teaching of the Greek philosopher Heraclitus, who said that war was the father of all things, to the struggle for existence of Darwin, to the struggle of the classes according to Marx, the insight of mankind into this profound law of his own being and becoming has grown. Mankind: a formative-annihilating battle of the titanic powers of the inorganic; a selective-negative battle of countless millions of cells, from the gigantic mass of infinitely small pygmies of the animated! A destroying-creating battle of millions of brains and hands, from individuals, from organized masses, from competitive classes of the enlivened and conscious! An eternal, rising and falling life, never resting, becoming on the background of an unceasing dying, struggle over being and not-being, struggle for a better existence in a waterglass as well as on the hardened ball of fire in the universe that we call earth—what a drama![20]

The intellectual storm and stress of Bauer's syntheses of Austrian politics won him early prominence. His study of the Austrian nationalities, written in his twenty-fifth year, elevated him to a leading role as a political theorist within Austrian Social Democracy. By his twenty-sixth year, Bauer was secretary of the Austrian Social Democratic faction in the Austrian Parliament, the editor of the foremost Austrian Social Democratic theoretical monthly, *Der Kampf*, and a doctor of law. In his thirtieth year, he was named editor of the *Arbeiter-Zeitung*, in charge of trade union affairs. Besides these responsibilities, Bauer was a teacher at the workers' school in Vienna (a two-year course, with two meetings a week), and he spoke almost every evening at the Arbeiterheim, a social center for workers.[21]

Bauer's rise to the top of his intellectual and social world, Austrian Social Democracy, was marked by an obsessive preoccupation with socialist theory and activities. His day literally existed only for the vision offered by Austrian Social Democracy and Karl Marx. One of his coworkers on the *Arbeiter-Zeitung* provided a glimpse of one of Bauer's average days:

A typical working day for Bauer: He went in the late mornings to Parliament, and took a lively part in all the debates of the Social Democratic faction, read papers on political and economic issues, and helped draft and revise legislative measures for the afternoon sitting of Parliament. In the afternoon, he participated in all the affairs of the Social Democratic faction in Parliament, staying there until evening, and if there were no special committees he went home for a short time. As a rule, he then went about 9 P.M. to the editorial offices of the *Arbeiter-Zeitung.* . . . There he discussed the lead articles with the editor-in-chief and his fellow workers, advising himself on the most important articles and reviews, and giving advice to others. . . . By 11 P.M. Bauer was usually finished with his article. He then went into the office of Austerlitz [the editor-in-chief] and discussed domestic or international affairs, or read a newspaper. In the meantime the proofs of his article had arrived; he read them thoroughly, and occasionally revised them. He never got to bed before 1 A.M., quite often later. Many times he sat with Austerlitz till almost morning. But this is only a rough outline of his daily productivity. How often he went to the workers' school at 9 A.M. to give lectures on national economy for two hours before the sitting of the Social Democratic faction.[22]

How was Bauer able to make the day so productive? He answered this question: "You know, the whole secret of my political activity is that I travel by streetcar and not by automobile, and second, every day in my room I walk back and forth for half an hour. That gives me the possibility to think everything over."[23] The creation of pseudo-history, as well as dramatic tensions and strategies, is the fruit of such tense reflection. Bauer's neglect of personal activities that would engage him in leisure with others, or any form of nonpolitical sharing or personal reflection, had to have repercussions in his emotional and mental life. We can assume that his needs beyond those allowed by his role as intellectual vanguard of the class struggle would announce themselves by linguistic intrusions into the theory he espoused and behavioral intrusions within his activities and action plans.

The great energy that propelled him through a day was surely robbed from the many domains of life that create a balanced individual. Bauer was restricted in his locus of power, although he did not realize it because he was rewarded constantly by his public family of Social Democrats. Bauer once stated that moral indignation gave him his power to fight for the worker.[24] Freud reminds us that hysteria is a moral disease, found only in well-educated individuals, who can turn emotional need through rationalization into a principled outrage at a person or event beyond themselves.[25] Bauer had much to be morally outraged over; besides his father's behavior toward the family, aspects of his father's textile business angered him. Bauer spoke of his contact as a youth in Bohemia and Moravia with the economically deprived classmates of the *Gymnasium* he attended, boys whose fathers were exploited by his father in the textile factory, and stated that this confrontration with the true source of his father's wealth created a moral conflict that was healed only by his engagement with Marx and Marxist activity.[26]

Bauer used as a pseudonym for many of his writings the name Weber, which in German means "weaver," thus reflecting his sense of guilt or perhaps kinship with the exploited workers of his father's textile factory. Bauer's moral outrage did, of course, have legitimate grounds in a public political sense. The test of health is proportion, however, and his adoption of the pseudonym "Weber" is one sign of a lack of proportion in relation to his adolescent anger. Bauer's kinship with the exploited workers in his father's factory was also a symbolic kinship with the elements of his own life that were "exploited" by the model of selfhood he had cultivated in the home of his father, that of the isolated, iron-handed "boss" of his own existence. All human interaction was to be directed to the profit of the owner. When Bauer thought of Czech workers, for instance, he would evidence anger at their laziness and lack of responsibility; he manifested thus a displaced anger at his own emotional life that wished more freedom and self-expression. The Czechs and other non-German workers, such as the Albanians, became symbols for his own emotional debts. Psychologists call such displaced anger at self onto others in the world projection.[27]

Otto Bauer's political personality reflected his childhood and adolescent development just as did Renner's. Bauer found a home in the Austrian Social Democratic party that fulfilled needs engendered in his youth. The party offered Bauer a basis for assimilation into the German culture in a leadership position; for Renner it was a basis for furthering the German culture among the Austrian nationalities under his leadership. The dominant place of language in the party, the emphasis on theoretical discussion, allowed Bauer to find security from an anti-Semitic public culture in a linguistic substitute for nationality. He experienced the insecurity and loss of esteem of all Jews in Austria as a daily tribulation. A political party that supported a revolution in society was a secure public institution that allowed him to redefine himself and his social reality. For Renner, the Austrian Social Democratic party was only an instrument for acquiring personal status in the status quo of Germanic cultural hegemony.

Bauer went through life in a purposeful haste, denying the angers, frustrations, and emotional warmth that he craved by dwelling solely on his plans and projects. His communication with others was always about the business at hand. He developed an intellectual arrogance that chilled and disturbed those around him. Julius Braunthal states:

Bauer appeared to other intellectuals very uncommunicative, in fact, repelling; he could, as had Marx, break out into a show of arrogance with the others if he considered the discussion unfruitful. His penetrating, critical, inexorable logical understanding rebelled against half-thought-through arguments, and if the discussion centered around matters which he believed had a deep meaning for the working class, he could put down his opponent with obstinate harshness. So he appeared to his fellows, as Friedrich Adler said at his burial, as a "severe man," who "merely was concerned with the unconditional validity of the ideas that he held, ideas that he would use for the awakening of society."[28]

In matters of spirit or intellect, Bauer believed himself to be a purist. Theory was not a matter for idle discussion, for theory had a unique force with redemptive qualities: "Only theory frees us from the bewildering influence of the bourgeois environment, only theory straightens us out when the changing events of the day make us irresolute. Therefore, every theoretical contribution, even when it is understood only by the few among us, in its long-range effect, is a benefit to us all. For 'theory too will be a force when it seizes the masses.'"[29]

Whereas Renner found solace for his ethnic strivings through expressionistic theoretical creations, which sought always to justify the existing state of German *Kultur* and Habsburg hierarchy, Bauer's peace of mind, if he ever had any, was approached only in the "expectational" products of theory, of future, nonexistent possibilities. Theory for Bauer expressed always the "not-quite-ready-yet," the becoming of things. The present was always surpassed through the voice of the half-heard angel that freed him from the morass of the extant. The Marxist concept of social revolution was sufficiently vague in its future predication to permit all Bauer's nameless expectations to reside within its boundaries.

As a student of law, Bauer gave himself fully to Marxist theoretical involvements. It was as if, having discovered Marx, he must translate every area of his immediate world into the projective renderings of a theoretical geometry that could subsume all his life needs.

Bauer wrote to Kautsky in 1904:

I am a law student in the third year. I became acquainted with Marx in the *Gymnasium*. Disturbed by the Bernstein discussions, I felt the need to win methodological clarity over the questions. Therefore, I devoted much time to philosophical studies, Kant and Hegel, and also familiarized myself with the discussions over the materialistic conception of value. . . . In order not to lose myself completely in questions of method, I have concerned myself at the same time with economic history, and with the modern manifestations of competition—banks, cartels, and so forth. In my involvement with the latter sphere, I came upon the problems of economic depression, and sought in the theoretical literature of this area a deeper understanding.[30]

Although engaged in the architecture of the future order, Bauer sought at the same time to maintain contact with those masses for whom he would provide the New Canaan. Bauer's exposure to the proletariat was in the role of pedagogue, a role as important to him as that of theoretician. He saw the need to develop two languages—one for the scientific pioneers of the socialism and one for the mass of humanity that would follow their footsteps. The creative realm of theory was inappropriate for common consumption: "For theory is a difficult matter that presupposes extensive *Bildung*. Theory must seek its readers in the circles of the learned, not in the masses of the people." A special language and a special effort must be used to reach the people, to impart the truths won by theory, because the undistilled scientific phraseology was beyond their comprehension: "Social Democratic writers have the duty, not only to avoid foreign words for which another expression could be used, but also to accommodate their phraseology to the needs of the reader, who is accustomed to plain speech. . . . Naturally, this is a difficult sacrifice for us, the denial of so many means of expression; but we will be repaid for this renunciation with the handsome privilege of being able to take part in the education of our youth, to have a voice in the thought and will of the working class."[31]

By slow steps the worker would be initiated into the mysteries of Marxist language and at some future time would be in a position to use the original sources of socialist research:

Quite often the worker takes a good, but difficult to comprehend work, whose comprehension the lack of a previous *Bildung* makes impossible; and disappointed, the worker despairingly lays the book aside and loses all desire to read. Therefore, it is not sufficient to suggest good books to the worker; we must tell him *in what order* he should read them; we must guide him in an *organized* reading program, so that he learns through his studies the simple and clear, and is able to prepare himself for the more difficult. For one must teach him also to read.[32]

Bauer devoted a series of short discussions to this theme in the first issues of *Der Kampf*, suggesting specific reading lists on various topics. Then in 1910 he drafted the plans for a special school wherein "advanced" workers would be exposed to the full impact of Marxist method. Bauer's plans for this school and the reaction of many of his students when the school was realized provide ironic commentary on the infinite distance between the inorganic figments of Bauer's imagination, the proletariat, and the actual workers with whom he wished to communicate but whom he never really saw through the furor of his subjective dialectics. Bauer proposed a schedule for the special school that took on the aspect of his own average working day. The school would last one month; classes would meet six days a week. The mornings would be devoted to the four main subjects, political economy, theory of state, social politics, and Austrian law. One hour each day would be allotted to each subject, for a total of twenty-six hours in the month. Bauer conceded that these broad categories included too much for twenty-six hours of lecture, so he limited them as follows:

(1) *Political Economy*—The decline of manual labor. The development of small business. Capitalism and the capitalization of agriculture. The growth of industry. Stock-holding organizations, cartels, and trusts. Banks and the exchange. The protective tariff and colonial politics. The socialization of the means of production.

(2) *Theory of the State*—The origin of the modern state. The bourgeois revolution in England, France, Germany, and Austria. The development of the Austrian constitution, and its political parties since 1848.

(3) *Social Politics*—Theory and practice of unions. The basic principles and developmental goals of the worker's insurance and protection laws.

(4) *Austrian Law*—Laws concerning the Austrian workers.[33]

The afternoons were free for "recuperation" (*Erholung*). Then:

Two hours every evening will be used for seminar exercises. In the seminar, the teacher should provide the students with a general view of the literature of socialism. He should guide the students to the collections of agitation materials, and instruct the students in the sources and method of statistical tables. The students should learn to deliver lectures and to lead discussions, to give lessons on speaking, and to compose short reports on group gatherings. Perhaps, in addition to this, our experts in political organization will visit the seminar and lead a discussion on political organization.[34]

For diversion, one weekend in the month would include a short trip into the countryside to a place of educational interest. In the second year of the summer session, this trip was to a nearby tobacco factory, a lead mine, and the local museum.[35]

The effect of this titanic *Bildungsarbeit* was measured after every summer session in an article in *Der Kampf*. These articles, written, to be sure, by fellow members of the party oligarchy, provide a glimpse into what actually occurred in the program. We read, for instance, that at the first session Otto Bauer taught political economy and Karl Renner (of course) taught the theory of the state. Bauer's lectures in political economy were praised, although the author of the article, Heinrich Wissiak, adds that the subject matter was so difficult and so vast that little time was left for discussion. Wissiak goes on to say, however, that Bauer's teaching method did enable one to ascertain to some degree what was learned by the stu-

dents. What was his teaching method? Bauer would have a student reca-
pitulate what he had lectured on—the rabbinical method.[36] Thus we see
the indoctrinary nature of the school, with its understanding of the class-
room as a ground of absolutes to be learned by rote rather than as a creative area for mutual exchange. An article by Oskar Helmer, after the second year's summer session, criticizes the quantity of material for stifling
any opportunity for discussion and requests that in following years more
seminar time be allowed because "the teachings in the classrooms clearly
confuse a great many of the students. It is difficult to find one's orientation. One doesn't wish to disturb the lecturer, therefore the seminar
should be available for these questions."[37] Considering the quantity of
additional *Bildung* expected of the seminars, however, one wonders how
much time or attention could have been devoted to the students' morning
problems in the evening seminars.

The question that none of the critics ever raised was that of the basic
assumption of the school that the task of education was memorization
rather than mutual investigation. The implicit acceptance of the view that
socialist knowledge was a body of unconditional objective information
and method possessed by the oligarchic elite led to a syndrome of spiritual
"inflation" in the possessors of the treasure.[38] Inflation manifested itself in
a complete physical and psychic identification by the leading intellectuals
with the theoretical products of their ideology. Thus a physical illness or
psychic depression in the individual could be projected onto the whole
environment and be seen as a sickness in the worker's movement or a
depression in the state of socialist activity. This psychic phenomenon is
the key to understanding much of Otto Bauer's later political behavior.
For the world when viewed through the transformative screen of his projections became truly a stage on which he was producer and director. And
so that his play might have a perpetual run, Bauer never forced a confrontation between his world of the abstract "becoming of things" and the
world in its immediate reality. Thus Bauer's critics, especially in the
1920s, when he was the leader of the left wing of the Austrian Social
Democratic party, accused him of hypocrisy, underlining the fact that
Bauer's radical phraseology never corresponded to his actions, which were
without exception compromise with the bourgeois world. Indeed, one
critic went so far as to publish a pamphlet psychoanalyzing Bauer's tendency to project his subjective state upon the world and thus involve him
in the syndrome of violent words and nonaction.[39]

Overt signs of a hysterical symptomatology affected Bauer's physical
and mental life particularly in times of political tension. In the years from
1910 until 1914, when the progress of Austrian Social Democratic principles in the Austrian Parliament was stymied because of the nationality

conflicts that paralyzed parliamentary action, Bauer became subject to violent migraine headaches that forced a halt to his activities periodically.[40] Moreover, his conceptual relation to Austrian states of affairs became increasingly dramatic; revolutionary politics seemed the only reasonable option, as he projected his own condition upon the body politic. He wrote to Kautsky:

Nothing new with the party now. In general we are in a very unpromising situation. The complete breakdown in the internal and external political scene saps the courage of the people, and the workers think that nothing can be done in any direction in Austria, that all endeavor is hopeless, and thus fall back into complete indifference . . . thus, all in all, a very depressing situation. The most reasonable tactic now would be, perhaps, a propaganda campaign that would direct the workers' hopes toward the dissolution of Austria. But that is not yet possible because a sudden break with the past by the party, and a consolation with the hope of not only far removed, but not too certain future, would not be readily accepted by the masses.[41]

Bauer's family pressures had intensified by 1913, thus compounding the reason for a hysterical relationship to his environment. His mother died that year, and his father developed what Bauer asserted was an abnormal dependency upon him. Bauer wrote to a fellow Social Democrat that he usually perceived his family's troubles as his own, "and therefore it occurs that I am pursued [verfolgt] by the misfortunes of my family which cause me to lose time, and destroy my capacity for work." After his father's death the same year, Bauer complained that even in death "the unfinished business of my father robs me of time."[42]

Bauer found solace in a marriage in January 1914. He married Helene Landau, née Gumplowicz, the niece of the sociologist who influenced the writings of both Bauer and Renner. She was ten years older than Bauer, was married herself when he began their relationship, and had three children. One might say that Bauer had found an ersatz mother, yet Helene Bauer was to provide the basis for a normal relationship that had been lacking in his life. Bauer's statements concerning her indicate a deep emotional and physical sharing. He wrote to her after being captured by the Russians, after the opening months of the world war, "I build upon you . . . we will find each other again in the heat of our old passionate love." Moreover, Helene Bauer was an intelligent partner who shared his Marxist theoretical interests. She wrote her doctoral dissertation on Eugen von Boehm-Bawerk's revisionist profit theory, which supplied a Marxist answer to Boehm-Bawerk's criticisms.[43]

The question remains: to what degree did this match create a home that might serve Bauer as a place of amnesty from his mental struggles?

In the light of Bauer's later writings and political behavior, the answer appears to be that his marriage did not completely free him from the furies that drove him into intellectual flight. Socialism remained for Bauer a choice of career that fulfilled the function he once wrote it served other intellectuals: "There are intellectuals who join the workers' party because they are drawn by the great historical conception of socialism. What they wish is the social revolution. The working class to them is no more than a force which is called and capable of destroying the capitalist order, and realizing the socialist ideal of society; the working class is merely a tool for the realization of this ideal."[44]

5

Bauer's Cultural Dialectics

Otto Bauer concerned himself with the same themes as Karl Renner—nationality and other tactical questions of Austrian Social Democratic policy. His extroverted nature inclined him toward the immediate events of Social Democratic politics. He had the ability to abstract issues and find organizing concepts that clarified the relationships of events to broader historical causes, but the emotional pressure of his life kept such studies in a deductive rather than an inductive mode. Inductive analysis of historical life requires the gathering of data and deliberation of alternative explanations. Bauer's mind dwelled continually at too high a level of abstraction for such research. Moreover, even these deductive studies of events were interrupted with equivocations that prevented him from completing a study that had clear arguments and definite recommendations. Leo Por wrote of him in the early 1930s:

A leader of the so-called left wing of Social Democracy is the well-known Austrian politician, Otto Bauer. Often in his writing, and especially in his public addresses, he superabounds in radicalism, but then follows a *reservatio mentalis* with Bauer, wherein the positive radicalism is conditioned with short or long explanations, sometimes with historical parallels, then again with arguments derived from specific tactical considerations, and then finally with the devil only knows what exhalation like "but please, on the contrary" [*aber bitte schoen, doch nicht*]. There is no speech, no article, no study, no work from this man who writes and speaks so much, in which this ambiguity, this state of contradiction is not present.[1]

His first work, *Die Nationalitaetenfrage und die Sozialdemokratie* (The Question of Nationalities and Social Democracy) (1907), reflects the strengths and weaknesses of his intellect and personality. The book, which was written in Bauer's last year in law school, was lauded by his contemporaries as a brilliant study of nationality. Bauer's incisive syntheses of diverse national expressions seemed to bring Marxist interpretative clarity to the present strife within Austria. Looked at more closely, however, the eclectic nature of the work is evident. Bauer borrowed his psychology and sociology of nation from Ludwig Gumplowitcz, as did Renner, and relied on Renner's proposed solutions to the nationality question. The book was written in haste and for motives of fame as well as science. On January 26, 1906, Bauer had written to Karl Kautsky that he might "write sometime a few articles or a pamphlet on the nationality question; to be sure, I am interested in other things much more, but it will perhaps be necessary that finally a Marxist tells the practical politicians and journalists exactly what is the origin of it all."[2]

Kautsky must have encouraged Bauer, for in February 1906 Bauer began to concern himself with the question that ten months later filled a book of 576 pages. Bauer's capacity for work seemed boundless. One week before beginning the book he had passed his final doctoral exams in law, and in the months that followed, he studied until 2:00 P.M. every day preparing for his entrance exams to the Austrian bar.[3] The book evidences an intensity of style that reflects his obvious passion for the subject and opens many secret compartments to his personality. One of these compartments contained the heart of his eclecticism. Bauer's intensity expressed an element of haste born of the desire to be the first Social Democratic intellectual to contribute to a theme. This desire is evident in the letter to Kautsky and in others, such as the one he wrote to Kautsky before the publication of his "Marxismus und Ethik" (Marxism and Ethics), wherein he pleaded with Kautsky to publish his review as soon as possible, for others would soon publish on the theme, and he would be merely a "camp follower" (Nachzuegler).[4] This haste prevented Bauer from ever treating a topic in depth; the words that first entered his mind seemed sufficient to render a topic completed, and these words inevitably were gleaned from men such as Max Adler with whom he had discussed the theme previously. Thus whereas other men arrived at a statement slowly from the history of a limited area which they had explored in depth, Bauer scooped the surface of their conclusions for his own purposes, considering the result an adequate original contribution. Indeed, his party fathers praised the universality of his interests; Kautsky wrote to Victor Adler in 1909: "We suffer from the "idiocy of specialization" [Fachidiotismus], which is unavoidable in many of the contributions of our intellectuals; but we need more people who are at home in all saddles, who create intellectual wholes that contain all the little pieces. Such a man is . . . Bauer."[5] The problem with such a mode of creation, which Kautsky also evidenced, is that whereas the works of specialization were consistent in all their parts, allowing the reader to follow the thinker through all the steps to his conclusions, the writings were filled with finished conceptions that when traced to their individual premises were often contradictory. Obviously, men like himself never challenged Bauer's eclectic inconsistencies, and his work passed for genius because it contained all the latest theoretical slogans in a readily digestible form, admirably suited for men who were too concerned with the future to waste time in grounding their thoughts in the particulars of the present.

Bauer gives the reader three possible etiologies of national character— a genetic, a cultural, and a psychological. At times these three causal modes are united into one supposedly consistent theory, and at times they are separate and at odds. Writing on the genetic etiology, Bauer represents national character as inhering in the germ plasm: "One can read . . . how our organs reproduce in their genesis the history of our animal ancestors. Similarly we can interpret national character. In the individual character-istic that every individual has in common with his nation . . . is the history that his [physical and cultural] ancestors portrayed, his character is congealed history."[6]

Bauer adds another etiology, however, that can be traced in the cul-tural history of economic development: "He who studies the nation as a national community cannot limit himself to studying *a specific material*— as the germ plasm inherited by the children from their fathers—and seek to make this the basis of nation; rather one must study the history of production, and the modes of distribution of goods carried on by our ancestors in their struggle for existence; only in this way can the inherited characteristics of the later generations be understood."[7]

Bauer seems to reify the economic Marxist metaphor into a separate and competing mode of genesis that is not passed down in the germ plasm but in the language of the culture:

We have discussed two means whereby individuals are molded by the conditions of their struggle for existence into a nation. One way is that of natural inheritance. The conditions of life of the ancestors give the later generations their qualitative characteristics through the germ plasm, thus through natural selection. . . . But the character of the individual is . . . also determined by the inheritance of a traditional culture . . . the product of the inherited cultural products passed from mouth to mouth through the education that he enjoys, the laws that he is subject to, the morals by which he lives, the views of God and world, of moral and immoral, the beautiful and the ugly which he inherits through religion, the phi-losophy, the science, the art, the politics . . . above all by the manner in which his forefathers earned their living in their struggle for existence.[8]

Bauer saw a dichotomy between the products of body and mind, in-cluding the physical activity of making a living in the products of oral

transmission. Bauer, whose life was based on the mind, conveniently ignored the determinism of germ plasm and the bulk of the oral tradition
when discussing the Jewish nation, from which he was removed by only
one generation of Germanized ancestors. When developed to their full
implications, Bauer's considerations would make him a quasi-German at
best. Perhaps sensing this problem, Bauer included an escape clause that,
although contrary to the development of germ plasm and tradition, permitted him entry to the German nationality on the strength of Marxist
cosmopolitan theory: "National character changes. Community of character forms a nation during a definite period of time; the nation of today
is in no way linked to the ancestors of two or three hundred years earlier.
Where we speak of a German national character, we mean the common
characteristics of the German during a specific hundred years or decade."[9]

As if to avoid the inconsistencies inevitable in developing an example
of one national character on the basis of these etiologies, Bauer tells the
reader that he is not interested in showing how national character arises
but in the way it develops culturally, in the *"formal* process of how a national character arises out of a cultural community, not . . . the derivation
of a definite content with national character."[10]

The tautology inherent in this task is obviated by Bauer's belief in the
formal laws of the dialectic that seem to stand outside the entity of national character, conditioning it yet not being part of it. Bauer used this
distinction as a basis for developing a series of "laws" concerning national
character, such as "every nation . . . which is based upon the common
inheritance of their forefathers [*Stammvoelke*], carries within themselves
the germ of dissolution [*Zerfall*], the inclination to divide into several nations from the one originally common nation." These "laws" are used as a
psychological introduction to why certain individuals leave the nation
they were born into and join others or establish their own. The inclination
of dissolution is the antithesis that lies hidden within the thesis of national
character; certain conditions in a culture, such as a new economic development, will unleash the inclination toward dissolution leading to the creation of a nation on the basis of class. The original national character and
community is called the community of destiny (*Schicksalsgemeinschaft*) and
the new one, such as class, is called the community of character (*Charak-
tergemeinschaft*): "One such community of character is the class. . . .
Within all differences, the common class characteristics of the German
and English, the French and the Russian, the American and the Austra-
lians shine through; the same joy of battle, the same revolutionary urges,
the same class morality, the same political desires."[11]

Bauer then arrives at a narrower definition of national character based
solely on one's inclination. National character "does not mean the whole

of the physical or intellectual characteristics, which are part of a nation, rather it means merely the difference in directions of will, the fact that the same stimulus creates many different responses, and that from the same basic ground many different conclusions can be drawn."[12] Whatever the individual or group of individuals will is national character. Bauer had managed to clear the ground for a very important discussion: why the Jewish nation no longer existed and thus why Otto Bauer could be a vanguard in good standing of the German intellectual tradition, even more a German than the bourgeois intellectuals who did not believe in the proletariat or the socialist state.

If national character was determined finally by one's will, then the next step was to identify certain people who exhibited no will at all, and they would not be a nation. Here Bauer ushered in Gumplowicz and the distinction between active and passive nationality (see Chapter 3). Obviously, Bauer could not ignore the germ plasm and tradition of ancient people such as the Jews on the basis of his definition of willful national character, for they did have a language and a history of physical and cultural inheritance; but he could say that as a passive nationality they no longer expressed these entities in their lives and that germ plasm and tradition lay dormant in their consciousness. When Bauer turned to his father's generation of Jews, the categories of active and passive nationality seemed to be consistent with his definition of national character; that is, the Viennese Jews seemed to have no relation to the Jewish ghetto culture that immediately preceded them, and yet many of them had not with active consciousness fully adopted the German cultural tradition. One may object that Bauer's father and uncles were respected Viennese professionals, but Bauer inserts an even narrower definition of national character that demands awareness of one's historical identity and conveniently excludes them from German nationality: "National consciousness is the awareness that one shares certain characteristics, physically, in cultural products, in the individuality of certain desires, which differentiate him from others that do not share these particular qualities: looked at more profoundly, it is the awareness that certain people like myself have the same history. Thus national character in no way demands a mutual love for a nation, or even the will for the unity of a nation; it only identifies the consciousness that one belongs to a nation."[13]

One must ask, however, how Bauer dealt with the Jews of the ghettoes of eastern Europe and movements such as Zionism that were contemporary with his writing. Did these not represent an active nationality? Bauer would answer that a distinction must be made between nations with a history and nations without a history (*geschichtlose Nationen*). The latter, though perhaps willing to maintain their identity, had been disinherited from the ranks of genuine nationhood. A nation with a history is one that controls its own territory and thus the means of production. Such a definition of history presupposes that one has a history only insofar as he is identified with the economic development of society. Hidden behind this neologism peeps the head of Bauer's real nation and real home, the Marxist metaphor, which is given the power to reshape Bauer's family tree. Thus when Bauer discusses how it was possible for the Jews to remain a nation for so many hundreds of years in Europe, he seems to forget that he has just called them a nation without a history and gives them a new history—an economic one. His somewhat confusing discussion of the Jews in Europe runs:

The Jews could become a historical nation, if they were able to remain a nation long enough; but the capitalistic society will not allow them to remain a nation. Here we use the shibboleth, the Jews cannot remain a nation while they have no territory on which to prove their identity. If one asserts this statement in the broadest general terms, namely that a defined area of settlement is the presupposition for the maintenance of a nation, then he goes astray. The history of the Jews, who for so many hundreds of years existed as a nation without a territory contradicts such a statement. But we know now how this was possible: The Jews, as representatives of a money economy within the older natural economy that formed the basis of the world at large, in spite of the fact that they lived in the middle of the other European peoples, had maintained a very loose contact with that world, and thus could maintain their identity as a nation.[14]

Bauer constantly exhibits in his writing the characteristic of attempting to hold onto the saddle of the horses that suddenly appear between his legs in midstream. The Jews, it seems, had a history once on the strength of their nascent capitalism, but no longer, for they have ceased to be spokesmen of the capitalist economy and as a nation can no longer go on without a territory.

Bauer also denies the Zionists the right to existence: "In the last decade a movement has begun that is inimical to the process of assimilation, one that desires to make the Jews again an independent historical nation. This new movement is driven by the same impetus that has awakened the cultural life of the other 'nations without a history,' that is, the social awakening of the lower classes of society, the awakening of their self-consciousness; the Jewish workers no longer feel inferior to the rich and educated Poles or the rich Jews who have assimilated Polish education." Bauer here places the Zionists within the frame of the economic metaphor and identifies them with the proletariat; thus they could be sentenced and executed on the basis of the dialectic:

The German worker wishes the same for the Jewish comrade as he does for the Czech comrade: higher salaries, a proud self-consciousness, and the ability for international class warfare. In order to arrive at these goals, the German worker must allow the Czech in German territory to preserve his own national autonomy; but in the interest of the same goals, he must deny the Jewish worker the same rights. The rights of national autonomy for a minority nationality, while further- ing the class struggle when we speak of the Czech worker, is only psychologically harmful to the class struggle in terms of the Jewish worker. This is because any maintenance of Jewish identity reinforces the mentality of the Jewish merchant in the worker, and hinders his assimilation into the modern class structure based upon modern industry.[15]

Judaism is wholly identified with the mercantile mentality of the ar- chetypal Shylock; no other culture really existed as far as Bauer was con- cerned. Thus when Jews within the Austrian Social Democratic party demanded the right to parochial schools, Bauer had to refuse their desires because they had no culture apart from the peddler atavisms of the ghetto. Bauer's definition at the beginning of his book of the traditional products of culture—the oral transmission of laws, aesthetics, morality, philoso- phy, science, and the manner in which one's forefathers earned their living in the struggle for existence—became in the case of the Jews limited to the struggle for existence. But this was necessary, for when Bauer turned to the New Man, the German national of the future, he had to be free from the cultural ghosts of his past. His reconstruction of cultural history allowed him to deny his Jewish heritage and thus indirectly separate him- self from his personal family. He used the economic determinism of Marx to dismiss the Jewish tradition as bastard capitalism, but he conveniently overlooked the success of his father's industrial activity and the fact that his father represented a new class of upper-middle-class Jews whose eco- nomic activity demonstrated their permanent place in Austrian culture. Through a gap in his logic emerged the glories of German *Kultur*, some- how not a product of economic determinism. The society of the future, and the New Man, would be a union of the proletariat and the German intellectual tradition; the proletariat was an expression of the historical destiny of the Austrian nation, the fruit of the immediate economic real- ity, while shining through the economic substratum, which otherwise de- termined all culture, was the German mother tongue and its reflection on the shields of the Social Democratic vanguard:

Socialism carries within itself the guarantee of national unity. It will make the German language the unified national language, the greatest portal to our cultural products, which even yet is like a foreign language to most of the masses. The German language will become the mother tongue of all in the socialized society;

it will be the determinant for the new community of character, and thus be the direction that must be followed by all who wish to identify with the new nation; it will make the cultural products of nation the possession of every German, and thereby make every German the creator of our cultural products.[16]

To initiate this new order, Bauer as a vanguard of the proletariat and the German intellectual heritage had a self-appointed social-pedagogical mission to fulfull—the education of the workers to their existence as proletariat and, their education to the treasures of German *Bildung*. As Bauer wrote in 1907, in a pamphlet entitled *Deutschtum und Sozialdemokratie*, "The greatness of a nation depends not only on its numbers, but also on the height of its morals and its culture. This greatness the German nation can boast of. Who will deny that German science, German philosophy, German poetry, and German art can stand their ground with any culture of any nation." He added, "But what do our German workers know of Kant, what to the manual laborers know of Marx, what do the German farmers know of Goethe?"[17] This hiatus in German greatness would be rectified by Bauer and his compatriots.

When Bauer speaks of socialism bringing the fruits of German *Kultur* to the people through the German tongue and of the New Man as being a worker who has the benefit of Goethe and Kant, one might suspect that he means only Germanic Austria. But Bauer laid a ground in his definition of national character that allowed him to include all the nations of the Austrian state in the Germanic heaven. Bauer calls the Czechs, Slovene, Romanian, and other nations of the Austrian state (with the exception of the German) "nations without history" but, in contradistinction to the Jewish nation, says that they can win back their history by participating in what he terms a "centralized unified state." Of the Czechs particularly, he writes: "Nationally [the defeat at White Mountain] of the Bohemian nobility meant that the Czech nation was transformed into the inactive state of a nation without a history [*eine geschichtlosen Nation*]. Politically, it meant that the way was cleared for their development into a modern centralized unified state [*zentralistischen Einheitsstaat*]."[18]

What Bauer seems to imply in the term "centralized unified state" is that by losing their culture the Czechs were open to receive the economic and political gifts of the German industrialized *Kultur*. Therefore, as evidenced by Bauer's later writings, they could be completely assimilated into the mainstream of German *Kultur*; even their language would be absorbed. The socialist development within the Austrian unified state would gradually transform all the differences of national minority groups, through common economic activity, into a united body that would speak one tongue. Of course, this conclusion was only implicit in Bauer's arguments, for in his book he had upheld Renner's personality principle and thus gave lip service to the preservation of distinct nationalities within a centralized administration. But when one examines Bauer's other declarations of what the new community of character would be and how it is always conditioned by the economic order, which gives essence to all cultural artifacts (with the notable exception of the German), one cannot fail to follow the direction of Bauer's thought toward a "Bauerization" of Austria. The impetus behind Bauer's transformation of all other cultures into the intellectual culture of German letters and Marxist metaphor was what he called the "narrower definition" of national character, that is, the recognition that an individual's will can draw original conclusions on the basis of a set of facts common to others. Bauer had created, in effect, his own national character and, in a projection à la Renner, made it the model for the society of the future.

But one cannot expect consistency in Bauer. When he thought of the German nation, culture was formed by language, and the other nations had an existence and a right to their language (except for the Jews). All one can understand from these shifting structures of explication is that images flowed through Otto Bauer's mind, and he was forced to shape his momentary argument in the pattern of whatever images immediately transfixed him.

Bauer's major article on the question of assimilation of nationalities, written in March 1912, contains just as many inconsistencies as his book of six years before, and the same images chase one another's tails. The article, written to aid in the framing of a German-Austrian Social Democratic tactic in the face of the Czechs' formal departure from Austrian Social Democracy the year before, was addressed to his fellow Social Democrat Ludo Hartmann, who had stated that there was no point trying to protect German culture in Bohemia or Moravia for the Germans there must in time by assimilated by the majority Czech culture.[19] Hartmann argued that the Czechs should be allowed to go their own way and that the German-Austrian Social Democrats should turn toward Germany if the Austrian state were dissolved by the centrifugal pull of the nationalities. Bauer objected strongly to Hartmann's pessimism regarding the preservation of German individuality in Bohemia and Moravia, asserting that if Hartmann really understood the laws of assimilation, which were an expression of the Marxist historical and economic dialectic, he would realize the Germans in Czech lands were not lost to German culture. Moreover, the Czechs themselves were not lost to Austrian Social Democracy, that is, German-Austrian–controlled Social Democracy, for in spite of present national differences, the industrial expansion of capitalism, and eventually socialism, must make all these neighboring nations brothers in culture. Bauer tried to establish why the German minorities would not be assimilated, whereas the Czech minorities, and eventually the Czech majorities, could be assimilated. Bauer lists twelve laws of assimilation, some borrowed from Gumplowicz's theory of nationality, others based upon the economic dialectic, and others that seem based only in Bauer's stream of consciousness:

1. The greater the minority, the smaller the attracting power of the majority; the smaller the minority, the more certain the assimilation.

2. The smaller the fraction of the majority in the total population, the easier the assimilation.

3. Assimilation is accomplished most easily where the minority is dispersed among the settlements of the majority; assimilation will be more difficult the more a minority settles together, and the more it separates itself from the community of the majority; assimilation is completely hindered if the settlement of a minority is completely separated from the majority and forms a language island [*Sprachinsel*].

4. National assimilation is easier, the more similar the majority to the minority in matters of race, culture, religion, and speech.

5. Assimilation of working classes [*arbeitender Klassen*] leads to little change in the oral tradition and morals of assimilated people; assimilation of a minority people by a dominant majority will create an amalgamation of the two people that will produce a *new nationality with a new language.*

6. If the social conditions of the majority change, then the conditions of assimilation of minorities to that majority also change: a) The governing class is assimilated to the majority nationality, where they are in constant contact with that nationality and allow that nationality a share in the governing. b) Nations that participate in a money economy, and exist within a people who are mainly adherents to a natural economy, will preserve their identity; they will only be assimilated in proportion to the proportion of people in the natural economy who change to money economy.

7. Slavery will never force assimilation; serfdom will promote assimilation.

8. Proletarian immigrants of the agrarian-domestic type assimilate to another nationality more easily than proletarian immigrants of the industrial-capitalistic type; the reason is that the higher the economic development of an immigrant's home, the higher the qualification of his work, the higher the level of culture.

9. The greater a nation's population, gross product, power, and culture, the greater its attracting power over minorities in its own area, the greater its resistance to the attraction of other nationalities if it is a minority in another nationality's area.

10. Minorities only assimilate if within the majority nationality they find their class, professional, or cultural counterpart, i.e., the farmer can be assimilated only through the influence of another farmer.

11. Assimilation proceeds more rapidly the greater the increase in population of the majority in proportion to population increase in the minority.

12. All conditions that serve to bring the minority and the majority in con-

tact with one another serve to further assimilation; all conditions that serve to hinder the contact between nationalities make assimilation more difficult.[20]

The potpourri of these "laws" witnesses Bauer's manipulation of concept into the web of his own character. As a final stroke to his gerrymandering of the Czechs into the corner of his logic, Bauer added three "universal" categories wherein he examines the various genres of minority nationality, in the world at large, and in Austria:

1. The first group is assimilable minorities. As for example: the German minority in North America and in French Switzerland, the Czech minority in the German areas of the Sudetenland and the Alps, the Jewish minority in Galicia. The national assimilation of these minorities is an unavoidable process of nature. . . . We must not permit these minorities the right to their own schools, although we must protect these minorities against infringements by the majority nationality, which would only slow down their natural assimilation.

2. The second group would be the nonassimilable minorities: They are protected against assimilation by the size of their population (as the Czech mining colony in Northwest Bohemia) or through their enclosed settlements (as all genuine language islands) or through their class situation (as the German bourgeois minorities in the South Slav areas). These minorities must be guaranteed their rights, their right to live their own national life.

3. The third group make up the assimilable and nonassimilable minorities. To this group belong the Czechs in Vienna or the Germans in Prague. These nationalities should be given schools that teach in both the majority and minority language.[21]

Bauer stated that Ludo Hartmann's desertion of the Germans in Czech lands would violate the natural laws he had outlined and that minority nationalities in Groups 2 and 3 of the above categories would be forced to assimilate against their nature, being deprived of the schools that would ensure their language. At the close of the article, Bauer adds to all the other "laws" an afterthought that seems to open new areas of ambiguity: "A great hindrance to assimilation is the difference in race. As soon as the Czech is assimilated into the German nationality his Czech origins are concealed [verdeckt] . . . but it is different in cases where the race of the minority is not similar to that of the majority. Thus the assimilated Jews are still obviously Jews according to their facial characteristics. Race instincts and race prejudices live on after assimilation."[22]

What does Bauer mean by "race"? He seems to refer to elements of ethnic inheritance that affect physiognomy, feeling, and thought, if racial prejudice and racial instinct are assumed to be manifested in thought. Odd that once assimilated the Czechs' racial differences are concealed or covered [verdeckt] yet the process of assimilation fails to hide something in the Jew. Facial characteristics cannot be concealed or covered; perhaps, then, Bauer refers to racial instincts that are concealed. These reflections on an apparent afterthought by Bauer are of moment for we will find that Bauer's relation to the Czechs can be unraveled by following the delicate threads of his metaphorical addendum. Keeping in mind his reference to race and the Czechs, let us observe a statement of Bauer's about Czech national character made six months earlier:

The Czech worker, who works on German soil, is not a pleasing présence for the German nation. . . . The whole manner of the Czech worker has a provocative strangeness. For the essence of the robust Czech proletariat who roams [continually through the German lands] in search of employment, having been driven out of the hunger-stricken land of Bohemia by the expansion of capitalism (*Konjunktur*), is quite different from the race of German worker who spends his life in the quiet, remote [*weltfern*] retreat of his mountain village dreaming and musing. For the German in this still corner of his existence [*stillen Enge ihres Daseins*], socialism is a profound inner belief, not a loud cry. In proletarian boldness and defiance the Czech outdoes the sedentary German. In the battle against the common foe, the Czech, therefore, is a wonderful comrade. But in questions of reason and policy, the Czech appears to the German as ignorant, rash, and unbridled. Thus it is difficult for the two nations to understand one another. And the kind of worries these foreign comrades have! The Germans think on the great promise [*Verheissung*] of socialism which will free mankind; the Czech interrupts him with national solutions, minority schools, the language of administrations [*Amtssprache*], and railroad signs! The German who has not had to work in foreign countries cannot understand the problems that the Czech brings to him. And when the Germans see how more and more of these strange people come into their valleys, and begin to make demands on behalf of their nation, year in and year out, then the Germans become anxious for their homes. Shall this beautiful piece of land in which my parents are buried, and on which the cradle of my child sat, this land that was for hundreds of years German, become the prize of people so wholly different than us?[23]

Thus Bauer puts words into the hypothetical mouth of the common German worker in an attempt to draw a compassionate picture of the German antipathy to the Czechs. But seen in another light, the exposure of metaphor, the question of Czech separatism and its threat to Austrian Social Democratic unity becomes an allegoric vehicle for the civil war of emotion and ego defense which Bauer constantly engaged in.[24] Within his self-consuming struggle were concealed the racial instincts attributed to the Czechs. Bauer, who attempted to force all his existence into a serfdom (not slavery) to the intellectual masters of Marxism and the Austrian Social Democratic party, who had isolated himself in an intellectual island of language, as removed as the quiet mountain retreat of the idealistic

Germans, was threatened by the foreign, unbridled, rash, irrational, and to him ignorant [*unwissend*] elements that invaded his German land. The issue of Czech separatism became a possessive picture of Bauer's being, usurping his vision of the external for its own hungry ends.

In the same article, Bauer suggests that to heal the increasingly aggravated split between the Germans and Czechs in the labor unions of Vienna and in the state in general, a "double organization" be created. This double organization was based on Renner's concept of the personality principle wherein the economic affairs of all unions would maintain an international, that is, unified party character, whereas the Czechs should have their own language rights and the Germans theirs. In an impassioned wail to fate, Bauer closes:

If my way proves to be invalid, then the working class will be forced to suffer the difficult, painful path of separation, a path which will cost the Austrian worker many fruitless years. But this way will lead finally to the goal [of unity], I do not doubt that. For just as surely as the unified party is not possible today, just that surely will the essential unity of all proletarian interests finally overcome all difficulties, which are our inheritance from the tragic history of our state. Damned through the malevolence of history to live in a state whose inner contradictions poison and contaminate thought and feelings of its inhabitants, we will only be able to achieve the kind of unity won by workers of other lands through long, difficult internal battles, only with inexpressible sacrifice of time, patience, and energy.[25]

In the light of such expressionistic language, one can gain a clearer understanding into many of Bauer's other proposals to settle the conflict between the Czechs and Germans. His proposals were cloaked in figures of speech that mirrored many attitudes toward this internal separation. At times, he desired unity so strongly that he would make major concessions to the Czechs; at times, he sought means to bypass the Czech nationalists and win support of other elements in the Czech lands (Czech Marxist internationalists); and at times, he damned the Czechs and suggested a separate German socialist party and state. For instance, Bauer's creation of the third category, the class of assimilable and nonassimilable minority nationalities in his article on the conditions of national assimilation, is, in terms of the world, a hapless effort of symbolic logic; but seen in terms of Bauer, one realizes that he admitted by creating this category that in the major metropolises of the state in which he lived it was not clear which nationality would win in the battle of cultures. Thus he suggested that the language of each nation be guaranteed in the schools of Vienna and Prague, allowing the individual national to decide the culture he would follow when given both alternatives. Once the Czechs were exposed to the obvious superiority of German letters and science, they could not fail to choose the German way.

In 1911, Bauer sought a more drastic means to bridle the Czechs and their desires: he encouraged the Austro-German Social Democrats to support the efforts of a separate Czech socialist movement that was nonnational in its aims.[26] Victor Adler discouraged this approach, for according to a letter Bauer wrote to Kautsky, Adler believed the Czech nationalist demands were the life force of Bohemia and Moravia and that the new Czech Marxist Internationalists would "give birth to a stillborn child."[27] During the early months of 1911, Bauer fumed under the conciliatory hand of Adler, calling him "a fanatic for unity," but by July 1911, after the Czechs had officially left the central authority of the Austro-German Social Democrats, Bauer joined Adler in attempting to bring them back and gave up the hope of the Czech centralists as fruitless. Bauer stated in a letter to Kautsky on July 8, 1911, "The struggle against separatism ends practically in a nationalistic baiting [*Hetze*] of the Czechs, in an actual struggle of German and Czech workers with each other—not only figurative—with knives! That is a poor means to propagate Internationalism."[28]

As George Eliot once wrote, every battle without is also a battle within. By the summer of 1911 the Czechs, who had functioned as a metaphor for the personal turmoil of Bauer's life in these years, began to lose their symbolic pregnancy. The first indication we have of this withdrawal of energy from the mirror of the Czechs is the article "Zu neuen Formen," where Bauer urges all Austro-German Social Democrats to close ranks and "go their own way" and expressed the desire for a recollection of all German elements in the empire "to form a new body."[29]

As long as a possibility of healing the separation existed, Bauer manifested his syndromes through the Czech problem, but when other civil wars were evidenced, as they soon were in the Balkan states, Bauer shifted his attention and his pen. As if to clear the ground for a new center of involvement, Bauer wrote an article about the Czech question that appeared in October 1912 in which he not only expressed satisfaction with the state of separate Social Democratic national organizations within Austria and the wish that they remain separated in the future but also attempted to show that there had not been realy party unity within Austrian Social Democracy since 1897 and as far as the Czechs were concerned, since 1887—before Austrian Social Democracy had been established by Victor Adler.[30] Thus, as done with the Jews, Bauer reinterpreted history in order to establish a new body of facts that would allow him either to generate or withdraw his projection of personal needs within the real world. His desire to establish "a new organization in new forms" was a metaphor that expressed the need for a new historical situation to serve as a projective scapegoat for his internal struggle, as well as the political need of Austrian Social Democracy in the wake of Czech withdrawal.

Foreign policy commanded all Bauer's attention between the summer of 1912 and the outbreak of World War I. Almost every month he published an article in *Der Kampf* on existing wars, future wars, the state of the Habsburg military, or the military policy of Austrian Social Democracy. The basis of all these articles was the statement in the July 1912 article entitled "Bourgeoisie und Militarismus": "There is no doubt that the fatherland needs protection against the external enemy that threatens its borders and protection against the disturbers of the peace internally; therefore the duty exists that every able-bodied man learn to use weapons."[31]

Above all other foreign threats, Bauer feared Russia and her influence over the southern Slav peoples within the Austrian state—other "nations without a history." Yet, although the southern Slav peoples of the state were placed in this inferior category, ostensibly because of their lack of a capitalized economy, Bauer granted them a superiority over their language brothers outside of the Austrian domain. This distinction is especially clear in an article written at the time of the final annexation of Bosnia and Herzegovina into the Austrian state in 1908 in which he attempts to explain why an expansion of the Austrian state into the Balkans could be beneficial and should not be viewed as an imperialistic evil. The expansion of an industrialized *Kultur* brought with it the treasures of *Bildung*, and although there was always the threat of capitalist exploitation, such expansion was a necessary evil for a nation without history. Bauer admonished the "blind hatred and fear" of the Austrian rulers, who insisted on treating the southern slavs as an inferior people and, instead of giving them national autonomy within the realm with the beneficial access to all that was best in the culture, alienated them, treating them as serfs. The southern Slav "irredenta" were in danger of revolting and following Pan-Slavism, Bauer asserted, because they were not treated as first-class citizens. As he succinctly put it, "Fear of the irredenta creates the irredenta."[32]

In November 1908, Bauer expressed the policy that would be best for the Balkan lands, both within Austria and not yet within Austria. He adumbrated the role the German *Kultur* of the Austrian state must play on the European continent, especially to the south:

Greater Austria [*Grossoesterreich*] is not primarily the satisfaction of our personal demand [as a Social Democrat], but rather the necessary final product of an already observed tendency of development. These existing tendencies, therefore, must define our own politics and set their direction. . . . Must not Austria, when she has developed her national autonomy earlier and more fully than her neighboring states, exercise a great attracting power by the nature of her constitution on her comrades across the border? . . . Thus, the idea of a Greater Austria, as paradoxical as it may sound, can become part of the oldest traditions of our political thought: its realization appears as a tool of European Democracy against *czarism*, and as a step toward the final completion of the principle of nationality.[33]

Fear of Russia justified expansion of Austria on the Continent. Moreover, one senses Bauer's metaphorical possession when he imagines that political and cultural forms of the Austrian Germanic state can "complete" the principle of nationality in the "comrades across the border." Historians differ as to Russia's actual force in the Balkans before World War I and whether she was a real threat to Austria. Oscar Jaszi stated that a Pan-Slavism initiated by Russia in the Balkans made war inevitable; Carl Schoerske, an expert on German Social Democracy, held that after the 1905 revolution in Russia, most of the party no longer saw the czarist culture as a bastion of reaction or a major threat to Europe.[34] In December 1909 Bauer again warned that military preparation was necessary and that Austrian interest must be protected, especially in the Balkans: "The advance of capitalism has created a world of enemies armed against us. Hatred of Austria unites Italian democracy with czarism. True, the wounds Russia has suffered from her war with Japan and the revolution [in 1905] are not yet healed. But in a few years Russia and czarism will have a powerful army again at her bidding. *What then?*"[35]

But as with all his writing, Bauer's statements regarding foreign policy in the Balkans are contradictory, either in the same or another article. For example, in an article written in September 1909, Bauer urged that Social Democracy fight every attempt at Habsburg expansion in the Balkan peninsula as an evil of capitalist imperialism. Instead of bringing *Kultur* through capitalism, Bauer emphasized that "free trade" with the Balkan lands was necessary to "take away the nourishment [*Naehrmittel*] that fed the voices of hatred against Austria, and thus avert the danger of war." In this article, Bauer saw the Balkan situation in different focus than in earlier articles; he concentrated on the customs war Austria had waged with Serbia since 1906. This aspect of the southern Slav situation seemed to allow Bauer to be more open to the non-Austrian Slavs than he had ever been but for the purpose of averting war and taking away the nourishment of their hatred. In the same article, he speaks of "tearing down the dam our agrarian egoism [*Selbstsucht*] has erected against the Balkan people." The Balkan people, like the Czechs, provided an excellent mirror for Bauer's ego defense against his emotional past and present. As in the

Czech question, Bauer's contradictions voice the manifold, shifting attitudes toward his own existence.

Even more pregnant in this vocabulary of civil war was the presence of Russia, an evil genius that carried every element of existence antithetical to Bauer's ego allowances. Thus Bauer's desire to tear down the dam of agrarian egoism erected by Austrian powers was mainly to keep Russia from taking advantage of the economically oppressed Balkans. In the same article Bauer employs his favorite tactic of self-justification when he condemns Russia as "the bastion of all reaction"; he builds an argument within the frame of a chronological history that would seek to give his subjective attitude a place in the objective flow of time, preferably a time with a foundation of at least one hundred years. Scattered dates and the authority of economic determinism are characteristic presences that give depth and continuity to Bauer's momentary impressions:

Marx and Engels during their life . . . sought always to mobilize the energies of European democracy against Russia. The war against Russia would serve as a European revolution, analogous to the war the French waged against the united princes of Europe. The war against Russia was urged by Marx in 1848 when he called upon the Germans to lead it, in 1853 when England carried the banner of his hopes; and even in the years from 1860 until 1890, Engels hoped that Germany and Austria would begin a war against Russia, for they knew Russia to be the bastion of all reaction.[36]

Thus the "bastion of all reaction" served as the evil threat that could organize Bauer's emotional reaction. The southern Slavs, even more than the Czechs, were excellent material for the emotional reactions to a repressive logic. The southern slav national character was much stormier than the Czech, and their secret societies and political murders provided Bauer with more than adequate material for his expressionistic forays. Perhaps the most fascinating and repelling people among the Balkans for Bauer were the Albanians; although a non-Slav nation, they were lumped in Bauer's mind together with the rest of the Balkan "nations without a history." In an article written at the time of the first Balkan war, Bauer dwelled at length on the national character of these people, whom he considered the most barbaric in Europe, describing the custom of political murder in Albania and treating in almost fond detail the tradition of family venegeance and the meting out of law by vendetta. He was fascinated by the political and social structure of Albania, its division into five districts on the basis of family, and how these five families marry exogamously, thus transforming the nation into a complex of family relationships—a nation truly organically united. After spending the first four pages of a six-page article on the culture of Albania, he says it is a country without a culture and a people without a will to one. The Albanians are condemned as a nation without a history, who have not yet awakened to their lack. As an example of their lack of culture, Bauer mocks the absence of a written language on the model of the Germans, completely overlooking the existence or importance of their oral culture. The Albanians had an oral epic literature that has been compared to the Homeric epic in its richness of tradition and educative function. Nevertheless, Bauer writes:

The Albanians, too, are a nation without a history. They have had no literature, no written language, not even an alphabet in which to write their speech . . . and not only do they have different languages among their own nation, they also have different orthographics composed of different alphabets. One person writes down the Albanian language in Latin characters, another with Greek, another with Arabian letters. One could jest about Albania "they have more modes of literating than literates" [*mahr Alphabete als Alphabeten*], that is, more means of writing than those who can write.[37]

Yet in later articles Bauer manifested a curious concern for the cultural integrity of Albania. He expressed the desire that the country be left alone by the European powers, including Austria, which wished to stretch its railroad nets (*Eisenbahnnetzen*) into Albania, acting as Albania's protector, but also giving itself an outlet on the Adriatic Sea. Here he contradicted his previous statements about the need for capitalist development in countries without a history, especially those on the mission of German *Kultur* and his allegation that Albania was the most culturally deprived country in Europe. Again Bauer was ambivalent about the primitive spontaneity of the southern peoples. In one breath he defended their right to autonomy and in the next demanded that this autonomy fit the conditions of his definition of culture. His ambivalence can be understood when we scrutinize his wording closely. His depiction of the interference of Austria and Italy in Albania brings to mind the childhood scenes he must have witnessed between two warring adults struggling for the favor of their children. The sentences are built from clauses that never seem to complete their point, that clash to a final conclusion. The clauses and the conclusion are always in the future conditional tense (if only one could avoid this state of affairs, Bauer seems to sigh):

If the Austrian and Italian governments support the capitalists of their countries in the competition over the Albanian market with political means of force; if each of the two governments seeks to place the conflicting parties of Albania under its control, and have them do service for it; if the two governments, filled with jealousy and mistrust against each other, meddle in the internal turmoil which the

Albanians cannot avoid, as their own palace coups and civil wars create new crises that involve Italy and Austria, then will Albania become an increasing threat to the peace between Austria and Italy.[38]

Bauer's desire for freedom and independence for Albania is expressed with words that recall his childhood struggles for personal freedom and pleasure:

There is a general interest of European democracy, of European culture, of European peace to stop a catastrophic outbreak of war between Austria-Hungary and Italy. Therefore the proletarian democracy on this side and beyond the Alps must demand that the solution of "Albania for the Albanians!" must be seriously attempted, and that any interference in the affairs of Albania by imperialistic politics on Albanian soil must result in Albania's real freedom and independence, even against the Austrian and Italian lust for domination [Herrschafts gelueste]. "Hands away from Albania!" [Haende weg von Albanien!] must be the watchword [Losung] among Social Democrats in Austria-Hungary and Italy.[39]

His concern with the Balkan peninsula (Balkanhalbinsel) must be considered, in part, a phallic metaphor for his continuing struggle for an identity free of the manipulative presence of his parental model. These expressionistic intrusions into objective politics were always controlled by a reality principle for Bauer; he managed to keep his deliberations within plausible boundaries of Social Democratic politics. He closed the subject of the Balkans and Albania in an article a few months later with the insight that fortunately Albania would probably be industrialized by other Mediterranean or Balkan nations in the near future, thus being brought into the civilized nations by another force than Austria.[40]

Bauer's relationship to Austrian Social Democratic participation in Parliament was as ambivalent as his attitudes to Balkan politics. He maintained a theoretical distance from unquestioning participation in a "bourgeois" government, yet as secretary of the Austrian Social Democratic faction in Parliament after the universal suffrage of 1907 he was active in parliamentary politics. His objection to participation never reached a pitch that would discontinue such involvement. An expression of his position in 1908 is reflected in an article he wrote for Der Kampf in which he states that the Austrian Social Democrats have a choice of two roles: they can be a critical minority, in constant opposition to the bourgeois parties, or they can engage in the tactics of obstruction, participate in committees, and accept the minister's portfolio.[41]

As long as Parliament was somewhat viable as an organ of political change, Bauer continued to work within it, making statements of qualification as to the role of such participation in Austrian Social Democratic policy and the future socialist state. He found personal meaning in his involvement with everyday political realities, and the activity of Parliament provided such political realities. Thus he could subtly justify Parliament in a more fundamental manner than his initial caveat would suggest:

> The great task of transferring the means of production into the possession and the administration of society, and the disciplined new ordering of societal production and societal consumption will naturally be led by the representatives of the whole society, thus *must* be led by a parliamentary body. Can parliamentary action be enough to fulfill this great task? Where democratic laws have created a democratic organization of autonomous local administrations, and a democratic military body, where the powers in control have no weapons to use against the parliamentary majority, there is the fate of the capitalistic society decided, and completely through the proletarian conquering of Parliament.[42]

Conceived as a military campaign, full participation in Parliament was justified. Bauer could allow himself to become absorbed by this body.

The continuing failure of the Austrian Parliament to pass social legislation between 1907 and World War I caused a great hardship for Bauer because he was not prepared to take the revolutionary alternative of direct action beyond Parliament. He needed the responsibility and interaction of an authorized forum; he was not a revolutionary. The loss of effectiveness in an everyday forum threatened his stability. In an article whose title signified his own gradual unraveling in the several years before the war, "Die Lehren des Zusammenbruchs" (The lessons of breakdown), Bauer bemoaned the stalemate of Parliament, which had been dissolved twice during the first six months of 1909 because of national obstruction. He saw only two alternatives for the future of Austria: "National settlements and reform in the order of parliamentary business by Parliament itself or bureaucratic *Oktroi* [the dissolution of Parliament by order of the Emperor]!—these are the alternatives! Shall these problems find a democratic solution through Parliament or a bureaucratic one dictated by the government?—That is the question . . . that will determine our whole internal development.[43]

Bauer's psychophysical development was tied closely to the meaningful structure of Parliament, which for him and his associates was the only alternative for Social Democratic realization of policy. The bourgeois way of life necessitated peaceful settlement of disputes. One must view a book review he published in 1911 on the Austrian politician Adolf Fischhof as a piece of dramatic irony, produced and directed by Bauer's warring state of existence, his unconscious. Who was Adolf Fischhof? "In 1848 [Adolf Fischhof] represented the bourgeoisie in the academic legion and the academic legion in the bourgeoisie; he sought to overcome the opposition between the bourgeois and the worker, between the moderates and the radicals; he was always and everywhere the "middleman," and the "politician of moderation," who sought to walk "the middle line" between the parties."[44]

Fischhof had attempted to find a constitutional solution that would resolve the German desire for a centralized Austria ruled by the Habsburgs and the Slav desire for a crown land federalism.[45] Like Bauer, Fischhof devoted his life to the political struggle of opposites in Austria. Bauer wrote: "Fischhof's example shows that the method of compromise has its dangers, that not every compromise is unavoidable as its generation believes it to be. . . . There are in Austria tendencies with which no compromise can be permitted, tendencies that must be fought until society's development removes them." Fischhof was guilty in Bauer's eyes of falling prey to the inherent contradictions of the Austrian state and not adequately exerting his will or perception to solve "the problems presented by the necessity of political and national compromise and the boundaries of its necessity." Bauer evidences a deep compassion, however, for Fischhof; after all, he says, one must recognize how hard it is not to be compromised by the monster of the Austrian state:

It is not accident that in Austria not only responsible practical politicians, but also the writers who show the necessary direction, whose job is really not at all the conclusion of compromises, rather the production of principles, must be content with seeking the "middle line" between the conflicting forces. . . . The most fearsome crime of this state is that every political idea, every political movement, is forced to make deals with its opposite and compromise itself. Therefore other nations have their Danton, Robespierre, Bonaparte, Cobden, Gladstone, Fichte, and Bismarck, while we—we have our Fischhof.[46]

Then, in a short description of the span of Fischhof's career, Bauer writes his own epitaph: "Fischhof's political effectiveness began on the 13th of March 1848. After the collapse of the revolution he accompanied the history of Austria as a political commentator until the year 1893 with countless brochures, articles, and letters. Thus his life image is intertwined inextricably with the social, political, and national struggles of two generations."[47]

6

Max Adler,
the Eternal Youth

Max Adler never became an active politician within the Austrian Social
Democratic party, although after World War I he represented the party in
the Austrian Parliament.[1] Adler did, however, represent the purity of the
Marxist ideal in the sense Karl Marx lived it—except for a brief period
during World War I he never compromised principle with the class enemy.
As a youth of twenty-one, Adler wrote of the danger that beset the Austrian intellectual: "The chief characteristic of the . . . student proletariat
[is] their goal to work themselves out of their difficulties into a good bourgeois position. . . . Thus the greatest frequency in the betrayal of youthful ideals is to be found with students. This feeling of belonging to the
bourgeois class, if only as reflected in the hope of eventually bettering
one's position, separates the intellectual proletariat from the industrial
proletariat."[2]

Max Adler never permanently fell prey to the trap he described, but
his failure to violate his youthful ideals excluded him from an active role
within Austrian Social Democracy and thus isolated him from the only
people who were interested in his ideas. In creating a Marxist platform of
principle on which to base his existence as a man of truth, Max Adler
picked a vehicle that demanded a Fischhofian willingness to mediate. But
Adler, enveloped in a Kantian categorical imperative of his rational creation, demanded that the world meet him on his own ground of truth.
Adler avoided the eclectic pitfalls that cost Otto Bauer his ethical and
psychological freedom only to fall into the opposite abyss—a proud, self-
created "objectivity" that used the personal metaphor as a bridge of concept on which he demanded that all his contemporaries walk if they were

to reach the promised land with him. Adler's contribution to theoretical Marxism was new, but it was a foundation, not a bridge; and his thought was in motion, not an encyclopedia of concepts that adherents could use for their own theoretical or practical thought. Adler expected a rigor in practical politics that matched only his own conception of events, thus making agreement difficult for others. Theory became metaphor for him as he assumed the role of defender of the faith:

If socialism is a science, then its techniques cannot be mere utterances of a political party, which would then not have universal validity. The statements of science are objective; that of a party, dictated by their interests, necessarily limited and one-sided. . . . To be sure the proletariat represent a definite interest, but not in the same sense as other political groups, who follow their interest as blind men. The proletariat, in contradistinction to such groups, act through clear, scientific knowledge of the existing situation. Thus they are more pioneers of science than members of a political party. . . . The procedure of the socialist party must be determined by scientific knowledge, not from blind obedience to class interests or subjective passions; and from such a basis Social Democracy—for it is scientific socialism—stands over all parties, as is always the case with a science.[3]

Little wonder Max Adler came increasingly into disfavor with his fellow Austrian Social Democrats and never soiled his hands in the swamp of the Habsburg Parliament. For Max Adler, socialism permitted the full flowering of an individual's human potential, but it could be arrived at only if the vanguards of socialism acted and thought as archetypes of the New Man of the future in their immediate existence within the Austrian state.[4] To be such a New Man demanded of the individual a selfless devotion to intellect and the denying of all "egoistic" passions:

Under [the concept] "individualism" one understands first the *free development of every individual*, in which all his potentialities are developed without contradictions, that is, harmonic for oneself and harmless for the other. Second, the word "individualism" can also mean the licentious satisfaction of the individual's egoistic passions. . . . The distinction between these two definitions of personal development has been beautifully and grippingly investigated by a poet who plumbs the depths of the soul, Henrik Ibsen, in the two forms of *Brand* and *Peer Gynt*. Only *Brand* arrives at a true individualism, that is, cultivation of character; Brand's motto "to thine own self be true" demands a self-imposed duty to society, whereas *Peer Gynt*, with his motto "to thine own self be enough," recognizes no duties whatsoever, is a plaything of his moods and the accidents of circumstance; *Peer Gynt*, thus, never achieves a strongly defined self, and since he is worth nothing, he can only be repoured by the button molder.[5]

In this critical appreciation of Ibsen, Max Adler bares the core of his personality. Adler feels that only Brand, the man who demanded ethical consistency from himself and others, who gave the cold love of spiritual principle, the black and white of self-imposed law, can truly be called a human individual; Peer Gynt, who followed the self-imposing law of passion, who gave only that which immediately arose, no matter how base its substance, to those around him, for whom black and white were but two invisible possibilities of the rainbow's manifest spectrum, was judged as one who had failed as a human.[6] Adler's critique is revealing of his own limitations, for Ibsen had written *Peer Gynt* immediately after *Brand*, as if to show his insight into the limits of ethnical consistency and the greater depths of human illusion and the human soul.

The world of egoistic passion, of Peer Gynt, was the hallmark of Austria to Max Adler. It was the sign of the times:

What is it that this generation alone can understand? In this question lies the source of all evil, the peculiar limitation of the bourgeois age, and the primordial ground of all its understanding; *that is, it conceives nothing other than its own self, that individual ego of the everyday, the narrow, small, transient personality* . . . the whole world is there only so this egoistic individual can be whatever will make him personally happy. What he cannot understand, and does not serve his egoistic goals, does not concern him. . . . Thus this generation sinks into the egoistic passions and complete absence of ideas [*Ideenlosigkeit*] or irrationality [*Verunftwidrigkeit*] which are only two sides of the same principle.[7]

Only through an uncompromising objectivity with oneself and complete repression of the egoistic passions that threatened to turn one into the sloppy-thinking, pleasure-loving Viennese, for whom all might be hopeless but not yet serious, could one raise himself to the status of New Man and be capable of leading others to these heights. It is not strange, then, that Max Adler was inspired by Nietzsche's image of the *Uebermensch*, the transcendent man:

The "transcendent man" [*Uebermensch*] is . . . a struggler for self-discipline—a thing that lies apart from a hunger for power over the state or other people. And if Nietzsche praised the warlike virtues, he did not mean them to be warlike in the interest of an actual war or for actual power, rather a war that should be waged with one's own commonness and baseness, with all the instincts and impulses [*Trieben*] that always tear us down from the heights of the "transcendent man" into the depths of the "subhuman" [*Unter-Menschliche*].[8]

Adler saw himself as one of the transcendent men, a champion of the spirit, qua intellect, that lived in an age of death as a germ of new life:

The present generation is . . . a transition period, a phase of time when all that is old is destroyed and the new is formed. All the forms of the old way of life in which reason was embodied now dissolve, but there are not yet new forms in which societal reason can find a home. . . . An empty freedom, an empty law, an empty science are the idols of this time: an empty freedom because it is only the freeing from the old law, without a creation of a new, free form of society; an empty law, because it contents itself with the formal literal view of equality before the law, instead of attempting to create equality within the laws themselves; an empty science, because it is only concerned with the categorizing of experiences, without attempting to employ in a useful manner that which it has collected.[9]

Adler states in this passage his intention to support through socialism positive policies and programs of social change. As a Social Democrat, he believed society needed not simply an "empty freedom" or an "empty science" but a definite direction and new social forms. Adler's idea of the social a priori in human consciousness was the new insight that might guide the creation of new social forms of interaction. He based his thought on the Kantian categories of human consciousness, which create the essential structure and horizon of concept by which we organize our experience.[10] Adler stressed in the social a priori the Kantian category of community, the reciprocity between agent and patient, that is, the interdependent nature of each experimental moment.[11] Whereas Kant had implied a field of others toward which one must relate each isolated moment, Adler gave a more definite social wholeness, in the sense of human community, to his definition. He extended this notion of community to base all human interaction in a social transaction, with even seemingly isolated human experience requiring a social communication to oneself in order to clarify its meaning. Thus to be accurate, each moment of human understanding must recover the social nature of each experience. Society had been unaware of this essential social structure of knowing and being in its historical development, and thus its social organizations had not adequately reflected the necessity of interdependence and the social nature of judgment in its hierarchies of meaning, communication, and authority. If the society began to incorporate the implications of the social a priori into its institutional arrangements, social organization would become truer to the nature of the human being, thus healthier.

The implications of the social a priori were enormous, and so was the work to be done if society was to be restructured. Among the implications was the need for new sciences of social structure and a new pedagogy that would help individuals see and use cooperative forms of living. Such fields as group dynamics and the phenomenological study of social systems may be said to be presaged in Adler's notion of the social a priori.[12] Adler realized that a lifetime would be required to transform the entire culture to his still somewhat inchoate vision, but he felt that one's life was of value only if spent in the pursuit of such purposes:

What does the "historical personality" mean? It is the vehicle with which the spirit can go its way, it is only a stamp which the spirit employs to impress its image upon the material of history. The personality is necessary because the consciousness of man can only survive in this torpid, divisive, relating constantly only to itself, form of the ego. . . . But like a mold that falls away from a bell, after the pouring of the bell itself has been completed, so in the greatest works of the historical personality, after it has performed the necessary service as historical carriers of the kernel of the idea that will create new societal forms, it falls to the earth and passes away leaving behind its true work. To be sure, there is no great creative work possible without a personality behind it; but this limitation is only a spatial and temporal one, in which the becoming of spiritual effect completes itself, but which in itself belongs to no individual personality, rather is the immediate spiritual possession of all thinking beings.[13]

As might be expected from Max Adler's view of the historical personality, he gave little moment to the everyday affairs of his own life, and the chatty autobiography such as Renner wrote was inconceivable to him. Adler served the higher ends of a new societal creation that permitted him little extra attention for the mundane passions and anecdotal affairs of life. It is perhaps this syndrome that led one of his biographers to remark in 1959, "Even a sketchy biography of Max Adler does not exist today."[14]

The curriculum vitae that Adler completed in 1919 on assuming a teaching position in the law faculty at the University of Vienna provides perhaps the most complete statement of his personal history:

I . . . Dr. Max Adler was born on the 15th of January 1873 in Vienna, and has lived there ever since. After the normal completion of the *Volksschule* and *Mittelschule*, I passed my *Matura* in the year 1892, and enrolled in the fall of 1892 in the law faculty of the University of Vienna. At the university I followed the usual course of study of a law student, and concerned myself at the same time, from the very beginning, with philosophical and sociological studies, as well as with disciplines that touched on the border of these areas, namely national economy and natural science. In the summer of 1896 I acquired the doctor of law degree. I had to concern myself immediately after my graduation with practical life, for I was compelled to earn my own living. After completion of my apprentice years in court service, I began in 1897 the activity of a law clerk until I established myself as a lawyer in the winter of 1904, which has been to the present date my occupation. Nevertheless, this practical professional activity absorbed only a part of my interest, for the major current of my interest was and is devoted to science. My involvement with philosophy (as early as my last years within the *Gymnasium* I came under the influence of the philosophy of Kant) has been the deciding factor of my whole existence [*welche zum betimmende Moment meiner ganzen Dasein wurde*]. From that point of departure, during my university years, I made the acquaintance of the writings of Karl Marx, an encounter that dominated all my later theoretical activity; on the ground of Marxism I have since that time not only sought in my studies to penetrate the theory and history of socialism, but also to establish the intellectual-historical relation of socialism with the classical German philosophy, specifically with the legal and societal aspects of this philosophy, that is, the so-called practical philosophical elements. By this path I arrived at my preoccupation with the epistemological foundations of any study of society, especially in connection with the materialistic conception of history given to us by Karl Marx.[15]

Few other facts about Adler's activity during the Habsburg era are known. He was born of Jewish parents and thus experienced the bourgeois milieu of the Viennese Jewish intellectual with its stress on the essence of the German language as a cultural island.[16] The autobiography of Karl Renner and comments by his compatriots tell us that Adler was a leading force in the establishment of the Freie Vereinigung Sozialistischer Studente, an organization which he headed for more than a decade.[17] One also reads that Adler participated in the foundation of the Zukunft Verein, a group of intellectuals who established in 1903 a workers' school and engaged in other pedagogical activities.[18] He had a wife, who was a physician, and two children.[19]

The presence of a family that he cultivated is important in our analysis of Adler because the one problem that prevented him from completing his philosophical projects and turned idea into metaphor was what Jung has termed the "eternal youth" (*puer aeternus*) syndrome, in which the individual refuses to accept his mortality.[20] As a family man Max Adler knew mortality—birth, aging, and all the changes a person undergoes in the social world—but as a thinker he refused to accept the finitude of ideas, and as a Marxist, the necessity of translating thought into policy. From his role as a family man, Adler undoubtedly gained the strength that allowed him to maintain a normal balance in thought and action through such difficult periods as World War I, but as a public contributor to thought he evidenced an unwillingness to complete the necessary research his constant prolegomenas promised and thus to offer a finished body of work to be judged. If.he remained an "eternal youth," his work could always show promise, and he could point out limitations and errors of thought in others; only as a finite thinker with a finished thought could he be judged in the light of historical contributions in his field. It was not cowardice to produce that made him a *puer aeternus*; it was the force and newness of the idea that was his charge, coupled with the introversion of his natural attitude and the norms and pressures of mixing ideas with political timeliness that produced his neurotic relationship to philosophy and politics.[21]

Thinkers such as Nietzsche and Kafka had struggled with the awesome task of articulating new ideas that were somewhat akin to Adler's notion of the social a priori;[22] whereas their lives were shattered in their *agon*, Adler preserved his in his refusal to bring the social a priori to its mature diversity of expression. Adler was, after all, a self-identified protagonist in the effort to educate a new type of person and build a new society. He could have been expected to provide ideas thorough enough in their development to stimulate new realms of research, social planning, and pedagogy. The foundation of such a new beginning for social thought was established by Adler in his first major work, *Kausalitaet und Teleologie im Streite um die Wissenschaft* (causality and teleology contend over science), published in 1904; after this work; which contained all the ideas he was to consider over his lifetime, he did little but refine his terms.[23]

The directions of thought he might have taken required planned cultural study and a rigorous schedule of introspection, modes of research that would have involved him in historical artifacts of social thought and creativity and a deep concentration on his own thinking and valuing in the midst of social interaction. The neurosis of the *puer aeternus* prevented him from undertaking either an open study of historical statements, which would place him in history with certain limitations, or a thorough analysis of his own mode of operating as a social being. The neurosis of the *puer aeternus* causes a hesitation to live fully in history, offering instead the allure of a timelessness of authority and value created by the psychic energy that feeds the syndrome. Positively, the Jungian idea of the *puer aeternus* connotes the emergence in the person of a new idea of individuality, an idea whose implications are not only personal but collective, in that the entire culture could benefit from the conception of individuality. Jung calls an idea with such universal potential an *archetype*.[24] Neurosis results if the individual who harbors this idea identifies himself with it, rather than learning from it or using it to understand others. The person who feels that he has a special ownership of the idea will experience an inflation or deflation of ego, similar to that which Otto Bauer experienced when he projected his internal reality onto the cultural environment. The inflation or deflation of the *puer aeternus* is in the face of an idea, a psychic force, that has collective, public meaning, but the person must separate his own learning and ego from that collective potential. If his ego becomes too closely identified with the idea, he will experience the megalomania Nietzsche knew in his identification with his cultural idea of Zarathustra. If the ego is deflated, the idea has proven so powerful that the individual becomes enchanted by it and serves it selflessly. Either pole leads to impotence in one's thought, and the idea itself suffers. The idea ceases to be individuated into a thought that is part of the world; it remains only a notion. Similarly, the individual ceases to individuate, for only by grappling with the idea and making it into a variegated reality in the history of thought and its established formats can he become the many-sided thinker and active person the idea promises.

As Adler stated in the speech honoring Kant in 1904, he viewed one's historical personality as only a "mold that falls away from the bell, after the pouring of the bell itself has been completed"; the bell is one's contributions to culture. In 1936 in his last work, *Das Raetsel der Gesellschaft* (The riddle of society), the same thought on the secondary importance of the historical personality is voiced and this time called the "dross" of life: "The person was and is only a historical form—dross [*Schlacke*] of the past—in which an impersonal, enduring spiritual content appears, which often does not show its full importance, until it is freed from that element that is called the historical personality." But when one belittles one's historical person, the vehicle of the tensions and decisions of life, one's own ideation suffers, and unrealized potentialities of one's mind and spirit intrude in conscious work, as we have seen with Renner and Bauer. Adler refers to Goethe's praise of the historical personality and turns the thought into an attempt to justify its disparagement:

Usually the value of the personality is not questioned, and seen from the perspective of Goethe's words: "The greatest happiness of being human is only the personality." Even with Goethe this was not without question, and it can be turned into its opposite when one sees the personality also as a limitation. And this is true not only in the sense of its incomplete or problematic character, as expressed by the comforting saying "Where there is much light, there are many shadows," but rather in principle, as the individual bound by the greatest personality must perceive himself as a single, one-sided, and incomplete person.[25]

These words show Adler's *puer aeternus* yearnings to be free of the historical limitations of a definite self with its moral character and fallible incompleteness. The irony is that only through accepting the reality of one's personality can a narrow outlook and individuality be expanded. Adler correctly intuits that any definite self will have a shadow side of unrealized potential. Carl Jung in discussing the *puer aeternus* in its positive meaning as an archetypal idea of growth and a symbol for a new integration of more elements of one's person points to the "shadow" symbolism that accompanies the process of individuating one's personality.[26] Shadow symbolism followed Adler his entire life. In the fall of 1901 he had reviewed a play, *The Shadow*, by M.E. Della Grazie, presented at the Burg Theater. The play dealt with a poet who became possessed by the appearance of a shadow side of himself because he neglected his work. Adler said that a man possessed by such a shadow must have been very weak in his conscious life, lacking the strength and courage to realize his ideas, or such a state of possession would not have occurred. Max Adler had perceived what was to be his problem—the failure to realize his ideas fully. In his review, one of the two chief reasons for his failure was made evident as he discussed the role of introspection in a life:

The hours of contemplation of oneself are seldom; yet they provide wonderful moments of the most profound inner possession, in which all those things that otherwise filled our lives and seemed to be our only interest suddenly appear to be inconsequential, lying outside us, only the most incomplete of means by which we could help our real value, our subjectivity, our true being to express itself. At such moments the soul, in comparison to its usual activity in daily existence, seems to have returned to its home from a foreign land. . . . At such times the mind seems to ask itself, "Is the many colored manifold of my external life in which all the powers of the intellect, all the feelings of the emotions, all the im-pulses of the internal by which the soul expresses itself, the sole extent of my life?" That is the anxious question that every genuine return to oneself produces.
    But the real condition of the soul is not comprehended by this question that attacks the mind of man. Where thought and action flow from a strong, secure character, where the entire being of the man is as consistent as a single substance, then this question is not one of despair. It is only a play of the intellect, in which the intellect tests its own strength. When the quiet hours of thought come, one is often tempted to paint a picture of oneself that portrays one's character as a differ-ent possibility . . . dream wishes emerge and longings, in a self-deceptive fantasy, or one is seized by subjective possibilities that open vistas outside of real life; but the hours of dreaming pass away; the images of longing flow by, the nightmares of imagined horrors disappear before the clear conscious knowledge of oneself, and certainity of one's actual inner being, a knowledge . . . that knows what and why every longing is. . . . But it is quite different with people who lack this inner certainty, who exist in a conflict of thought and action from the very begin-ning. . . . Such a person would stand in the center point of the "shadow."[27]

    In this passage, Adler expresses an ambivalence toward introspective thought. On the one hand, it is a return to certainty to feel and reflect on the stable values and purposes of one's person, but at that moment "the anxious question that every genuine return to oneself produces" occurs, which is, "Is the many colored manifold of my external life in which all the powers of the intellect, all the feelings of the emotions, all the im-pulses of the internal by which the soul expresses itself, the sole extent of my life?" That anxiety and question blocked Adler from the phenome-nological reflection that would have been necessary for disciplined thought upon the possible categories of social interaction that made up the social a priori in cultural life. Phenomenological reflection is the turning over in one's mind of the perceived transactions or objects of life in order to see them more fully in reflection and to develop a logic of their meaning.[28] Late in his life Adler admired Edmund Husserl, the father of modern phenomenology, and saw the structured introspection of his thought as the key for understanding the meaning of social transactions.[29] But he was never able to practice the extended inquiry of reflection because of the intruding anxiety that overcame the contemplative moment. He found it necessary to challenge the possibility of inquiry with what he knew, a diverting of attention to his certainties, instead of the agony of an open search for specific meanings in the morass of facts derived from close observation of human interaction. The *puer aeternus* cannot probe the facts of his consciousness, for such control of attention and logic toward his own person will secure the specificity of his personality. The neurosis diverts the possibility of such a dwelling in personal thought to ward off self-knowledge.

The second reason for Adler's failure to develop his ideas lay in his resistance to securing evidence for his thought from careful study of cultural artifacts or behavior patterns that might reflect the social a priori in operation.

The laws of consciousness are known only in their empirical appearance in human performance. Then one can either reflect on one's own experience, abstracting the rule of consciousness from it, as in phenomenological reflection; or one can find in the products of human performance, through inference and deduction, the laws of social interaction inherent in human thought. Adler recognized the necessity of finding thought's laws within their historical expression: "An action of thought is not an empty abstraction, as it manifests itself directly in empirical action. For only because the person in his historical presence thinks with passion, need, and haltingly with a search for understanding, does one's pure will become the teleological and ethical striving of empirical life (Kant calls this thought's pathological associations)."[30]

Adler tells us that one can see the social a priori only as it is interpreted through a specific reality of a time and place, through the "pathological" lack of understanding and vulnerability of one's consciousness seeking to solve a life moment through decision and action. Any analysis of what the social a priori might be in its various delineaments would have to interpret it through its historical incompleteness and skewness of expression. Here he stopped short of the clear tasks before him. Georg Simmel studied not only artistic expression in cultural periods in order to ferret out the laws of consciousness that were incompletely expressed, such as his study of Dante's psychology, but also lifestyles of his own culture, such as those of the adventurer, the stranger in a community, or the miser and the spendthrift.[31] Simmel showed how human action and expression were given peculiar shape within the social interactions of the person with the norms and social institutions of his environment. Simmel did not link his insights to a historical epistemology, such as that of Kant or any other philosopher or psychologist. At the time of Simmel's death Adler praised the ingenuity of his insights into social interaction but condemned him as a shallow thinker.[32]

Adler could have improved upon Simmel by founding his own cultural analyses upon the Kantian base of the detailed schemata[33] of the social a priori, but he failed to carry out such a project because of his *puer aeternus* condition. He could not study artifacts with an empirical thoroughness that identified definite cultural norms for such an identification would have rooted him in history and recognized his own mortality as a thinker and activist. As a creative social thinker, he would have had to define his own generation's limits and "pathology," in the sense Kant meant the term, when he saw how the social a priori was being realized by his associates. The limited social interaction and patterns of communication would have forced him to account for his manner of operation. The closest that he came to such study was in the early 1920s in his *Staatsauffassung der Marxismus* (conception of the state in Marxism), in which he discussed the correct Marxist interpretation of democratic forms of political structure, including the organization of a party, the state, and the dictatorship of the proletariat.[34] His analysis in this work, written in the heat of the possibility of a socialist state in Austria, fails to relate to his pre–World I reflections on the necessity of founding new social organizations upon a deeper knowledge of the social a priori of human consciousness. All his arguments are derived from the reification of class conflict, without an analysis of how social communication and interaction are limited or furthered by particular forms of social-political organization. To develop the nuances of social communications and interaction as they would be guided by an increased knowledge of the social a priori, he would have had to make thorough models (schemata) of social discourse so as to demonstrate the social appearance and the rule of each form of human interaction. He would have had to explore how the limited understanding of the particular social culture set norms of interaction and communication that were more or less adequate in their accord with the timeless guides of the schemata.[35]

Instead of undertaking these studies, he complained of thinkers who did them. His objection was either that they did not go deep enough, that is, to the laws behind the cultural artifact,[36] or that men who made such studies were interested in practical matters, whereas he was a theoretician. In the first argument, he expressed his own guilt at not making a better study; in the second, where he objected to an overly practical orientation, he expressed his own fear at mixing his study with a body of evidence that would determine who he was and how he should be acting in order fully to meet his cultural obligations. His attack on a fellow neo-Kantian, Rudolf Stammler, for his study of legal norms used both arguments—that he was too shallow and too practical:

An original way to look at a thinker is to realize that the thinker's will is not the only thing that sets the course of investigation, but the thinker's limits, which cannot be overcome. The will to thought of Stammler is essentially *practical*. . . . He does not raise the genuine theoretical question in relation to social problems: What is it? What is happening there and why does it happen in that manner? rather [he raises] the practical question: Is that which occurs right? [*Ist das, was da ist oder geschieht, in Ordnung?*] How can I make it right? [*Wie mache ich alles recht?*].[37]

The slovenly expression in which the practical questions are phrased in the German deliberately obscures Adler's understanding that recognizing the social a priori required study of how things were done in real situations and that such a recognition not only gave the possibility of theoretical understanding but created the entry to a program of cultural change based on the adequacy or inadequacy of what exists, given the rule contained in its expression. Stammler sought to show how the legal norms of a given culture were based upon adequate or inadequate understanding of the imperatives of ethical consciousness, seen from a Kantian perspective. Stammler saw his own work as akin to Karl Renner's study of legal norms, relating the legal expression to the social consciousness of its formulation.[38] Adler expressed his own limitations that could not be overcome, not Stammler's, who was both theoretical and practical.

Consciousness became a shibboleth for Adler, an island that kept one safe from the shadows of uncertainty. Being certain was rooted in ideas that became fetishes, and research became a practical falling away from theoretical purity. Adler made consciousness into an object with powers that guaranteed one a "companionship" with a force that had godlike qualities—omnipresence, omniscience, and possibly even immortality. On consciousness' omniscience and ubiquitous presence, Adler wrote:

We can only think of an end to consciousness by means of consciousness itself, and therefore the thought that there could be no consciousness is a logical impossibility in view of consciousness itself. The condition of sleep, for example, is known only in those cases where dream life initiates consciousness, and the condition of deepest loss of consciousness such as a dreamless sleep must remain as foreign to us and the internal condition of a lifeless body. Thus for man there exists really no state wherein consciousness is not present, uninterrupted, and no end to consciousness can be thought of.[39]

Adler's casuistry takes on the aspect of a lawyer pleading his case for the innocence of consciousness in the face of a nameless crime against existence. His overemphasis on consciousness' constant presence in the phenomenon called man seems to be a compulsive need rather than merely an excursion of logic; behind his insistence seems to lurk a fear of the state in which his consciousness might be at an end. The concept of death, which Otto Bauer asserted haunted Adler,[40] was indeed a specter behind his preoccupation with consciousness: "Whether we believe it or nor at some time we will cease to be. As Socrates stated when he found that he did not fear death: As long as I am, death is not, and when death comes, I am no more. This 'ceasing to be,' however, is a mere word to consciousness, and, therefore, *genuine* thoughts of death *never* occur to man when he is in physical and mental health, no matter how much his thought dwells upon the idea when in a depressed or confused state. To the strong mind the dying organism, itself, appears as but a physical illness."[41]

Adler's insistence that the dark thoughts of the melancholic and despondent nature are not signs of a true condition and that even if a true condition of dying were present, the strong intellect would be able to sublimate them into a nonfatal condition gives us a clue to the crime of consciousness he defended. His conscious grasp on the logic that protected him from deeper involvement in research, and a concomitant social policy, refused to die. He resisted accepting his mortality and working to complete his finite tasks. Thus he was poised always at the edge of a specter of death, for to cease to become *puer aeternus* of intellect, he would have to die the philosopher's death every day, as Socrates states, in order to know through experience and inquiry his mortal limits.[42] He would have to turn his eyes from a worship of intellect and use it as a tool for the tasks to which he professed to be dedicated—the transformation of individuals into more knowing persons and the reconstruction of society into a social ground with greater opportunities for developing human potential.

By 1910 it was evident to the party fathers and Max Adler's Austro-Marxist peers that he overemphasized an approach to theory that avoided exploration of the cultural facts of the present. Otto Bauer, in a criticism that sums up the party oligarchy's attitude to Max Adler, called his wooing of the young intellectuals "an optimistic attempt to create a mystical sect of those who long for the future" and recommended that Adler dwell more on the economic conditions of class than on the realm of pure idea.[43] Adler had a brighter vision because he did intuit the idea that could provide a genuine basis for new forms of social judgment and social institutions. As we explore his writings, we will see the promise of that idea of the social a priori which was metaphorically abused by him but which had substance.

7

Max Adler, the
Incomplete Theoretician

In his theoretical writings Max Adler pondered a theme central to Marxism—individuality within an interdependent world. According to his interpretation, Karl Marx had inherited the problem from cultural fathers such as Kant, and Marxism was a political expression that relied on epistemological and social-psychological principles integral to Kant's thought. In fact, the conundrum of human freedom within the laws that bind man to nature and society is as old as historical philosophy; the idea of individuality within interdependence can be traced from Plato through the whole of Western thought. Adler recognized the historical nature of the problem and thus gave himself latitude to provide an answer for his generation and the future. Had he fulfilled his promise as a philosopher he would have stood on a par with the many thinkers he celebrated in his writings. Adler's value as a social philosopher is twofold: as a historian of social philosophy, he clarified the origins of socialism as a solution to the realization of human potential, and as an epistemologist, he laid the foundation for a study of social discourse as a setting for individual judgment.

His attachment to Austrian Social Democracy can be seen only as destructive for his thought. He had no dialogues with fellow party members on his explorations of individuality and interdependence that could make genuine contributions to a future socialist state. His only dialogues with his Social Democratic peers concerned the party program, a practical concern that elicited in him a shallow adherence to untested shibboleths. As we explore the Kantian-Marxist basis of his social thought, we will encounter the reified nature of class conflict and the dictatorship of the proletariat as championed by Adler, which cheapened the significance of his own theoretical writings. Austrian Social Democracy was an ersatz realm of action for a man who needed to pursue active research to find evidence for his ideas. His party work as a contributor to *Der Kampf* and in the political education of the young separated him from the accomplishment he wished to give to the world—a truer foundation for social living based on a deeper consciousness of social experience. Human energy is finite, and the heightened relevance of being a contributing party leader insulated him from dialogues with other social thinkers that might have stimulated his research. There is a laziness (*Faulheit*) in his thought, which he accused others of at times,[1] an indolence bred by the easy role of being accepted as a leading Marxist theoretician by a circle of party activists who saw little relevance in what he said. To accept such a position was to settle for an inauthentic role for his individualilty. Adler's real aspiration was projected onto the thinkers he admired, such as Kant:

A strong and tortured consciousness of poverty permeates all Kant's works. Pouring forth from his works is a moral indignation that his most intense labors still bear the stamp of failure, and that while every other science increasingly progressed, metaphysics "which would be knowledge itself, to which all men turn as if to an oracle, continually marches in place, without advancing one step." There is a Faustian feeling of the impossibility of finding Truth in the old paths. [Kant] turned away from the philosophical heritage of the past, in the clear consciousness that the way must be sought anew:

"Shall I, perhaps, read in a thousand books
That men have everywhere been miserable,
That now and then one has been happy?"
No! Even if the dreams of metaphysics had not added to our knowledge, at least its error had borne some fruit—a conviction that one had to make a regression on the false path back to the starting point, and there find a compass to orient oneself. This compass is—*The Critique of Pure Reason*.[2]

In his curriculum vitae Adler had called Kant "the deciding factor of his whole existence," whereas Marx was an "encounter that dominated all my later theoretical activity," a "ground" that served to develop his social ideation. One can interpret this succinct self-definition, written in his forty-sixth year, as a realization that his real mission was to develop a new, radical approach to social judgment and not merely to contribute to finished social concepts and an established social program.

Faust was to be archetypal figure for Adler,[3] Faust, who wanted to change the world, not only to know it; yet if it were to be changed, it had to be seen as no one had yet known it. Faust makes a pact with Satan and is guided through the nether world. For Adler it was necessary to traverse the frightening realm of introspection as he made a phenomenological study of social experience. As Adler stated this goal in *Kausalitaet und Teleologie*:

First, regressively, through reflection the concept "truth" is arrived at in its pure existence as knowledge; on this foundation all historical truth lies, in that the foundation established by reflective knowledge makes it possible for historical "truth" to be named. Through all the changing contents of history, the formative and self-establishing laws of consciousness, the thought necessity, act as the determinant of historical truth. This concept of truth established unconditionally the value of all judgments in which a historical truth is expressed. . . . Upon its basis the practical notions that make up world views are derived.[4]

At the end of his life, in his last work, *Das Raetsel der Gesellschaft*, he expressed the same phenomenological goal as the basis for social change: "There was and is another metaphysic possible wherein . . . the development of [society] is shown to be nothing other than the logical conditions of the individual development of consciousness; where the essence 'behind' the self-consciously acting intellect—whether beyond this consciousness there exists such essence or not—is exposed within the 'grant' of this consciousness."[5]

Adler had become acquainted with the phenomenological thought of Edmund Husserl by 1936. He began a dialogue with Husserl in *Das Raetsel der Gesellschaft*, pointing out the Husserlian promise of a logical exploration of the hidden realms of thought which conditioned experience:

The conception of a descriptive psychology has arisen where the life of the soul is not merely broken into its parts, and "scientifically" categorized, but is viewed in its totality and the whole context of its purposeful functioning. In this method there is, to be sure, an analysis of the parts of consciousness, but only insofar as the forms of the conscious functions are concerned. It is clear that in the direction of this descriptive discipline not only phenomenology but also epistemology can play a role. Only that epistemology here would not be concerned with the forms of the psychic [*Formen des Psychischen*]), *rather with the psychic experience* [*Erfahrung*] and the functions that condition it.[6]

Husserl's approach to psychic experience seemed to promise not only an array of established concepts that might help Adler more completely discover and define the schemata of the social apriori but an introspective journey that had a safe conclusion. In *Das Raetsel der Gesellschaft* Adler rejects Freud and the "unconscious" as a mystification of experience.[7] (In his first work, *Kausalitaet und Teleologie*, in his use of Faust as a representative of the human search for truth, Adler articulated the intellectual method of the Freudian search for health.) Freud's insistence on the psychobiological facts of selfhood and accepting one's mortality may have been too strong a medicine for Adler, but Husserl might have indirectly helped him to bring his thought to fruition. In his appreciation of Husserl, Adler cut out for himself a "study of psychic experience and the functions that condition it," whereas Husserl would name the psychic forms. Adler thus was poised for a phenomenological psychology that probed experience in society.

Husserl was always available for Adler; he had written his *Logische Untersuchungen* (Logical investigations) in 1901, and in 1913 had finished his *Ideen*, which outlined the new discipline of phenomenology.[8] Why hadn't Adler formed an association earlier? The problem was that thinkers such as Husserl were not actively engaged in radical social change, and one did not openly exchange ideas with bourgeois thinkers. The rich source of non-Marxist, neo-Kantian thought was likewise closed to Adler during his active party years because of the emotional screen of class warfare. Thinkers such as Ernst Cassirer, whose *Life of Kant* and *Freiheit und Form* could have aided Adler in the use of Kant's *Critique of Judgement* as a tool for developing the cultural studies that would uncover the facets of the social a priori, went unmentioned in Adler's works.[9] When he did debate other neo-Kantians, his stance was aggressive and belittling, as in his critical review of Rudolf Stammler.[10] The bourgeois thinkers were at fault, abstaining from the Kantian notion of the "socializing" (*vergesellschaften*) nature of man and refusing to explore human reality from the perspective of interdependence.

For the liberal bourgeois thinker, social change was a product of increased knowledge about life, which would occur through the free choice of a democratic people. For the Marxists, knowledge was closely tied to political programs, and discoveries were instantly seen as the property of their party, not of humanity in general. Adler was enchanted by the syndrome Schorske defines in fin-de-siecle Austrian politics as politics in a new key. One thought for the benefit of humanity but not of those with an opposing political point of view. The aggressiveness associated with a philosophic position among Marxists before World War I curtailed the mutual interpenetration of ideas between thinkers who could have aided each other.

According to Immanuel Kant, it is the concept of antagonism between thinkers and proponents of conflicting social positions that leads to human progress. Adler used the concept of antagonism to link Kantian thought to Marxist thought. In Adler's understanding of life in the world, the concept was fundamental. He quoted at length from Kant's Fourth Thesis in the *Idea for a Universal History* to introduce the idea that was to become a justification for class conflict and a basis for his notion of the social a priori:

By "antagonism" I mean the unsocial sociability of men, i.e. their propensity to enter into society, bound together with a mutual opposition which constantly threatens to break up the society. Man has an inclination to associate with others, because in society he feels himself to be more a person, i.e. in the developed form of his natural capacities. [*Der Mensch hat eine Neigung, sich zu vergesellschaften, weil er in einem solchen Zustand sich mehr als Mensch, das ist die Entwicklung seiner naturan-lagen, fuehlt.*] But he also has a strong propensity to isolate himself from others, because he finds in himself at the same time the unsocial characteristic of wishing to have everything go according to his own wish. Thus he expects opposition on all sides because, in knowing himself, he knows that he, on his own part, is inclined to oppose others.[11]

According to Kant, this contradictory disposition in man to associate with others in order fully to feel one's human capacities, yet to withdraw in order to know one's own mind and will, was an anthropological law. Through the conflict in oneself and among others, one reached a coherent view of life that embraced ideas and realities beyond oneself. The encounter with others tested one's ideas, and experience enabled one to correct the restricted limits of one's vision. Kant felt that nature has a plan in so constructing the dialectic of approach-avoidance within the human being. The plan was to drive men to develop their full capacities by means of an internal gadfly creating constant movement and change.[12]

Adler saw the antagonism that necessarily kept individuals linked yet at odds as the heart of what Marx saw in the class struggle of society in every period of history.[13] Kant had added in the Fourth Thesis that "one cannot tolerate his fellows, yet one cannot withdraw from them."[14] Adler saw the structures of the social-economic world as a proof of the interrelatedness of people at odds who were inextricably brought together to earn their livelihoods. Both Kant and Marx saw history as a progression toward more equitable, broadly shared benefits within society, a progress won as the majority of people within a society saw a more rational, efficient solution for their mutual plight. The antagonism and conflict taught hard lessons, one of which in the modern age was the necessity of increased self-consciousness in social planning. Instead of the conflict of blind wills that gradually brought improvement through trial and error, a conflict of social theories would more quickly bring human beings closer to a system of living that promised to nurture their capacities. Kant and Marx saw history as a gradual realization of a society that was genuinely healthy in the sense that it furthered the natural competencies of each of its members.[15]

Marx's dialectical materialism, according to Adler, was to be understood as the movement of social institutions through the antagonistic encounter with others in work and dialogue and the redirection of one's energies as a result of these encounters.[16] The interchange of thought and action in culture broadened one's position so that he could see opposing ideas and resolve differences within a new perspective. There was no magic force beyond humans that moved history. History was the dialectical action of men in antagonistic force and counterforce, creating, then recreating, social organizations to embrace their varied visions.

The dialectic itself was the process of thought that could be exercised by the scientific thinker. Not all men could clearly see the opposing forces in the antagonistic social world. Dialectical thinking would identify the ideas and things of the social world and find a logic to relate them in an organization that brought progress rather than conflict, progress being a healthier state of affairs for all who shared that social world. But one could not simply apply schoolbook logic; the real experience of the world had to be approached with a phenomenological insight: "The dialectic is the methodological attempt to transcend the boundaries of merely logical thought by means of a regression to the lived experience of total consciousness. It strives to reorder, more or less by force [mehr oder weniger gewaltsam], the fragmentary expressions of isolated logical thought into the original flow of undivided experience, which to be sure is never fully expressed in practical thought, but nevertheless lives in each consciousness, and can be shown there in its presence."[17]

The reordering of experience in phenomenological reflection was equivalent to the Freudian effort to bring a patient to a recovery of what actually occurred in a particular situation. The new view was initiated by a logical understanding of the components of the experience in a deeper, more authentic manner than in the original living of it. By redefining the protagonists and the meaning of the actions, one could see "the original flow of undivided experience, which to be sure is never fully expressed in practical thought, but nevertheless lives in each consciousness, and can be shown there in its presence." In other words, just as Freud helps the person to see what he "knew to be the case" but "repressed," Adler's dialectical vision brings one to a reconstruction of actual experience.[18] Adler, however, did not allow this unconscious element to suggest the subjective abysses of Freud; rather, he saw it as a reservoir of the concrete world. Adler's understanding of a regression to the original flow of undivided experience was guided by his own educated inference into the sketchy statements of Karl Marx then available on the role of consciousness in social experience.[19] Consciousness would contain only what was encountered in external life.

The regression to what had actually occurred was accomplished by a search within the remembered events for the logic of their occurrence. Ordinarily, one's vision of external events was distorted by one's inherited cultural concepts so that one saw only the delineaments emphasized by the values and norms of the time. Seeing correctly was a complicated process, but it could be achieved. First, one must find the word that most accurately defined what had occurred. This process involved the individual in a review of the experience in question—a "phenomenological" review—for one sought to recover the full set of elements that made up the event and determine the logic of their interaction. An antagonism was created by the insertion of a new concept that reordered the significance and order of events because one's understanding of an event was part of a world view that ordered all events. The searching dialogue initiated in the analysis of one event would lead inevitably to a change in the point of view one brought to all past and present events.

One's own logic might be wrong, however. The rationalizations of an individual tend to falsify facts in order to preserve coherence. To arrive at a true judgment, one must use two measures to balance one's own phenomenological reflections. First, one must engage in discussions with others about the reality one is attempting to define; the antagonism of their viewpoints will help one avoid a solipsistic position. Second, as the result of a formally defined phenomenological psychology, one could be informed by a causal interpretation of what should have occurred in an event, given the psychic forms that govern perception and reaction. In these measures of truth, Adler proposed a form of personal analysis that would have had similar methods and outcomes as psychoanalysis.[20]

Adler's concept of social therapy developed over the course of his life, although the best example appeared in *Kausalitaet und Teleologie*. He depicted Faust in his cell deliberating upon the Gospel of John, about to begin a translation of the original Greek into German.[21] The translation was a focus for decisions Faust must make about his own life. Faust felt that simply reading about life in the world provided an insufficient understanding and an incomplete basis for his own action: "Shall I, perhaps, read in a thousand books / That men have everywhere been miserable, That now and then one has been happy?" Faust enters a dialogue with himself that creates the inner antagonisms Adler believed were critical for recapturing the "undivided flow" of facts truly experienced. The passage begins as Faust arrives at a mental impasse when considering the first line in the Gospel of John, "In the beginning was the word"; Faust states that if he is to be enlightened by the passage, he must translate it differently. His insight is that the passage should read, "In the beginning was the intelligence [*Sinn*]." "Intelligence" causes the word to occur; it initiates activity. Faust seeks a more active life, and intelligence seems a more powerful agent in a history that the passive word. But then Faust sees that it is power he is seeking. "In the beginning was the force [*Kraft*]," thus displacing the still but potent presence of the intelligence with the vital, animal energy of human presence. Faust is on his way to an existential view of creative experience. He arrives at a point of view that gives him peace of mind when he finally translates the line as "In the beginning was the act [*Tat*]."[22] Adler stresses Faust's deliberation in making these changes, seeking the expression that was in concord with reality as he knew it. Adler's assumption that Faust arrives at the truth is a weakness in the example. Adler ends *Kausalitaet und Teleologie* with the quote from Marx's *Theses on Feuerbach* that "philosophers have only interpreted the world in various ways; the point, however, is to change it."[23]

Adler strongly identified with Faust's position. In the process of recovering true judgments of social experience, Faust need not be right in this first stage of reflection. He could enrich his understanding in conversations with Wagner and Mephistopheles (given that the latter would exhibit goodwill in his answers).[24] A further check would be the application of a phenomenological psychology to Faust's deliberations to see if they corresponded to anthropological fact.

This first stage of reflection was a reconstruction of experience by Faust that had the certainty of a balanced viewpoint considering the history of his understanding. His deepening of comprehension as to how things "began" was the product of a healthy deliberation in its tensions of thought and counterthought, with judgment satisfied only with as thorough a view as possible. Was it a Freudian model of healthy deliberation? It was in the antagonism of one view against another until all the opposing meanings were seen. There is also an interesting parallel between Freudian word association and the dialectic of word selection used by Faust to expand his understanding of the actual cause of the beginnings of things.[25] But Faust's reflections lacked an essential Freudian basis of health, the anthropological standard of what indeed gives rise to origins. Freud based truth on the structures of human nature and weighed judgments on their proximity to these facts. Adler, too, sought a firmer basis for truth in a judgment than its thoroughness. As much as he admired Faust for his efforts, he indicated that there was a model for truth in the laws of consciousness that condition how we know and shape experience. He interjects an analogy into the discussion of Faust that opens this deeper insight into judgment. He speaks of an engineer who is called upon to help repair a fault in a construction. While walking through the site, he points out where a pillar must be placed. His judgment in the visual moment is based on his translation of what he sees into a broader, more scientific understanding, informed by his knowledge of the plan of the building and of engineering. He sees the invisible but present truth of the situation through his reflection on the immediate facts.[26] Adler used the Faust example and the analogy of the engineer to debate the neo-Kantian teleologists, such as Rudolf Stammler, who insisted that value judgments and ethics, as well as goal statements, were arrived at in the freedom of a practical judgment that was stimulated rather than conditioned by facts. Adler, on the other hand, felt that every value, ethic, or goal statement is caused in a twofold manner: it is conditioned by the logical network of one's existing point of view, as exemplified in the Faust example, and it is caused at a deeper level of consciousness by schemata of consciousness that organize perspectives and actions in the social world.[27]

Adler based his thought on Kant's critique of teleological judgment in which Kant points out the teleological thought is connected to the determinative judgments of the categories of understandings at some supersensible level of mind.[28] The connection assures that value judgments, ethics, and goal formations are not arbitrary but are connected to structures of understanding that condition how we shape and interpret the factual world. *Kausalitaet und Teologie* contains this argument: if one's values and goals are rooted in a transcendental structure of the mind which also provides the categories of understanding whereby we identify and use facts, then a science of society is possible which identifies the best values and goals in the light of these structures of understanding that guide human development. Existing judgments and social organization would be measured against ideal but real possibilities. Adler was debating the neo-Kantian teleologists who claimed an exact social science was impossible because society was the result of the value decisions and goal formations that were not directly linked to any physical cause but made in the freedom of reflection. Adler pointed out that Kant saw reflection not as an isolated free act but as inextricably linked to the forms of causal understanding.[29]

Again, Adler approached a Freudian understanding in his consideration of the "boundness" of individual judgment by deeper levels of causality within consciousness. As in his dissection of dialectical thought, wherein the original vision was reconstructed to show its true delineaments, corresponding to the Freudian recovery of the actuality of memory, in his discussion of teleogical judgment Adler replicated Freud's view of the "rationalization." Freud shows how a logical argument of goals and values can always be traced to a causal understanding that creates the field within which the person perceives meanings. The "perfect" logic that justifies choices may be traced to the vision of reality which constitutes the person's pathological "world."[30] Adler quoted Spinoza on the "perfection" of reason in making a seamless argument to justify its judgments.[31] He used this example to caution the teleologists to find a firmer ground for their values, ethics, and goals than their individual judgment. No individual can escape the delusion of reason. Only a science that identifies the constituting structures of the person's entire field of meaning can bring objectivity to judgment.

Perhaps it is more than chance that Max Adler and Sigmund Freud had parallel views of the delusive nature of teleological judgment, unless it is traced back to more fundamental causal structures in consciousness. Immanuel Kant clearly links the "wishes" of the teleological judgment—the goals one strives for, the preferred states of affairs one seeks—to the faculty of desire in man. Kant states in the *Critique of Judgement* that when the individual feels incapable of realizing a task, or undoing an unpleasant past, or annihilating a delay that keeps him from the wished-for moment, he will represent objects in his thought that substitute for the desired goal. These wishes, Kant says, can be traced back to their causality, which is not the object one appears to desire but the faculty of desire itself: "But why our nature should be furnished with a propensity to consciously vain desires is a teleological problem of anthropology. It would seem that were we not to be determined to the exertion of our power before we had assured ourselves of the efficiency of our faculty for producing an Object, our power would remain to a large extent unused. For as a rule we only first learn to know our powers by making trial of them. This deceit of vain desires is therefore only the result of a beneficent disposition in our nature."[32]

We may reasonably infer that Freud was stimulated by this passage. He had read Kant, though his only reference is negative, pointing out the ethical categorical imperative as typical of a repressive, domineering superego.[33] Yet Kant, in discussing teleological judgment, which is the faculty of ethical formation, shows that desire is the force with which ethics struggles. Kant does not claim that ethics is capable of taming desire; on the contrary, he sees the faculty of desire as an anthropological force that impels man to develop all his powers. Freud is less positive about desire, which he sees as a force bent only on pleasure, pain, reproduction, or extinction. Nevertheless, Freud and Adler clearly following Kant, both seek a casual mechanism in human nature, articulated through the laws of consciousness, that initiates and shapes the teleological judgment.

Adler felt that a phenomenological psychology which identified the "forms of psychic experience" and the "functions which condition it" could be the means of arriving at true judgments about cultural goals, values, and ethics. For a Marxist this meant that social policy and planning might have a basis that more quickly arrived at the anthropological health toward which Kant implied our desires prodded us. Instead of a blind groping, through individual and collective goals prompted by frustrations, impatience, and pathologies of personality and culture, individuals and communities could probe their policies for abnormalities that deviated from a standard of healthy interactions based upon the ideal models discovered among those psychic forms. The implication of the social a priori and its constitutive schemata, that is, forms of psychic experience, was that there were classic forms of healthy interaction as human process. For example, one might say that Marx's identification of the human need to exchange the products of one's labor was the discovery of a schematism of the social a priori and that a society that protected this need by guaranteeing its opportunity and equity established a cultural norm that was healthy in its accord with the schematism. Marx used a Hegelian language, but his intention was the same enduring standard of health as Kant, Freud, and Adler desired:

> What causes me to alienate *my* private property to *another* man? Political economy replies correctly: *necessity, need.* The other man is also a property owner, but he is the owner of *another* thing, which I lack and cannot and will not do without, which seems to me a *necessity* for the completion of my existence and the realisation of my nature. The bond which connects the two property owners with each other is the *specific kind of object* that constitutes the substance of their private property. The desire for these two objects, i.e., the need for them, shows each of the property owners, and makes them conscious of it, that he has yet another *essential* relation to objects besides that of private ownership, that he is not the particular being that he considers himself to be, but a *total* being whose needs stand in the relationship of *inner* ownership to all products, including those of another's labour. For the need of a thing is the most evident, irrefutable proof that the thing belongs to *my* essence, that its being is for me, that its *property* is the property, the peculiarity of *my* essence. Thus both property owners are impelled to give up their private property, but to do so in such a way that at the same time they confirm private ownership, or to give up the private property within the relationship of private ownership. Each therefore alienates a part of his private property to the other.[34]

Marx's notion of alienation would also classify as a schematism for he develops it within his writings as both a social-psychological consequence of human transactions and an ontological condition of human creativity.[35] The schematism provides a logical form of human operation with a universality that allows it to be found in any culture; it reflects the processes of human consciousness in their interaction with reality. The goal of social scientists or natural scientists who accept the possibility of identifying the schemata of human operation in the world is to arrive at laws that are anthropologically definite, not relative to the conditions and forces of a specific culture. Kant, Marx, and Max Adler shared a belief that the individual found his full capacities, thus health, within the social milieu. Marx defined the individual as "not the particular being that he considers

himself to be, but a *total* being whose needs stand in the relationship . . .
to another." Kant said the same thing when he described how one must
associate with others as a condition of his full capacities. Adler's potential
phenomenological psychology would have been identification of the schemata that constitute the necessary interaction between the individual and
his milieu and identification of abnormal forms of that interaction within
any given culture.

Adler's brief published flirtation with artistic criticism might have
been an avenue whereby he could have solved the relationship between
the teleological judgment of the individual against the background of the
causal forms of understanding. The arts, according to Kant, contain perhaps the truest expression, in symbolic form, of the union of the teleological judgment and the causal forms of the understanding, arrived at in the
free play of the artistic imagination.[36] The artistic judgment seems to capture a vision of temporal-spatial organization that is true for its age and
perhaps for every age. The sensous elements of the medium allow a concrete, individual relationship yet carry an idea that may be applied in
countless individual judgments to different times and places. The schemata of an a priori would have to have both the timeless quality of idea
and the temporal-spatial sensuousness in its articulation that allowed individuals to find their particular relation to things with its guidance. Adler
could appreciate the timeless quality of an art work, but for him that
quality was found not in the material senuousness of its form, but rather
in its idea. The idea of the artist linked him to all active minds, not the
colorful vision by which that idea was expressed. As Adler exclaimed: "It
is the thought, the idea itself, which forces its way to appearance".[37]

Art, then, is for Adler a means of selection and orientation that saves
man from the colorful manifold of life. To strengthen this aesthetic crite-
rion Adler brought some of his German fathers into the lists with him: he
quoted Schiller and Grillparzer in an attempt to give added value to the
notion that the idea is the prime moment of art, but as will often happen
when one resorts to a great mind for support, Adler exposed the narrow-
ness of his own position. Schiller is quoted as saying: "Everyone who is
capable of translating his emotional condition into *an object*, so that this
object compels me to introject myself into it, and feel the life that is called
forth, I call truly a poet, a creator." Grillparzer is quoted as saying: "Ideas
do not make the true attraction of poetry; the philosopher has perhaps a
higher task; but the cold thought-provoking qualities of the ideas in poetry
contain a reality that transports one. The corporeality [*Koerperlichkeit*] of
the poem makes [the idea] an effective force." Adler overlooked Schiller's
stress on "feeling into" the object and Grillparzer's emphasis that the "true
attraction" of poetry is the body, that is, the senuous quality of the poem.

Only the cold idea, the universal thought, was important to Adler, and even the hint of this in the memory of his *Bildung* was employed as a buffer against the spontaneity of the actual. Why? Adler states: "An ideal . . . preserves reality for man . . . it provides a force to stop him from skidding into the void [*ein Nichts*]."[38]

Adler would not have experienced a void had he relaxed his one-sided view of art as solely idea. He would have felt the corporeality of the work, knowing his own emotion as well as that of the artist. With the tangible evidence of the medium's earthly qualities, he could have realized how ideas are symbolized through mass, line, shape, sound, rhythm, the colorful manifold that harbored the view of how the individual personality expresses itself when in touch with causal understanding. Only by honoring the historical personality of himself and the artist could he truly see the interplay of teleological freedom and causal ground. Personality is extremely important in the act of creation because the interplay between the givens of a conceptual field in which the ego is situated and the struggle of the artist or thinker to make a statement in that field require a coherence of personal vision, a personal identity, a memory of purposes, and a sense of what is distinctive in one's acts. The object of art is the creation of an antagonism between the fallible human subject, who, one step at a time, reacts against the boundness of the laws of perspective, composition, and human motility. The product is a vision of eternal organizing principles as experienced by an individual who has made his own statement in and through those laws. Thus the law expresses itself in a particular individual, and the individual shows his freedom in the use of the law. Here the social a priori as it is known in an individual life might have become apparent.

Adler's inability to see a more nuanced context behind the literal meaning of words in a poem was an indication of his tendency to overemphasize literal meanings. A metaphorical abuse of idea resulted from his reification of words: "War is hereby declared upon the *words*, the old hackneyed concepts that heretofore mobilized thoughts are under attack: but only so that one can better arrive at *things* themselves, so that they are viewed uncovered in their true . . . essential reality."[39]

The war was to capture the organizing principles of understanding behind the words, to expose the schemata that gave rise to them, and to coin new words that better expressed the true state of things in the environment and in consciousness, or to preserve those words that really articulated the state of things. Had his inquiry been carried out through research into cultural practices and mental forms, he would have concentrated on vocabulary as the final step in preparing social policy for his party. In this case, however, the beginning was not in the word but in the

act of research. When Adler confronted the tendency of his party to engage in bourgeois forms of political expression, such as a revision of the
party program in 1901 to soften the harsh specter of class conflict and
allow for moderate forms within the existing system of society, he defended the words that secured the reality of the class conflict but ignored
the only statistical evidence on the question of improving the condition of
workers. He took a scholasticist position that held that the definition of
the thing was sufficient to prove its reality. Even if class conflict was not
immediately evident, it must exist as an illness that temporarily has no
symptoms but works its destruction unseen.[40] The Parteitag of 1901 was
to revise the Hainfeld program of 1889 in order to make the wording of
its Marxist format more compatible with the growing respectability of the
Social Democratic party within Austria.[41] The planned revision was to
extend the basic principles of the party to cover new areas of concern and
rephrase what it had previously written. Two changes were particularly
evident to Max Adler: the removal of the so-called "pauperization theory"
(*Verelendungstheorie*) and the failure to emphasize a need to save the "will
and consciousness of men from its 'degradation' by economic necessity."[42]
The Hainfeld program had stated the "pauperization" theory in strong
Marxian didactic terms: "Those who possess the working power within
the society, the working class, become slaves [*Sklaven*] to the possessors of
the means of production, the capitalist class, whose political and economic
rule is expressed in the present state. The individual possession of the
means of production, as it means also politically the class state, means
economically the increasing poverty [*steigende Massenarmut*] and the growing pauperization [*wachsenda Verelendung*] of broader areas of the people.[43]

The revision of 1901 omitted the emotive words "slave," "poverty,"
and "pauperization."[44] It also omitted something even more important in
Max Adler's eyes: whereas the Hainfeld program had stressed the role of
the revolutionary workers' party in helping the individual proletarian to
realize his individual will and thus in himself combat the growing misery
of his condition, Adler felt the revision of 1901 ignored the theoretical
importance of individual will, within either the Austrian Social Democratic party or the masses, in combating the evils of the capitalist order.
Adler stated that the omission of the "pauperization" clause was evidence
of the greater sin of the planned revision of 1901, for these pejorative
words had underlined the principles that forever isolated the individual
worker from a bourgeois consciousness and designated the position the
Austrian Social Democratic party must take in matters of policy and action. Adler argued that the proposed revision failed to stress the essence
that justified the very existence of the vanguard of the proletariat in its
form as Austrian Social Democracy; that is, the rigor of its intellectual

task as pedagogical molder of wills. The language of the revision of 1901 was called a concession to the "popular" understanding of Marxism, a phrasing that had lost the "precision" and "purity" of the Marxist message. In pandering to the goodwill of the general public and the comprehension of the non-Marxist, the party oligarchs had sacrificed the spirit that made them a living force in the environment: "One should not forget *for whom* the program of the party is drawn, that is, for Marxists. [A party program] must not concern itself in the least with those who are not Marxists; it must only concern itself that its own teachings are clearly expressed. Most particularly, the Marxist should realize that in such a program he need not contradict the false views of Marxism, for even in an indirect involvement, his language will be influenced by the false conception."[45]

The purpose of an authentic education is to aid the student to make the truest judgment. Indoctrination was not the real spirit of Adler's intention, yet his insistence on the shibboleth distorted his aims. The worker as an individual must discover if in fact there was an unbridgeable gulf between his interests in society and a bourgeois life, or whether there were points in common between himself and his "masters" that might allow cooperation. Even more significant is the thralldom of will Adler would impose by insisting that in areas of practical judgment a limited vocabulary be accepted without testing. In his philosophical deliberations, Marxism became a fluid set of concepts that pointed to new directions of thought, but in his practical involvements it became a rigid text.

Adler's rigidity grew as he experienced the antagonism inherent in developing his thought with his peers and party fathers within Austrian Social Democracy. At thirty-one years of age, in 1904, he was a bright star on the horizon. He had an array of ideas to bring to Social Democracy. In 1901 his critique of the proposed changes of the party platform had won him the respect of the party fathers. Victor Adler had exclaimed in a letter to Karl Kautsky: "I will print most of your article, but even that won't completely answer Max Adler. He's quite a fellow! isn't he?" Kautsky answered: "I wanted to write to you chiefly in order to ask who Max Adler is. A splendid fellow! If I had been aware of his critique, I probably would not have written mine. He said . . . essentially all there was to say. So, there is a Marxist *Nachwuchs*! A good feeling, when one can say that there are people who will continue our work. We must win him for us. Hopefully, I will get to meet him in Vienna."[46]

But by 1910 Max Adler was openly criticized in *Der Kampf* by Otto Bauer as a "metaphysician." In April 1918 Victor Adler dismissed the idea of having Max Adler speak on the occasion of the hundredth anniversary of Karl Marx's birth in the name of Austrian Social Democracy with these words: "Many do not like Max, above all me: I detest the court chaplain of Marxism. From his oily overflow all of us will go home spotted with grease."[47]

In 1904 Adler might be compared to the figure of Faust sitting in his narrow cell about to begin the translation of the Gospel of John. He saw himself giving a new translation to social thought that would begin to expand his knowledge of the world in order to develop all his thought and person, but as Faust he risked his historical personality in the hubris that misused idea for personal immortality. By accepting Faust's change of "In the beginning was the word" to "In the beginning was the act," Adler sacrificed the careful progress of his thought for the fruitless debates and the alienating party identification of Social Democracy. The "word" should have preceded action in his life. The social norms of Austrian culture did not legislate toward patient progress. Had Adler separated himself from party involvement, with its ready but empty support for personal identity, and pursued his research in dialogues with his true community of peers, the neo-Kantians who were interested in a more equitable society but who did not identify themselves as vanguards of the proletariat, he might have completed his thought. Thinkers such as Karl Vorlaender, Paul Natorp, Franz Staudinger, and Rudolf Stammler could have benefitted from his view of the social a priori and its implications for social development.[48]

He conducted an arid denunciation of Stammler for several years before World War I, but there was no actual dialogue between the two men. His polemics with Stammler had just and unjust bases. Justly, he demanded of Stammler social scientific certainty. Stammler was content to speak of trends in cultural norms without referring them to an epistemological or psychological set of constants that would permit causes and effects to be isolated and thereby permit social planning. Stammler's relativity reflected a movement in social science shared by peers such as Max Weber. Adler represented in his criticism the insistence for anthropological certainty that motivated the work of Kant, Marx, and contemporaries such as Freud. Stammler justified his position by interpreting Kant's critique of teleological judgment as a document that said no knowledge is possible of how goal formation and ethics are affected by the categories of pure understanding, even though one might surmise that they are; therefore, phenomenological introspection upon one's experience was not likely to expose this mystery. Instead, Stammler turned to the artifacts of his culture, such as constitutions and legislation, seeking, as Kant had in his *Idea for a Universal History from a Cosmopolitan Point of View*, the evidence of thinking that reflected ethical autonomy or thinking that violated it.[49] Stammler measured the cultural law against Kant's categorical imperative—that each man should be treated as an end, not a means.[50] He rightly understood this activity to be a genuine discovery technique of the legislator's social consciousness. He was wrong, as Adler pointed out, in believing that such a discovery was sufficient to show an adequate law for the development of human potential. Even Kant saw human planning through laws as only the expression of a hypothetical imperative that might create conditions for the best anthropological development of man. One might find the categorical imperative in oneself or in the intention of another, but to formulate principles that actually elicited human freedom was a practical precept, not a law.[51] Max Adler, however, felt that deeper investigation of the human mind in its processes might reveal those a priori laws of consciousness, the schemata, by which the individual articulated his here and now understanding of culture. With the deeper insight into human knowing in the moment, one could determine those human perspectives which more or less adequately expressed a healthy anthropological standard. With this new phenomenological psychology, Kant's intuition that man was a socializing creature, as well as an autonomous one, would be developed through research so that new categorical imperatives could be formulated that expressed the law of man as a cooperative being.

Max Adler's thought remains as challenge. Can exploration of the human mind through its artifacts and attention to its processes arrive at certainty as to its nature? Is a major dimension of its nature inherently social? Discovery of the social forms of human knowing will found the possibility of an education that ends the self-alienating norms in which Adler began his thought.

8

The Party as Father
for Friedrich Adler

For Otto Bauer, Karl Renner, and Max Adler, the Austrian Social Democracy party served as a transpersonal father, providing a thread of hope in the labyrinth of the Habsburg state. For Friedrich Adler, Austrian Social Democracy was the Gordian knot of his existence. Whereas Renner and Bauer found a sublimation to their family situations within Austrian Social Democracy, Friedrich Adler's family, personally and transpersonally, was truly the party, and any solution to his problems of personality could come only by a direct confrontation with the chimeric presence of Victor Adler as party leader and personal father, and not, as for Renner and Bauer, in a return to self apart from the party. For Friedrich Adler had no self divorced from Austrian Society Democracy; he depended totally on the world and presence of Victor Adler. And if a self could come to be for Friedrich Adler, it could arise only out of the ashes of destruction—the annihilation of the party and family patriarch that had usurped his life.

Not all sons of political leaders share the patriarchal possession experienced by Friedrich Adler. The unique quality of his origins can be appreciated only with the unfolding of his family's story. Friedrich Wolfgang Adler, the first son of Victor Adler and Emma Adler, née Braun, was born in their home in Vienna on July 9, 1879. He was named after Friedrich Schiller and Wolfgang Goethe, with possibly an allusion to Friedrich Nietzsche, whom Victor Adler venerated. The marriage of Victor and Emma was stormy in the beginning, for Emma, who was said to be fit as a bride for only the revolutionary nature of Friedrich Nietzsche or Victor Adler, was melancholic and subject to severe spells of depression.[1] Her tragic beauty and dark, passionate nature served as the model for creative work by artists of the society.[2] From the beginning of their marriage Victor controlled and suppressed the emotional abyss represented by his wife and present in his son Friedrich. Their honeymoon was a *Studienreise* (educational excursion) in Italy, in the manner of Goethe, after which they went to England, where Victor studied factory conditions.[3] Apparently, Victor, proud and protective of his rational existence, had picked his antithesis as a bride and proceeded to mold her to mesh with his planned existence.[4]

Victor seemed to have a genius for choosing professions and associates that expressed the dark forces of his own unrecognized self and channeling these factors into currents that would suit his will. Before directing the inchoate desires of the proletariat, he had studied psychiatry, and he saw his family as a mass that symbolized the irrational forces of nature that could erupt at any time. Of the three children of his marriage to Emma, one went permanently insane at seventeen years of age, and Friedrich, as we shall see, walked the edge of mental collapse continually.[5] Adler's patriarchal will within the family was frustraed by emotional illnesses he could not control and that compelled him to devote more attention that he desired to those immediately around him. The family could break through the abstractions of Victor Adler, party leader, only by exposing him to the violence and intensity of an emotional crisis.[6] When the house was quiet, Victor spent fifteen hours a day on Austrian Social Democratic business.[7] Friedrich, who grew up simultaneously with his father's other child, Austrian Social Democracy, in his thirtieth year wrote a letter to his father on the occasion of the twentieth birthday of the Gesamtpartei, which expressed the family life he had known: "You never took the slightest notice of your person, and its appendage, the family. I, who belonged to this appendage, who made you a great deal of care and trouble, I would like to tell you today that no matter what happens with me in the future, I am glad that you were a man and not a father. The highest that life can give one you would have taken away from me if you had had consideration of the family."[8]

To Friedrich Adler, the highest that one could experience was a life lived only for an intellectual ideal, excluding all personal affairs, all subjective concerns. This birthright granted by his father replaced and embraced all normal family life. As a child, Friedrich heard at meals the stories of the poor workers' families, which touched him so deeply that he would break out in tears. The emotional energy—the love—of his father was felt primarily through the vehicle of the proletariat world; the image of the suffering masses was the third person in virtually all contacts between father and son. Such an abstract emotional vehicle became an impediment to any genuine contact with his father or his own emotional self. Socialism became a vehicle that absorbed all the qualities of individual life. All feeling and the sense of meaning that is granted by an emotional presence were first known in the metaphors of a Marxist world. These metaphors embraced the entire spectrum of love and hate and all the hidden motives that would find an outlet as Friedrich matured. Even as a child Friedrich released his ambivalent feelings toward his father through Social Democratic events. In 1887, when his father was imprisoned for four months, we are told that Friedrich happily told the news to the first person he encountered. In 1893, when his father had been indicted for many political offenses, Friedrich "proudly" reckoned that his father could receive a twenty-year sentence, and "he could not understand why his mother admonished him for telling this to his sister." His biographer states that Friedrich's joy was "pride over his father who suffered for freedom," and adding that Friedrich was "a tender child from whom every aggressive impulse was foreign." That aggressive impulses toward his father remained foreign to Friedrich Adler's consciousness there seems little doubt, for his father appeared as a god, the one god. Nevertheless, the anecdotes of Friedrich's childhood contain the germ of his later behavior toward his father and his father's political party. Friedrich's later rebellion within Austrian Society Democracy was vitally connected to its essential truth and meaning content. Never did the metaphors of socialism cease to exert their force. As Friedrich Adler wrote to the Christian theologian Leonhard Ragasz in 1921: "Belief plays an extraordinary role in the life and activity of men . . . belief seems to me to be the most important human attribute, something that is given subjectively. . . . The belief in the realization of socialism is such a belief, but one that is throughout a human belief, one that is possible within . . . the framework of what can be experienced. . . . I am, however, of the opinion . . . that *knowledge* of the conditions of the development of socialism is not enough, that an *emotion* must also be present for it to be realized."[9]

The religion of socialism was a live force for Friedrich Adler from his earliest consciousness. At eight years of age he helped fold the first numbers of his father's socialist publication *Die Gleichheit*, which he considered a service in behalf of freedom. At ten years of age he was inspired by the tramway strike in Hernals (a section of Vienna) when workers and soldiers clashed in the streets. In the same year the first May Day parade was held, and Friedrich "could not forgive his mother for not permitting him to attend. He had expected on this day, after all he had heard, a great revolution." By his fifteenth year Friedrich considered himself a full-fledged "party comrade" and read all the socialist literature available, consuming daily the *Arbeiter-Zeitung* from the first to the last line. He took part in street demonstrations and spent all his free time outside of school in party activity.[10]

Victor Adler's reaction to his son's involvement in the affairs of Austrian Social Democracy brings inevitably to mind the image of his archetypal predecessor, Oedipus's father. Victor Adler did not want his son to have any part in the political life of the party. From his earliest years, Friedrich's education was tailored by his father to exclude activity in the party. What Victor Adler articulated as concern with Friedrich's weak and sensitive constitution, causing him to plan a quiet bourgeois existence for Friedrich, must be viewed as an attempt to emasculate his son.

Although Victor gave little attention to his family's everyday presence, the question of his son's education and general goals was a matter of concern. As early as his fourteenth year Friedrich was oppressed by his father's wishes for his future, which ran contrary to his own. Victor Adler planned that Friedrich would not follow the path of the normal bourgeois intellectual, which could lead to the party oligarchy. Friedrich was to attend *Realschule* instead of *Gymnasium* and then go the technological institute and learn a practical profession. This plan, formulated when Friedrich was ten years of age, was ostensibly to protect the boy's sensitive nervous system. After completing the first grades of the *Realschule*, however, Friedrich pleaded "that he could not live without higher mathematics" and begged to be allowed to take his *Matura*, which would permit him to visit a university. Victor consented only after a long conflict and with the qualifying condition that he must follow a practical profession as a chemist or engineer, or "if worse came to worse" as an academic professor. Friedrich was allowed to go to the University of Zurich because his *Realschule* degree excluded him from entrance to the University of Vienna.[11]

During the fourteen years between Friedrich's entrance to the University of Zurich in 1897 and his admission to the Austrian Social Democracy party oligarchy in 1911, a continual internecine strife existed between father and son. On the father's side this conflict was evidenced by constant undermining of Friedrich's attempts to establish himself in Social Democratic politics. Friedrich was kept outside of politics and outside of Austria, in a genuine exile, but the psychological center of his life remained within the compass of Vienna. And although during these fourteen years he made many attempts to establish a life apart from his father and Austrian Social Democracy, they all paled quickly, and the image of Vienna would again force its way into his desires.

While in the University of Zurich, Friedrich repeatedly threatened the life plan his father had constructed for him. In the first year he wrote to his father that he wished to leave his studies for a year to work in a coal mine and then in a factory so he could learn what a proletarian life was like. His father reasoned with him at first, then refused to hear of the plan. At the end of his second semester in Zurich, Friedrich informed his father that besides chemistry, he wished to study history, national economy, and philosophy. His father replied with a "categorical no." Friedrich proposed a compromise: instead of becoming a chemist, he would study physics and mathematics, which were more intellectually stimulating, and would forego subjects that smacked of political and economic preparation for a Marxist career. Thus Friedrich began his third semester working toward a doctor's degree in physics. To Friedrich the study of physics provided an outlet to the promised land. It became a focus for the path to his own self, Austrian Social Democracy. His concern with physics was centered on an attempt to find how the "mechanical materialism of this science related to historical materialism." During his university years Friedrich sought continually for a "unified world picture." He created models of organic life based on a dialectical use of Darwin and employed Marx's dialectical reasoning in the areas of his studies that dealt with cosmogony, embryology, and geology.[12] A satisfactory relation between historical materialism and the development of theoretical physics eluded him for many years. Eventually, however, he was to discover the magic key that could turn his scientific effort in physics into the living word of political Marxism.

As a student, Friedrich "did not drink, smoke, or lead a gay life"; he spent all his time discussing politics or studying. He was actively involved in the Russian Communist group of students at the University of Zurich and often discussed Marxist theory with them far into the night.[13] Victor Adler had sources in Zurich who checked on his son's activities. August Bebel, the German Social Democrat, who lived there at the time, seemed to share Victor Adler's opinion that Friedrich was not meant for a political career and wrote frequent letters warning Victor of Friedrich's activities.[14] On the basis of such information, Victor wrote to his son in his third year at Zurich: "You seem to require more of your nerves than they will stand. For God's sake, postpone your examinations, rather than tax your nerves to the degree that you are . . . whether you finish a half a year later or not is absolutely the same. *But you must remain healthy for me* [underlined twice] *for my sake* [underlined three times]."[15]

Friedrich received frequent letters from his father warning him about his health. His weakness became a fixed idea in the minds of father and son, and although he suffered no physical ailment until 1911, the grounds for a psychosomatic illness were well prepared by the paternal power of suggestion. When, for example, Friedrich finished the examination that would permit him entry into the technical field of physics, he begged to be allowed to continue his study in the area of epistemology, an interest stimulated by Engels's *Anti-Duehring*. His father replied:

There is no doubt that you are a talented person with an ability to work. How *far* your talents go, whether they are more than normal, I don't know, and you hardly know; that your physical strength, the strength of your nerves must be exercised with caution, is already known to you. But I am happy to believe that your talent and energy will suffice for normal goals. . . .

But you will not be satisfied with something normal, you wish the supernormal abilities could bring personal satisfaction.

And here begins my fear . . . that you will drop physics, become an aimless student [*verbummlete student*] . . . wander through other areas of knowledge, without a plan, without a defined goal, grasp your career in a merely improvised manner. Perhaps a few people have done that without going to pieces [*kaputt zu gehen*]. . . .

This new enterprise of yours I consider beside the point, it is simply crazy, you have already found an area to work in, and are happy enough! I consider it wanton and petulant to leave your involvement in physics. . . . You wish to undertake something where you have but *one* chance in a thousand to succeed without losing yourself.[16]

Then as if to soften the wound, Victor added: "But you do have this *one* chance in a thousand to survive. Perhaps you do have the abnormal energy, nerves, and ability to become a man of many fields, a worker without a definite area of work. Perhaps! After all, you are young, and you risk nothing but your own head."[17] But Friedrich dropped his plans to study epistemology and continued his work in physics toward a doctorate, another compromise with his father. In 1903 he acquired his doctor's degree in physics and assumed the position of assistant in the physics laboratory at the University of Zurich.[18]

In 1900 at the University of Zurich Friedrich had met the woman who was to be his wife, a Russian Jew, Katharina Jakoblewna Germanishkaja. The couple soon wished to be married. Victor Adler objected, believing Friedrich to be too young, but after he met Katharina (Kathia) he gave his permission. By 1905 Friedrich had two children, Johanna Alice and Emma Frida, and his assistant's position at the university proved insufficient to support a family. From 1903 to 1905 his work had absorbed him, sublimating the longing for a political career, but the necessity of assuming a more responsible position with higher pay forced him to make the overt step toward a Social Democratic career. His father again discouraged him, and Friedrich was compelled to accept a position as scientific assistant at the Deutsches Museum fuer Meisterwerke der Naturwissenschaft und Technik in Munich. He remained there from June 1905 until the spring of 1907. Friedrich was unhappy with the position and complained to his father that his real desire, to be an Austrian Social Democracy party worker, was frustrated mainly by patriarchial ill will. His father answered: "That you maintain a political longing I can well understand. . . . If I was really the force that kept you out of politics—a rather childish philosophy of history—then I wouldn't blame myself, rather I would consider it a service rendered."[19]

Apparently without his father's knowledge, Friedrich turned to Karl Kautsky and pleaded for a position on *Die Neue Zeit* as an editor; he told Kautsky that he had taken the job at the Munich museum "on the one hand out of the need to earn a living, but on the other hand, because I thought it would be reasonable to dress in bourgeois clothes once to show the party that I didn't come to them because no one else would take me."[20] But this argument, which sounded as though he was trying to satisfy his father's usual qualifications for party oligarchy, did not influence Kautsky, and Friedrich was forced to remain in Munich. In 1907 Friedrich accepted a position as *Privatdozent* in physics at the University of Zurich. He lectured in this capacity until 1910, when he failed to receive a newly established post of professor of physics. During these three years his research and lectures again returned to the theoretical physics that sought a Marxist base for pure science.[21]

When Friedrich Adler learned that his university career could go no further in Zurich, he "had the feeling of an enormous liberation" and wrote to his father, "What depressed me for months in a horrible manner was finally finished. . . . I believe now I must leave theory and seek a practical activity. And that *can only be a party activity* . . . that is important to me besides epistemology. To deny science *and* party, become *purely and simply* a family father, would never satisfy my energy." Although the answer to this letter is not available, it seems that Victor Adler once again attempted to discourage his son, for Friedrich wrote in his next letter to his father: "I didn't become the engineer you wanted me to be, because it contradicted my entire nature; I did not seek a position in the university as you wished me to; every step I took toward what I wanted to be was done against your will. . . . You shouldn't take this as a reproach, but realize the fact that I can take care of myself without your great circumspection."[22]

The opportunity to engage in Social Democratic politics finally came in the spring of 1910, but not from Austria. The Swiss-German Social Democratic party in Zurich offered Friedrich the editor's post of its daily paper, the *Volksrecht*. Because Friedrich had been active in political groups in Zurich since 1897, his nomination to this post was on his own merit. He had served since 1901 as president of the Association of International

Workers' Groups in Switzerland (Verband der Internationalen Arbeiter-
vereine in der Schweiz), an amalgamation of German and Austrian socialists, besides contributinng to the *Volksrecht* as a political commentator.
The editorship was seemingly the answer at least to his stated yearnings,
for it allowed him to devote his full time to practical and theoretical Marxism. Moreover, the condition of the Swiss socialists was reminiscent of
Austrian socialism in 1889; Friedrich was placed in the position of media-
tor between the radicals and moderates, as was his father at the beginning
of his political career. Friedrich wrote to his father soon after beginning
his activity: "I work like a horse, do not get a chance to sleep, but feel as
if I was re-born. . . . I am filled with the fire and flame of the thing, and
the people here are somewhat flabbergasted, for they are not used to this
tempo." He described how he had reorganized the paper and how he did
everything from writing the lead to articles to reporting on the affairs of
the day. He closed this letter with "It seems as if I was born to be an
editor-in-chief."[23]

Yet as promising as this area of activity was, it failed to fulfill Friedrich's needs. A short time later he wrote his father that although he was
satisfied, he was not sure that this post was sufficient for his wants: "I
cannot say that I will not make greater moves. Subjectively, the position
was good for me, but in the long run, there is still a question."[24] He spoke
of the editorship in the past tense; his present was still in Vienna and in
the hunger for activity within Austrian Social Democracy.

The call that he had waited for came on April 26, 1911, in a letter
from Karl Seitz, the vice-chairman of the Austrian Social-Democratic
party. Friedrich was asked to accept a position as party secretary, an opening created especially for him, and to help prepare for the election campaign of 1911. Friedrich was given the editorship of a small biweekly
party organ, *Das Volk*, besides the activities of election propaganda that
were part of the position of party secretary. He also lectured at the Arbei-
terschule, spoke at political meetings, and, in 1913, was appointed an
editor to *Der Kampf*.[25]

Why had his father relented? Because of his position on the party
executive committee, it is obvious that Victor Adler approved of Friedrich's entry into the Austrian Social Democratic hierarchy. Moreover, in
creating a special position for his son, Victor demonstrated that had he so
desired, Friedrich could have at any time begun Austrian Social Democratic activity. Victor Adler wrote to August Bebel in July 1911: "That
Friedrich (Fritz) is here is a true blessing, as you might imagine."[26] But
how can we explain these words that contradict Victor Adler's behavior
over many years toward Friedrich's wishes to return to Vienna and enter
the party? The answer to this enigma, which Friedrich Adler's biogra-

phers admit to be as puzzling as Friedrich's sudden lack of interest in Swiss socialism, can be suggested but never fully resolved.[27] Friedrich Adler's desire to leave Swiss socialism and Victor Adler's readiness to make it possible may be seen in Oedipal terms. As Friedrich wrote in 1910, the job as editor of the *Volksrecht* "subjectively . . . was good" for him, but he could not say that he would not "make greater moves."[28] Shortly after receiving this letter, Victor Adler had Friedrich called to Austrian Social Democracy. It seems that after Friedrich challenged his father with the news of his manifold creative activity and hinted that he was ready for bigger contests, his father accepted the challenge. Seeing that his son was proving himself not to be the sensitive, emotionally unstable, ordinary person that he had been trained to be, Victor brought him home for what may be considered an Oedipal moment of truth, facing his son in a last effort to make him into the person that his imagination desired. Victor's motives may be seen as twofold. On the one hand, Friedrich, like his mother, had to be physically limited to a dependent, unstable role. On the other hand, Victor constantly sought liberation from his self-made prison of reason, and a confrontation with his son might be the only way to win back his own projections. Either Victor would again vanquish his son or in his own defeat he would be freed from the self-made treadmill of his life.

Friedrich's acceptance of the challenge was, in a sense, a betrayal of his greater self, for he did not bring his wife and three children to Vienna in 1911. Thus in his attempt to win back his life from the metaphors of patriarchal Austrian Social Democracy, Friedrich recreated the one-sided father who had created him. His excuse for leaving the family behind was that his children were too weak and sensitive to come immediately to Austria.[29] In confronting his own myth, Friedrich began to perpetuate it. Perhaps because of his acceptance of his father's challenge without the presence of his own creations such as his children and of his wife, who might support him, Friedrich had a heart attack in September 1911.[30] His heart ailment, myocarditis, was a psychosomatic disease that recurred periodically and included among its symptoms a mental incapacitation.[31] Friedrich was forced to remain in bed for several months, during which time he suffered from depression and doubt over his ability to engage in politics.[32] By returning to Austria, Friedrich had exposed himself to the full power of his father and his father's organization. In matters of party policy, he could do nothing but follow his father, although in a manner that expressed the hidden struggle. His article in *Der Kampf* about parliamentary policy in June 1911 approved of "parliamentarianism" but made the distinction between the "potential" energy and the "kinetic" energy of a party; he stated: "One cannot fulfill *potential* constantly. There must be a phase of waiting. One must join leaders of the bourgeois and express a threat of what can be unleashed."[33] Friedrich's own kinetic energy was checked by the presence of his father's rule; his potential had yet to be unleashed. In such an environment, according to the Viennese psychiatrist Alfred Adler, a physical illness might develop created by an inferior (*minderwertig*) organ symbolizing the psychic inferiority felt by the subject.[34] Adler's hypothesis of the inferiority complex (*minderwertigkeitsgefuehl*) and its psychosomatic result has moment here, for Friedrich Adler knew of Alfred Adler and his theories. One might almost surmise that Alfred Adler had given Friedrich Adler a hint of the roots of his own condition. A month before the psychosomatic attack that incapacitated Friedrich mentally, striking at his heart but numbing his brain, Friedrich had written an article for *Der Kampf* entitled "Minderwertig in Internationalismus" (inferior in internationalism) in which he said that the idea of internationalism had been neglected by both Czech separatists and Austro-German Social Democrats; he stated that internationalism as a principle must be raised from its inferior rank in the national consciousness of Social Democrats to a more prominent place.[35] Internationalism, the one socialistic unit that could assert more symbolic power than Austrian Social Democracy, was the metaphor that would serve Friedrich as the foremost weapon in his struggle with Victor Adler because Austrian Social Democracy seen through its relation to the Second International was but one part of a greater whole.[36]

Friedrich recovered from his illness in the spring of 1912 and returned to party activity. His family had come from Zurich, and he began to gather energy and courage for the next assault upon his father's stronghold. During the two years between his reentry into political action and the outbreak of World War I, Friedrich retreated to the fallow ground of mental and emotional preparation and the nonassertive contemplation of his position that built up his supply of potential energy. His state of mind is revealed in the first article he wrote for *Der Kampf* after his illness, "Wissenschaft und Partei." Ostensibly written as a comment upon the ouster of Gerhard Hildebrand, a German Social Democrat, from the unified ranks of German Social Democracy because of his heretical views on colonialism, the article served as a forum for a debate with himself over his relation to his father in the person of Austrian Social Democracy. Friedrich compared the Social Democratic party in all lands to the Catholic church. The party program was viewed as the Eucharist, the manifest presence of truth and the means whereby the individual Social Democrat could partake of the spirit and matter of this truth. The metaphor indicates that Friedrich recognized his essential bond to the party program of his father and understood that his life force emanated from the transcendental presence of the party imperative. Thus there was no question of manifesting an individual will apart from the general will of the party in Friedrich's mind. He considered the ouster of the German Social-Democrat justified. Although Social Democrats had the free will to think for themselves, if they reached conclusions contrary to the party program they should consider themselves no longer Social Democrats and, like a Catholic who ceased to believe in the Eucharist, should leave the organization. No man might act contrary to the party program, although a man might attempt to transform the program through the proper channels.[37]

Friedrich committed himself to the existing order and hierarchical obedience in this article, yet he opened a door for his own possible triumph as an individual over the will of his father. For if his will could assume the same status as that of his father, having the same general validity for all Social Democrats, he could win the independence of person so long denied to him. If he could finally partake in the framing of Marxist law within the party program, then the old king would be vanquished and the new king would reign. Would such action, however, truly be a liberation from the clutches of his father's spiritual womb? Or would it not be a Pyrrhic victory, an independence that left him as emotionally emasculated as his father and as destructive to those around him? For with such a victory, Friedrich, too, would have limited his conscious life to a marriage with the abstract bride of Social Democracy, leaving his personal emotional life, his family, and his everyday affairs in the same dark closet as his father had done. Friedrich Adler was faced with a difficult path through the labyrinth. He could not turn his back upon Social Democracy, for only by confronting it could he face the metaphors of his own life and rescue them from the stupefying abstraction of Marxism; on the other hand, he could not rest with expressing his will through his own brand of Marxism, for this, too, would be a continuation of the alienation from self introduced by his father. At the outbreak of World War I, Friedrich began the first half of the liberation process, the exerting of his own will through the metaphors of Marxist principle and the tremendous effort to have his understanding of Marxist principle incorporated into the party program. The physical illness of his father no doubt aided him in his revolutionary stance. By 1913, Victor Adler had begun to manifest the symptoms of a fatal illness and was virtually unable to carry on party business.[38] A vacuum of power was created that would cause contention among the party oligarchy. Within this vacuum Friedrich Adler, in the single act of assassinating Count Stürgkh in 1917, created the potential conditions for a spiritual and emotional liberation from the curse of his forebears. But then, unconsciousness set in; the full magnitude of Friedrich's act was lost to him. The act became a vehicle merely to establish his own will within Austrian Social Democracy, to usurp the party from the will of his father.

From the confines of his prison cell, where he was incarcerated until the last months of the war, Friedrich gained increasing popularity among the rank and file of the party, which enabled him to influence the general policy of the oligarchy.[39] In the long run, however, he never replaced his father within Austrian Social Democracy. The reason was twofold. On the one hand, Otto Bauer's ubiquitous eclectic presence usurped the theoretical mantle from the shoulders of Friedrich Adler. Bauer, who had become a favorite of Victor Adler in the last three years of Victor's life,[40] managed to appear to the radicals as radical as Friedrich Adler, yet was obliging enough for the moderates to gain their support. On the other hand, after the death of Victor Adler, Friedrich seems to have lost interest in Austrian Social Democracy. He did not attempt to counter Otto Bauer's leadership over the left and left-center factions of the party or Karl Renner's leadership over the right and right-center factions; rather, Friedrich shifted his attention to the question of international socialism. After World War I, Friedrich created his own socialist international, an inter-European organization without any genuine support from national socialist parties; his organization had an office but no proletarian adherents. The Second International had collapsed at the outbreak of World War I, and international communism had found its most powerful exponent after the war in Russia, who established herself as the leader of the Third Communist International.[41] Friedrich Adler's organization, officially known as the Labor and Socialist International but popularly called the 2½ International, sought to become the leader of the Marxist center, a direction of thought that had no place in the post–World War I world of national socialism and the Russian Communist International.[42] In his involvement with the 2½ International, Friedrich Adler had closed his vision; he spent the rest of his life in the self-made darkness of intellectual fantasy. Victor Adler lived on in his son as a mocking spirit; Friedrich was to be a caricature of his father's hyperrationality and neglect of personal life. For Friedrich lacked the balance of real political presence in the organization controlled by his will, and thus the 2½ International became a bizarre arena for the play of his neglected emotions. It was claimed that in the years before World War II, Adler turned the 2½ International into a personification of his "shadow side." As a petty tyrant, he made his office staff answer to his will. His attention "compulsively" concerned itself with every detail of the International's activity from the placing of stamps on letters to the international principles that he had drafted, which defined in detail the action to be taken by socialists of all lands in peace and war.[43] And so when he finally knew freedom from the exile imposed by his father, his life became monstrous. His mission was still a force with the fulfilling energy of a religion, but a religion that devoured its disciple.

In 1944 Friedrich Adler reflected publicly upon the religious basis of his life:

Everyone has an a priori behind his political consciousness. He has assumptions upon which a political theoretical structure arises which he takes for granted, assumptions which for him could never be based upon illusion. Those deepest of all convictions can be affirmed through experience and scientific knowledge, but they themselves spring from a knowledge before any science; they are, as the psychologist Jung designates them, a religious experience—[44] religion in the broadest sense in contradistinction to scientific knowledge. . . . I will not judge of others, but will confess that for myself socialism was a religious experience for me long before I knew of or understood its scientific doctrines.[45]

Adler concludes that he knows he has realized fully the existence of his "personal a priori" through his life in socialism.[46] So might Oedipus have spoken at Colonus!

9

Friedrich Adler:
From Physics to Marxism

In his article in 1909 for *Der Kampf* entitled "Wozu brauchen wir Theorien?" (Why do we need theories?), Friedrich Adler stated: "A single individual can only have a limited amount of experience himself. He depends, therefore, on other people's theories concerning experience in his own approach to the manifold of life. . . . The child who listens to his mother when she says: 'Don't touch the oven, it burns, other children have already tried it,' can live a whole life without burning his fingers."[1]

At the time this article was written, Friedrich Adler was still under the thumb of his father, not yet having crossed the bridge to political action and Austrian Social Democracy. The article, with its major thesis that theory guides the individual through dark and possibly painful areas beyond his experience, can be read as the Rosetta stone of Friedrich Adler's, theoretical language. Adler's relation to Marxism is grounded in the mediating, protective role the theories of his "fathers" played in his life. Whether during the period when the words of Marx, his father, and the programs of Austrian Social Democracy were considered as holy writ, or during the period when he sought to add his own exegesis of them, theory was the omnipresent force that guided Adler's footsteps:

The animal who through a stimulus has a wish, an expression of will, arise in him, follows this will automatically and reacts immediately. The moth sees the lamp; he has the wish to come closer to it, and flies into the fire. The child reacts in the beginning like an animal: only gradually does he learn to use a *tool* that will serve him as a protection from injury: theory. The adult bridles his will, reacts in the first instance with his brain, tests the consequences of his action with theory. If he finds that the impulse of his will leads to a destruction of self, then he seeks to become master of this will; if he sees that his will leads toward a higher personal development, then he allows his will its freedom quite happily.[2]

Friedrich was the moth who circled nearer and nearer to the flame of his own life until 1917. The intensity of the flame, his life energy, was screened at first by the theories of Victor Adler and the influences of Victor Adler's world. But as Friedrich Adler got closer to this flame, the theories that served as a screen and a shield became his own, allowing more of the light to penetrate yet preserving him from dissolution in the fire. An examination of the theory of Friedrich Adler will show a development from the realms of abstraction most removed from his own life flame toward a theoretical construct that all but touches the living flame. For Friedrich Adler eventually involved himself in the area of phenomenology and in the immediate images of his existence. As with Max Adler, however, the full implications of phenomenology escaped Friedrich Adler, and he followed a derivative direction that spared him the trial of direct contact with its content. There were moments when his wings were singed, but on the whole, his theory kept the insect that sought warmth intact within the protective penumbra of abstraction. The freeing death, the fiery baptism, was never wholly to be Friedrich Adler's experience.

Friedrich Adler's writings before 1914 are almost wholly concerned with his attempt to discover the epistemological relation between physics and Marxism,[3] a relation that would create a bridge that led out of the abstract exile to which he had been condemned and toward the whole personality represented by the socialist ideal. If he could portray physics in its social origins, he would be able to win a ground that connected him with much of the body that had been denied him. After this ground had been won, Friedrich began with self-assurance to write articles on political topics. His tactical contributions to Austrian Social Democratic politics can be viewed as a corollary of this psychologically motivated search for a more direct contact with the ground of his existence. Thus we will first examine Adler's growth as a theoretical physicist and then turn to his more manifest relation to political Marxism.

As a youth Friedrich developed a love for mathematics, a subject that he stated he could not live without.[4] This passion that he used as a tool to force his father to allow him to prepare for a *Matura* and entrance to a university can be viewed as Friedrich's first step to escape from the world of his father's will. His love for mathematics, although an expression of his own will, at the same time removed Friedrich even further from the heart of his life, the life hidden within the domain controlled by his father. In facing his father and the source of his own existence controlled by his father, however, he had to divorce himself, at first, from the painful facts of the family situation. The abstract and eternal language of mathematics proved an ideal means to dwell painlessly and freely in a universe that seemingly belonged totally to himself.[5] As he grew older, this esoteric realm proved too limited, too lacking in the essential warmth that had been denied to him by his existence as an appendage to the will of his father. In the University of Zurich, first in chemistry, then in physics, he sought an exit from the pristine world of natural science to the world of man. The theoretical vehicles used in these first efforts to liberate himself from his intellectual exile were those of historical materialism.[6] The eclectic application of dialectical materialism to physics failed, however, to provide the bridge that he sought. Although Marxism remained the manifest goal of his attempts at contact with the world, its inherited language as expressed by the historical materialists ceased to be used by Friedrich as a theoretical tool in his efforts to free himself from the puerile abstractions of his academic studies. In his attempt to make more meaningful his engagement with physics, by showing how physics was an outgrowth of man's relation to his environment, Friedrich was simultaneously to transform the words of his spiritual fathers into syllables that reflected his own self.

The metamorphosis of physics, of Marxism, and thus of Friedrich Adler, began after he had acquired his doctoral degree in physics and had plunged into the epistemological studies so long denied him by his father. Through these studies, which lasted from 1903 to 1907, Friedrich became a confirmed follower of Ernst Mach.[7] The story of his conversion to the ideas of Mach is also the story of his conversion to a stance that permitted closer contact with the flame of his inner life.

Friedrich Adler's doctoral dissertation, written in 1902, while he was still a disciple of historical materialism, was entitled "Die Abhaengkeit der specifischen Waerme des Chrome von der Temperatur" (Dependence of the specific warmth of chrome on the temperature). The theme stands as a symbolic witness to the nature of his involvement with physics and his quest for warmth, which in its wake would bring a change in his physical constitution. Physics was still dominated by the conception of unchanging physical bodies. The physicists of his day adhered to the atomic theory of constant molecules; although some had postulated the existence of electrons, these more basic entities were held to be as indivisible and constant in their weight and characteristics as the molecules had been.[8] Friedrich's research into the dependency of the specific warmth of chrome upon temperature opened the question of the constancy and indivisibility of the molecular or electronic makeup of metals. The raising of this question, which touched on his own physical condition, led to the bridge that he had sought between physics and Marxism. Friedrich wrote his dissertation as a convinced mechanical materialist, that is, as one who accepted the notion of constancy and indivisibility in physical bodies; his study was only to determine the range of variation within the metal chrome. Although chrome was shown to change in its physical characteristics to some degree, it was still held to be a constant mass.

Ernst Mach had challenged the notion of constancy and indivisibility in physical masses in 1867. Mach first introduced the notion of relativity within physics, that is, the idea that the definition of a physical body depends upon the context within which it is investigated.[9] Whereas other thinkers in physics and in other areas of German *Kultur* grounded all certain knowledge within a unified system, Mach's proposition of relativity asserted that no systematic knowledge of the universe was possible, because man's context of investigation changed constantly.[10] Adler wrote that in 1903, upon completion of his dissertation, he became attracted to Mach's thought but did not understand the seeming conceptual abyss opened by relativity and therefore set out to attack Mach. The point of attack was to be Mach's definition of mass, which Adler felt to be the keystone of his theory. Three years later, upon the publication of this study, Adler was a Machian.[11]

Adler's identification with Ernst Mach provides the key to his conception of Mach's thought, for Mach's disciples went in many directions.[12] Adler investigated Mach as a personality in a collection of essays that he published while in prison after having assassinated Count Stuergh. The book's title, *Ernst Machs Ueberwindung des mechanischen Materialismus* (Ernst Mach's vanquishing of mechanical materialism), gives some indication of the heroic role Mach was to play in his life. Adler wrote: "The advance in science accomplished by Mach was as all great advances, simultaneously a personal experience [*Erlebnis*]. This *experience* took place in the struggle between two powerful realms of thought." These realms were the critical philosophy of Kant and the mechanical materialism of physics. Mach stated that his personality changed in the process of transformation that forged these two separate ideas into a new unity that reflected his own new self. Adler dwelled on this process of transformation: "In the completion of 'this complete transformation' lies the heart of Mach's life work. His work had as its result the complete *vanquishing of his earlier standpoint* in physics, and at the same time the complete vanquishing . . . of his earlier attachment to Kant." Moreover, Mach's transformation of Kant and physics, not to mention himself, opened up horizons of theory that could deal with almost all of life's questions, not just those in his particular area of endeavor: "Mach was compelled not only to investigate physics in its whole historical development, but also the profoundly related areas in the realm of science, above all *physiology* and *psychology*. He wished, as he said, 'to gain a standpoint in physics that would allow him to view other fields without having to change his point of view.'[13]

As indicated by Adler's use of italics in the above quotations, he identified Mach's experiences and goals with his own life. He, too, sought a position from the field of physics that would allow him to deal with all the problems of his world, that would come from the vanquishing of an earlier set of opposites and their higher unity within a renewed personality. The earlier set of opposites in Friedrich Adler's case was reflected in the "two powerful realms of thought" that divided his existence—the Marxist corpus of ideas and the abstract world of theoretical physics. These two realms symbolized the separation of body and mind, physiology and psychology, in his person. Marxist socialism represented the body that was denied to him, and physics served as an intellectual escape from this dispossession. Thus, through the symbiosis of physics and Marxism, a possibility offered by Mach, Friedrich Adler hoped to transform the past modes of thought and himself into a new condition. The question, of course, is to what degree he was eventually transformed through Machian thought. Mach stated that anyone who would follow his thinking must undergo "a psychological process of transformation like I myself had to undergo, which is quite difficult for one who is young."[14] The necessity of this psychological transformation, which could bring a new physical relation to the world, is evident in Mach's teachings.

Mach introduced existentialism to Europe in the field of physics. He asserted that all truth is immediately given in the phenomena of the moment and that any knowledge of this moment is possible only as a description, not as an explanation of cause, because all statements about the phenomena were derivative experiences, that is, new phenomena.[15] Mach's ideas were similar to those developed by Husserl in his later years, but Mach never adhered to the strictness of the phenomenological method.[16] His investigations into phenomena were encumbered by the spirit of his age; he attempted to bring into his descriptions a mathematical language, which he felt would be the one pure means of immediate description, a notion that since the turn of the century has been shown to harbor a narrow view about the "objectivity" of mathematics.[17] Although he was not a true phenomenologist, the aphoristic style of his philosophic writings encouraged others to develop a phenomenology. Perhaps the most important concept that Mach introduced besides the notion of phenomenological investigation was that of the unity of subject and object in the phenomena of consciousness, that is, the understanding of the ego as merely a moment of a total field of experience. This insight was tremendous for his age, and in its existentialist basis antedated most of the cultural developments in science and literature in the Western world today.[18]

Such an insight could hardly have come from an eclectic reordering of past theories. It was part of the psychological breakthrough that Mach insisted all his disciples must personally undergo. Mach writes of this experience, which led to his revolutionary stance to traditional German thought: "Two or three years after reading Kant's 'Prolegomena' I suddenly perceived the lazy role played by the thing-in-itself [*Ding an Sich*]. On a beautiful summer day in the country it seemed to me that the world and my ego were one coherent mass of sensations, only a little more coherent in the ego. Even though reflection set in and changed the impact of my impression, this moment was a definitive one for me in all my later experiences."[19]

Mach struggled to capture in the language of his age the sensation of being one with nature, of having dissolved the abstract barrier between himself as cognizing ego and the world as objective presence. It was difficult to phrase such a view, for the ego in Mach's time was assumed to be as indivisible and substantial as the material world. Even in the statement quoted above, Mach had trouble accounting for the change in perspective experienced by the ego and the role of the ego in this change. He found it necessary to maintain the concept of the ego even in the face of its seeming dissolution into the oneness of the immediate.[20] As his thoughts developed over this experience on a summer day, Mach conceived the ego in twofold manner. On the one hand, the subject could reflect on the material of the phenomenon as it was immediately given, which would create an ego that existed only as a subordinate element of reflection that represented the total field it was part of; on the other hand, the subject could reflect upon his own sensations within the field of the phenomenon, which would create an ego that had a history of its own.[21] For Mach, the ego, a troublesome conceptual inheritance from the past, existed always as a mode of reflection upon the flow of experience but never as an entity that could take objective positions over experience beyond its immediate place in the environment.

Mach used his insight to attack Kant's conception of the thing-in-itself, for he felt that in the immediacy of the phenomenological experience all of the "thing" is known because man's ego is part of this thing-in-itself. Thus with one stroke Mach removed all the epistemological problems that presented an abstract barrier between man and his touch with existence. Mach did borrow from Kant the negative helpmeet that man's culture is built upon the conceptual language of consciousness, that is, the derived statements that seek to interpret the original experience. Thus Mach introduced a third major innovation into his culture: recognizing that man is largely a product of inherited language which immediately interferes with the purity of the phenomenological insight, he reduced the whole of man's past knowledge to the value of time-bound hypothesis.[22] Gone was the nineteenth-century positivistic belief in the progress of Western civilization. All knowledge from the cave man to the present was considered equally profound. The main task of modern science, according to Mach, was to recognize this fact and strive to simplify language and develop a more accurate means of description to deal with the phenomena of the environment. In this Heraclitian view that saw all life to be a flow, a river whose water constantly changes, man's desire for an objective standpoint could be achieved only if he let go of all props and allowed the current to carry him. In this state of flux, language would be employed "economically."[23] Realizing that he could never return to exactly the same contextual moment to prove the observations of earlier moments, man must employ language that did not depend on a continuity of the same experience, as a language of cause and effect would necessitate. The problem arises, of course, as to what language could best fulfill this "economy" and still enable man to act upon his insights. Thus Mach turned to mathematics as a language of description for the physical world, and, as a language of description for psychological understanding of man, he employed an aphoristic vocabulary later used by Ludwig Wittgenstein, an Austrian thinker who carried Mach's path to more radical conclusions.[24]

We can now introduce the question, What did Mach offer Marxism? In what way could Friedrich Adler employ the path of Mach in his understanding of Marxism? The most obvious path of action for a Machian, as for Mach himself, would be a quiet, introspective life withdrawn from environmental commitments such as politics, for as we have seen in the case of Max Adler, an engagement in the full phenomena of life leaves no time for such abstractions as political programs.[25] This is by no means to deny the presence of a psychological and physical revolution for the Machian, for in recognizing the abstract basis of culture, man is thrown back upon his own truth, his own insight, and all action is based upon the existentiality of his every moment. Friedrich Adler used Mach's ideas literally and metaphorically. Literally, Mach's relativization of cultural truth permitted an "existential" Marxism, a radical posture to social development that encouraged revolutionary changes. Metaphorically, Mach became a support for an existential lifestyle, with radical breaks in the continuity of his associations and habits. Mach became a palette of aphorism that Adler employed in the expressionistic picture of his life. In his first contact with Mach, Adler was attracted by the concept of the divisibility of mass, the relativity of body.

As an example of the misguided constancy theory of mass, Adler describes the great efforts expended to keep the International standard measure of length unchanged. His description can be read as an extended metaphor for his father's efforts to keep him in an unchanging role, and the pain he must have experienced in this struggle. Theory, for Friedrich, always functioned literally, and symbolically for his personal drama:

At the International Bureau of Weights and Measures in Paris, in its own [*eigenen*] building, the fundamental measure of length is preserved—the archetype of the meter. The walls of the building are hollow in order to allow liquids of a definite temperature to run through them so that the warmth of the internal space where the meter is found may be kept constant. In this way it is hoped that the meter will remain a constant length. But that is not enough in itself to keep the temperature of the meter constant and protect it from extending itself; it must also be submerged in a bath of water of constant temperature; moreover, this bar of metal . . . must take a certain form to prevent bending, that of a cross. . . . We cannot here go into all the various measures taken to keep this bar of metal from changing. We see, however, that the physicists have engaged in an enormous amount of work and the employees of the "Bureau" also, in order that *one* body be kept unchanged. Thereby is this primordinal measure [*Urmass*] of length, aside from its practical meaning for measuring, the *clearest proof of the changeability of all bodies*.[26]

Mach's relativism was an idea that promised that all situations change, as well as the measure of what is truth for any situation. Just as the primal measure of length could not be kept from extending itself, so Friedrich could not be kept from growing out of the confinement of his father's house.

Mach's recognition of language as the medium that gives physical phenomena the illusion of being constant was equally important to Friedrich. But his use of this insight differed from that of Mach. Adler writes:

Only a relatively small part of the knowledge of a single man comes from *his own* experience; the major portion of it supports itself on the *statements* of others concerning their experience. This fact conditions the *particular belief* that the scientific investigator cannot withdraw from the belief in the statements of other men. This belief is not blind. The statements of other men will be checked over and excluded from one's knowledge if it appears that they contain faults of intellect or character. Thus there will occur many times a knowledge that is first formed on the basis of the statements of others, which later gains support in one's own experience. This does not change the fact, however, that the greater portion of one's knowledge comes from the statements of others.[27]

Adler used Mach's insight that man's knowledge of his own experience is constantly influenced by the inherited language of his culture to justify belief in statements beyond one's experience, that is, until one sees that such statements have a fault in "character" or "intellect." Adler laid the ground in this transition of Mach for his approach to the Austrian Social Democratic party and its program. He subtly raised the statements of others to a plane of necessity that the individual must accept until he is able to measure the statements with his own experience. The Machian emphasis that one must dwell in descriptive contact with his own experience because of the inaccurate abstractions of language within the culture loses its place in Friedrich's interpretation. But in the years before 1911, when Adler's lectures on Mach were first written (for a course at the University of Zurich from 1907 to 1910), he believed in the abstractions of Austrian Social Democracy of necessity, for within these statements beyond his experience lay the active unity he grew toward. As a corollary to his twisting of Mach's view of language, Adler added a comment upon the form that science takes wherein we see the raising of past language to an absolute state that negates the individual initiative opened by Mach: "The statements over one's knowledge can exist orally or be put down in writings. In the last case the same statement can find entrance to the knowledge of men of different ages. Under the concept of written statements . . . especially *printed books*, we understand the entity of *science*."[28]

Mach's major effort was to weaken the holy nature of the written word in his culture and to allow man to view science as merely timebound descriptions, which within German culture in particular had taken the presence of imposing shibboleths. Mach sought to free man from the printed word and return his powers of individual observation. Why, then, did Adler reemphasize the written word? The answer to this question emerges from the nature of the end to which he employed Mach—the vanquishing of his father's leadership and his usurpation of his father's power. To be a leader of Austrian Social Democracy was to have ink in one's veins, for the essential reality of this movement was that of the printed word. In a very un-Machian statement in 1917 before the Emergency Court that tried him for the assassination of Count Stuergh, Friedrich Adler was to give as his most basic motive his belief in the written principles of Marx and the Austrian Social Democratic party, adding, "Since I was in the *Gymnasium* . . . it was clear to me, and deeply and internally gripping, how holy was the written word. And that the greatest sin, the sin that could not be forgiven, was the sin against intellect."[29]

Thus Mach's work became another holy printed word and not primarily a method of life. Mach provided Adler with the belief that his fixed body and the fixed body of Austrian Social Democracy were relative entities, wholes that could assume new form on the basis of new definitions. But it was important that Austrian Social Democracy and its Marxist program not be too relativized, for then the major area of his struggle would lose its definition. Adler did not really desire the relativized ego preached by Mach; he merely wanted his own ego for the first time and used Mach as a tool for the dissolution of his ego-as-appendage-to-his-father so that his own ego might be established. An examination of Adler's interpretation of Mach's writings on the unity of subject and object, that is, the ego's existence as part of a whole field of experience, shows Adler's personal touch to the existentialist direction of Mach. Mach stated that the subject could reflect either on the environmental elements of phenomena or on the sensations of his ego as part of the phenomena. The ego in this twofold aspect was regarded, as outlined above, as a dependent moment of the total field of experience. Adler wrote in a further illustration of this essential point:

The entire world of experience in its development is for us a *tremendously complicated context of a huge number* of elements. A comprehension of the essence and the constitution of this complicated context [of subject and object] would be made easier if we employed for our first orientation a schematic picture. Such a picture would be a huge knot of threads, which was made up of smaller knots. . . . In this network we can differentiate certain parts that can be released [*ausgeloest*] from the total network, for example a cluster of threads [*Knotenbueschel*] that consists of one smaller knot, or a bunch of threads [*Knotenbuendel*] that consists of many knots. Every such release that separated these elements from the whole network without cutting the threads would create a series of knot branches [*Knotengespalten*]. . . . To this picture we tie on [*knuepfen*] the notion of a length of string between two (of the released) knots. This length of string would symbolize *an element* (i.e., the unity of subject and object); the knots themselves are *nothing other than the crossing place* [*Kreuzigungstelle*] of the lengths of string. . . . Every one of these released areas can be designated as a "thing." Certain of the "things" will be called "subjects," others will be designated as "objects." Subject and object are the released entities from the whole (original) network.[30]

The "schematic picture" of Adler's simplification of Mach is an illustration of a man who sought to unravel the mystery of his life. No more fitting metaphor could be used than this Gordian knot wherein subject and object were in the last instance the single thread—Austrian Social Democracy. In releasing the knots to bare the thread, Friedrich Adler was careful not to cut away any of the ties to Marxist socialism in Austria. Thus Mach became a delicate instrument to separate out those theories and political tactics that did not accommodate themselves to Adler's necessities and especially a tool to discover his own path through the tangled skein of his father's machinations against him. With World War I, Friedrich would find in Mach a basis for an ethic that would transform him for a moment into a true existential hero, but until that time he would dwell as a censor in the written words around him, gathering the critical strength needed to assert his will in politics.

An indication of exactly in what manner Friedrich Adler would manifest his will in politics and, at the same time, a glimpse of the major obstacle in his path to a complete freedom of movement is given in a letter he sent to Karl Kautsky in 1903: "We are Social Democrats insofar as we have a harmonious view over the development of *society*. The various methodologies which we bring from *other* fields to the study of society have nothing to do with the criteria of who should be considered a *party comrade*. A party comrade is he who recognizes the program."[31]

Adler allowed that an individual might bring new interpretations to the older Marxist dogma concerning the various spheres of culture in the natural and social sciences, but the program of tactical action arrived at every year at the Gesamtpartei meeting was too definitive. Adler stressed that a party program was imperative law and comparable to the Catholic Eucharist.[32] No matter what path one chose to the fount of all belief, the party program, one must not give the impression to others, especially the class enemy, that the dogma of Social Democracy was anything but unimpeachable—the holy word. All polemics were to occur within the privacy of the party, especially in party organs such as *Der Kampf*, whose name fit much more closely the internal struggles of the men within themselves and with each other than the class warfare that is implied. Thus even Friedrich Adler's moment of truth in 1917 was a private act, and all his attacks on the party during the years of World War I were within the acceptance of the party program. Adler never sought to rebel against the program, only to change it through the normal party channels. For whereas the Eucharist was the body and blood of Christ, the party program was the body and blood of Friedrich Adler.

Mach's understanding of relativity was tailored to this distinction between the absolute quality of the party program as opposed to the relative validity of the individual's research into the social world. In the years between 1907 and 1914 Adler published a number of articles in *Der Kampf* and *Die Neue Zeit* developing his relation between Mach and Marxism.[33] Four concepts were borrowed from Mach that formed the backbone of his symbiosis: accommodation (*Anpassung*), release (*Ausloesung*), function (*Funktion*), and unequivocality (*Eindeutigkeit*).[34] Adler understood by the principle of accommodation that man as a dependent element in a total field of experience must adapt his understanding to his particular context.[35] Adler showed the similarity of Mach and Marx in this regard: Marx's understanding of man as a creation of an economic set of conditions that changed constantly was compared to Mach's view of the ego as an element of the external flux of experience. The analogy was striking, but some critics wondered why Mach was necessary because his view was anticipated by Marx.[36] Adler pointed out, however, that for Marx every sphere of human capacity was determined by the economic context, whereas Mach allowed that different contexts create different qualities of human capacity and that man must learn to accommodate his understanding and language of description to the proper context. Thus the orthodox Marxist language tended to obscure many facts of being human because an economic language of description was proper only to a certain context, whereas many different languages of description were necessary for an objective view of life that would allow a better accommodation to the myriad contexts of existence. Again Adler's understanding of life appears in the analogy of the knotted threads, each knot within the major one needing a separate language of description. The second concept, that of release, designated the separating of the various contexts involved in human experience and redividing the sciences accordingly. For the Marxist, such a redivision of the spheres of societal study would allow a more accurate political and social knowledge. Moreover, the political program of Social Democracy would be allowed a greater range of application; it could comment upon and plan for all areas of human experience. Herein lay the third concept, that of function: Marxist socialism would be made up of individuals who devoted themselves to the various functions that made up experience. Gradually, as the Marxist scientists sorted out the various threads from the confusing bourgeois knot that passed for knowledge, the separate functions of being human could be studies in their particular integrity. Only then could true unequivocality, the fourth concept, be arrived at in Marxist dogma. A unified Marxist program could one day be drafted in which all areas of knowledge had been explored in their relation to man's changing experience and all could be seen in terms of their interrelatedness, for all of the separate functions studies were dependent upon their relation to man's ego and language. One day a language might be developed, presumably a mathematical language, that showed the functions of man's life in their interrelatedness; for the time being, however, the best language to use in a science of man and his environment would be one that satisfied the demands of the age. Adler suggested that the party, since it was dealing with human lives in transition, should accommodate the language of Marxist theory to the latest advances in scientific research concerning man, especially the biological sciences.[37]

It never seemed to occur to Adler that a reinvestigation of knowledge based, presumably, upon the introspective rigor of phenomenological investigation might negate the metaphorical assumptions of class structure and class warfare. Somehow Adler was able to accommodate himself to the contradictory stance of holding the socialist belief above the relativity of all other areas of human experience. A necessary accommodation was that Adler's freedom from the bonds of patriarchal possession could come only from his engagement within the holy circle of this unquestioned area; and from the direct contact thus permitted with his father, he then might release the manifold functions of his life from their undifferentiated torpor within the metaphors of his father's family house, the Austrian Social Democratic party. A release of these long-imprisoned functions would allow an unequivocal sense of self for the first time in Friedrich's life; such a release would bring with it a flow of energy that must transform completely the house where Friedrich made his home. Friedrich seemed to anticipate this possibility as a consequence of his course of development when he wrote in "Wozu brauchen wir Theorien?": "We go in the morning to that house where our place of work is found because in terms of our past experience we find ground to make the theoretical assumption that there we can exercise our accustomed activity. Perhaps, however, our theory is false, a condition has arisen that never arose before, for example, the house burned down. But in spite of this risk we will take the same way, that is, rely on theory. For because of this unknown possibility, not to go to our place of work would be much more impractical than to test it with our theory."[38]

Apprehending at the roots of this consciousness the future flame that promised freedom, Friedrich Adler prepared himself with a language with which he might secure it. It was only natural that in the following years he would find a biological language attractive for the revolutionary image of the Austrian Social Democratic man. Yet when the walls of his house did start to burn, it was a failure of language that prevented him from securing a home that allowed greater living space. In the moment of confrontation with the dissolution of his family house, Friedrich forgot the theoretical text that could have won him freedom and instead borrowed the dictionary of his fathers to defend his integrity.

II

1914-1918

This almost pathological striving after truth and after a way out from the present state of distress, and the attempt to grasp the one path through the myriad influences and interests that surround one, create in their wake unreconcilable opposites that are themselves projected upon the working class.

—*Karl Renner*, "Problems of Marxism," *Der Kampf*

10

Karl Renner as German Chauvinist

World War I disrupted Austrian culture, as war disrupts any culture. The complexity and range of everyday activities is truncated, and the inherent supports that social norms give to individual growth are lost in the poverty of the emergency environment. In Austria in this dearth, individuals whose prewar actions were guided by principles shaped by their own deliberation tended to remain balanced and consistent in their personalities. One's essential self came to the surface in everyday encounters of coping with social chaos. There were ersatz norms, just as there were ersatz products. There was chauvinistic passion in the early war years and hopeless cynicism in the later years. Individuals who normally found their identity in norms outside of themselves fell prey to several waves of behavior and emotion between 1914 and 1918.

The radical change in norms during wartime can heighten a person's sense of individuality, for the fabric of everyday life that has been taken for granted is threatened with dissolution. One is forced to question his peacetime values and principles and to arrive at new organizations of thought and action. The Austro-Marxists were thinking persons, yet they were also individuals with large areas of unconscious character. The change in the social reality and the tempo of everyday life thrust them into contact with dimensions of their person that were repressed in the normal environment but manifested themselves in a time of uncertainty. It was a time of self-confrontation for the Austro-Marxists. The war, indirectly, was a radical therapy. Each man had the opportunity to express his repressed desires and even to exercise his competencies toward either achieving these desires or understanding the implications of the fears and joys that swept over him in the face of long-repressed dimensions of himself. But therapy is not normal life. The patient may make strides within the analyst's office, but he must transfer his gains to the world outside. Self-realizing insights and activities occurred among the Austro-Marxists during the war, as well as activities that came frustratingly near to growth but were distorted or diverted by a failure of will or understanding. After World War I, with the gradual reestablishment of the normal social reality, the Austro-Marxists lost some of the gains they had made. Nevertheless, each man confronted himself during World War I and came to moments of truth that brought maturation.

Even though on the surface Karl Renner seemed much more satisfied with the pre-1914 state of affairs in Austria than his Austro-Marxist compatriots, some of his prewar articles bear seeds of a will toward violence. His pride in the German essence and suspicion of the enemy that lurked on the borderlines of the German soul were manifested in an article written in January 1909 entitled "Sympathien und Antipathien." Renner justified the annexation of Bosnia along with German expansion into Africa in the light of the imperialistic conquests of England and France. He states that in contradistinction to the anti-imperialistic sentiment in Austrian Social Democracy, the western European nations were much more greedy than the Germans, and moreover, the Germans brought education (*Bildung*) to the lands they influenced. In the same article Renner quoted Ferdinand Lassalle's comment made in 1859 at the time of the Austrian intervention in Italy to the effect that Austria was the greatest hindrance to the victory of democracy in Europe and added, "Whereas that might have been true before 1866 or 1905, for today and for the whole future of Austria it is false, exactly the opposite is true."[1]

But in peacetime such sentiments raised the eyebrows of the socialists of principle, and in later prewar articles Renner wrestled with his German nationalism, trying to find room for it within the pattern of life to which he was compelled to conform. A good example of the sparring with himself in which he was engaged before 1914 is provided by an article written for *Der Kampf* in January 1912:

The socialist places internationalism against nationalism because he is against militarism and war, therefore every expression of chauvinism is looked upon as a barbaric abomination, a sin against man; for the socialist the so-called patriotic virtues are seen merely as particularism. And this particularism is just as reactionary in the time of a world economy and a world culture as that of Bavarian or Hessian or Oldenburgian was designated a hundred years ago.

Yet now the shallowness of the thoughtless represents itself, and cries: What do you want [with this internationalism], a cultureless conglomeration of peoples, a disgusting mixture of white, yellow, and black, the inevitable decline of every individual quality, the road of socialist "equalization" and the other banalities connected with such notions![2]

The "shallowness of the thoughtless" represented an argument that Renner appropriated after August 1914; with the "Day of the German Nation" he no longer had to sublimate his personal shadow with such rhetoric.[3] He was at first eclipsed by his shadow but then extended his consciousness to the areas inhabited by dark forces he formerly could not admit to himself. These areas included personal and public dimensions of himself, for Renner found his identity within the affairs of the state as well as in individual capabilities. Renner desired to assume a leadership role in the Austrian Social Democratic party and in public life. He was forty-four years of age when the war began. The party "fathers" were in their sixties and prepared to pass the baton of leadership to their *Nachwuchs*.

Renner identified strongly with his uncle, Leopold Habiger, who possessed an enviable domain. He wished to overcome the dependency he inherited from his father and reverse the fortunes of his youth by taking and wielding authority. In such an assumption of power, he would cease to be a servant of his own fantasies of geography and would become the owner of territory. His extroverted personality and German Catholic background gave him the credentials of an Austrian German political leader for the majority of his nation. The war allowed him to assert himself, for he no longer had to be ashamed of his German chauvinism; his preference for an ordered state, which restricted diversity of opinion, was the norm during World War I. The patriarchal control of social policy toward which he aspired was the order of the day. Moreover, the inextricable constellation of his ego with the public world and the mechanisms of the state flourished in a society in which he need not apologize for national expansion.

Thus in his first major article of World War I, in which he defended the war and rationalized Social Democratic support of it, he used the psuedonym Josef Hammer.[4] Hammer means "powerful man." Charles Martel, who began the Carolingian dynasty, in which the personality principle was developed, was called Karl der Hammer.[5] Hammer was also the brand name of the bread factory (Hammerbrot) developed by Austrian Social Democracy, with the entrepreneurial guidance of Karl Renner, for the benefit of the party members' financial situation.[6] In "Was ist Imperialismus?" he introduced the notion that imperialism was a blessing to the worker. Using Rudolf Hilferding's *Das Finanzkapital*[7] as a basis, he pointed out that the industrial state no longer existed, that the economy could now function only through international cartels, supereconomic states embracing several lands, and that the standard of living and wages of workers were dependent upon the growth of such larger capitalistic organisms. Just as the capitalist gains a new image and body through this process of international economy, so the state must assume a new body. A war of imperialism necessarily dissolves the existing order and means of relating to one's environment. In the wake of such a war, society advances to a higher stage of economy.[8] What Hilferding had designated as an inevitable direction of economic development, which would create through its giant monopolies a class-conscious proletariat large enough to bring about the social revolution, was used by Renner to compel the worker passively to obey the course of events.[9]

A month later Renner turned to the question of international socialism in an article published under his own name. The bogey of international brotherhood must be dealt with if he was to find peace of mind as an Austrian Social Democrat supporting the German-Austrian war aims. Renner called the international organization of socialism that existed before the war a naive cosmpolitanism that had no basis in the reality of the nations it represented.[10] The only basis for an international organization of socialism, he said, was the actual state of economic life. The Second International previously had no real basis because economy was basically limited to national boundaries, but with the transformation to a truly international economy, it was justified but would have to assume a new form. This form could come after the imperialist war, when the new body of Europe was established.[11]

Meanwhile, each nation should concern itself with its own cultural values and development. Renner felt that the German culture must prevail within the European community because of the superiority of its ideas and education. In an article entitled "Was Siegt im Kriege?" (What is victorious in the war?),[12] Renner juxtaposed the "illiterate" culture of the Russian masses and the other nations east of Austria with the superior German culture of "Middle-Europe" (*Mitteleuropa*):[13]

German *Volksschule* build the intellectual capacity of the masses for the living of their lives. Other nations have *Volksschule*, though none that nourish the youth as wholly as ours. Not only the mechanical skills of life, but . . . the thorough *Bildung* of conceptual thought is also decisive, as strange as it may seem, in the hour of battle. When the German officer gives the order to his men to occupy a certain terrain, his men can fulfill this order in a third or a tenth of the time required by the Russian soldier because the German has learned to represent the state-of-affairs in a clear general picture and translate this picture immediately into action. When the intellectual capacity of the common soldier has reached such a height that he knows not only the meaning and goal of every movement of the war, but also the meaning and goal of the entire world conflict, a consciousness is created that brings with it discipline that continues from the first to the last day of the war, without any need of special compulsion by the authorities.[14]

Turning to the culture to the west of Germany, especially that of France, Renner developed further his understanding of German *Kultur* as the decisive factor that must lead to a German victory:

It is strange but many socialists and Marxists allow themselves to be deceived by the cultural lies of western European bourgeois culture. They should realize that often in history the small governing clique of a so-called barbaric land (Germany) is far more civilized than the governing class of an old culture (France). The so-called Latin culture is a noble culture and thereby distinguished in some respects, but it is a bourgeois culture. In this respect the Germans stand without a doubt higher than the Latin: The farmers and proletariat masses of *Mitteleuropa* are far more cultivated than any Latin land. The division between the two cultures is manifest in the distinctions of sensation and temperament, reason and feeling: In sensation and temperament the Latins lead, but in reason and feeling the Middle-European is out in front. The method of the Latin is the aesthetic, the aesthetic of the Middle-European is, however, methodology in all things. One may argue over which is best, but in our time without a doubt methodology determines the winner.[15]

Since the late spring of 1915 Renner had employed the term *Mitteleuropa* synonymously with the German culture. Yet in its inclusion of the Habsburg lands it also embraced non-German nations. And as Renner developed the concept of *Mitteleuropa* from the fall of 1915 to the fall of 1916, it became an even larger organism that was to extend from the Bosphorus to the North Sea.[16] The concept of *Mitteleuropa* was borrowed from the German National-Socialist Friedrich Naumann, whom Renner quoted in an article written in October 1915:

He who wishes to remain small and alone will nevertheless remain dependent upon the changes of conditions among the major powers. This is inevitable within a generation of . . . centralized technology and large armies. He who is not allied is isolated; he who is isolated is endangered. In this period of union between states into large mass states, Prussia is too small and Germany is too small and Austria is too small and Hungary is too small. Such isolated states can never win a world war. . . . Today a Middle-European state is not a contingency, it is a necessity.[17]

Renner added to Naumann's statement that of course such a state could not result from conquest; there must be a positive aim, which he identified as socialism.[18] With such a positive justification for expansion, Renner's dream of the organic state of *Mitteleuropa* knew no boundaries: "Everything seems capable of being united, the boundaries of possible communities of interest are infinitely wide. When the Germans can be united in life and death with the Turks and the Arabs of the Near East, should a union between the Germans and Poles . . . the Germans and the Czechs . . . the Germans and the Magyars and Romanians for the future be unimaginable . . . but one understands these things daily in the trenches."[19]

In the same article Renner praised the German nation for sending teachers to Turkey and Arabia to spread the German *Kultur* even during the war, making obvious the nature of the future organic culture of *Mitteleuropa*.[20] Just as the organic unity of this superstate would know no bounds, Renner's eloquence and excess knew no limit. Leaving all Marxist theory behind, Renner wrote of "nation" and *Mitteleuropa*: "Over the lands of *Mitteleuropa* for the last thousand years . . . infinite storms have blown, yet the national communities have only become more solid, and have changed increasingly less in the last few hundreds of years showing that the attempts of denationalize [*Entnationalizierung*] these communities are futile. . . . The basic function of national life fulfills itself *beyond* the state, for the final causal forces of national becoming [*Werden*] and life lie outside of the state, outside of political willfulness [*Willkuer*]: The nation is before the state and after it.[21]

Renner's affirmation of nationality as preexistent to superstructure is an obvious corollary of his personal road to engagement in the state and politics. His German hearth was a ground upon which his parents' suffering and dispossession prompted his incorporation of the threatening presence of the state into his identity. The Habiger *Scholle* (family soil) was the model of the homogeneous German community that the state should echo. German hegemony should be present in every relationship with other national communities.

During this period of the war Renner seems to have found a perfect symbiosis for his personality in the service of the German-Austrian state. Yet he was continually frustrated that his Social Democratic background caused those in power to ignore his intellectual assistance.[22] Renner bemoaned publicly his lack of recognition by the Habsburg government; he complained that in other lands men who had devoted their lives to the details of particular government problems and whose names were identified with those problems were called to government service in times of crisis involving those problems.[23]

Failing to find a position in the Habsburg regime that complemented his new patriotic mien, Renner became increasingly sensitive to criticism of him within the Austrian Social Democratic party. He had to remain in his first political house, and so he attempted to care more for the opinions of those with whom he must dwell. By 1916, however, Renner's Austrian Social Democratic home in Vienna was a nest of hornets. Any Social Democrats who still attempted to maintain contact with the prewar slogans of Marxism considered Renner as anathema. Friedrich Adler and Max Adler wrote barbed diatribes against Renner as the archetype of chauvinistic and class perfidy.[24] Renner was disturbed by the relentless criticism of those Social Democrats. He collected his articles into a book, hoping that his arguments supporting his passionate conviction would open the eyes of his critics; he titled the work *Oesterreichs Erneuerung* (Austria's renewal). In the foreword to this work he appealed to his comrades as Austrians, not simply as Social Democrats: "The work of renewing Austria can only be accomplished by the cooperation of all nations and all classes . . . the reconstruction of the state is in the interest of all classes and all nations. In this sense I do not speak merely as a man of party or a party comrade.[25]

Although his arguments had little currency with his party associates, his zeal for Austria finally got the attention of the heads of the Austrian state. Renner was given the opportunity he had desired for his entire life to be a political authority in the state hierarchy. After the assassination of the minister-president, Count Stürgkh (by Friedrich Adler), in October 1916, he was invited by the new minister-president, Count Koerber, to head the Ministry of Food.[26] The assignment was probably prompted by Renner's success in keeping the Hammerbrotwerke, the Austrian Social Democratic bread factory, alive and successful and his management of the Austrian cooperative association.[27] Renner devoted himself to this office until June 1917, when the Austrian Social Democratic party forced him to resign, deeming it unfit for a party member to participate in the war government.[28] By June 1917 the trial of Friedrich Adler, the February revolution in Russia, and the prolongation of a losing war had created a wave of sentiment that left chauvinists like Renner stranded upon a deserted beachhead. Whereas men such as Friedrich Austerlitz changed their tune with the times, Renner, who had reached almost full flower with his dual position within Habsburg service and the Austrian Social Democratic party, remained steadfast to a principle that truly expressed himself—a state socialism that preserved the German cultural hegemony.

The power of Renner's personality and persuasion won him gradual control of Austrian Social Democracy and its program. Although he was the scapegoat for the Austrian Social Democratic conscience from the spring of 1917 to October 1917, after the Parteitag of that month he again became the mouthpiece for the majority sentiment. Renner was able to make the German cultural desires in Austria palatable in the face of the new state of Social Democracy in Europe, for he was, above all, a master juggler of concept. His defense at the Parteitag in 1917 gives an indication of the spirit in which he spoke and wrote for the duration of World War I:

They say that I am a state fanatic. I am not. . . . But I say: Let us not speak in terms of abstraction, but of facts. The worker demands that the state shall stipulate the eight-hour day, protect the producer in the workshop in every regard, insure him against illness, accident and old age . . . protect the mothers, take care of the babies, ensure the health of children, do all that is possible for education and science, further agriculture, do away with anarchy in production, end the war. "The state shall!"—that is the solitary, every-recurring, *proletarian* imperative . . . In order to do all this it must be rich and strong. *How could it succeed otherwise?*[29]

To a war-weary Social Democratic rank and file Renner's argument made eminent sense. Yes, the state was necessary to bring back order, for their passivity that had encouraged the war was a quality that needed a state to act for them. Thus although the majority of the Austro-German socialists at the Parteitag of 1917 condemned the "ministerialism" evidenced by Renner and urged a peace without annexations as speedily as possible, most joined with Renner in desiring the maintenance of a strongly centralized state that preserved the prewar unity of nations.[30] Renner's position was aided by the Bolshevik revolution in Russia (which occurred shortly after the Parteitag of 1917). The violent, unorganized nature of the November revolution in Russia, coupled with the manifest threat to the eastern lands of the Austrian Empire by the Bolshevik demand for self-determination of all nations, destroyed the influence of Russian Social Democracy in the minds of most Austrian Social Democrats.[31] Moreover, the spontaneous uprisings in Austria during January 1918, encouraged by Bolshevik-oriented communists, forced the party intellectuals to realize that a social revolution could run its course without the planned development of their theory. Nothing good could come from such a state of affairs. Even the element within Austrian Social Democracy that opposed Renner's desire to maintain the unity of the Austrian state joined him in condemning the Russian way to socialism.[32]

As the separatist tendencies among Austria's nationalities became stronger during the spring and summer of 1918 and the Russian example of encouraging every nation to make its own choice of future affiliation influenced more and more Social Democrats in Austria, Renner's hatred of Russia increased, and he reached deep into his bag of concepts to maintain his authoritative role in the party. Not only did Renner have to contend with the Left and its advocacy of the self-determination of all nation-states but with those on the political right of Social Democracy who held that all non-German lands should be allowed to go their own way and that German Austria should make an *Anschluss* with Germany.[33] Renner contributed an article to *Der Kampf* in June 1918 in which he returned to the economic agruments of the organic superstate in trying to prove that the Donaureich was indivisible. Renner mocked the theoreticians who wished to divide up the multinational empire according to abstract theory, stating, "Space in itself, as a geometric concept, may be divided up as much as one likes, but one cannot do this to an economic space." Then, however, he spoke of the economic unity of the Donaureich in language that recalls the topographical-abstract images of his autobiography—the language of a man seeking to preserve his identity:

The middle Donau basin is in its western outlet (area of Vienna and Pressburg) the geographical knot of myriad lines of commerce which are dictated by economic necessity. This basin is unqualified inland . . . it lies in the center of Europe. The commercial highways, which extend in all directions of the compass and connect to the seas, are for all those who live in and adjoining this area economic necessities of life. . . . Thus the main highway of Vienna-Trieste is such a commercial artery, built by the Empress Maria Theresa, also the network of highways between Vienna-Prague-Dresden, and Vienna-Olmuetz-Weisskirchen-Ostrau built in the Josephinian and Francisian time. The so-called Emperor roads were also military creations, but not merely for those ends. The increasing internal commerce, and with the victory of world economy the world commerce brings about, necessitates, the creation of throughways. These were built in the beginning by capitalist entrepreneurs, then later were taken over by the state. Today no one can dispute that the system of nationalization [*Verstaatlichungssystem*] has succeeded. Great throughways are to be created by the state and to be administered by the state, as routes from Vienna-Adriatic, Vienna-North and Baltic Sea. . . . Therefore, no future order of the world, no modern economy is conceivable without a Donau basin that is connected with the two seas . . . and thus the problem: How is it possible to maintain a unified route of travel and a unified administration to control travel despite the four nations (of the Donau basin) and the colorful mixture (of peoples) within the areas crossed by these arteries?[34]

If Renner were writing strictly about Austria's railroads or commercial highways, one might hold that he was attempting to give a partial history and prognosis of those entities; but the title of the article in which this topographical excursion appeared translates as "What Must an International Program Accomplish?" and it was presumably written as an aid to creating a future policy for Austrian Social Democracy's economic and social relations with the various nations of the Austrian state and other nation-states.

The emperor of the Austrian state ended Renner's dream of a Donaureich temporarily on October 16, 1918, when he published a manifesto that gave all Austrian nations the initiative to form their own legislatures. Although the emperor intended that the nations remain within a Habsburg multinational structure, the nations used this manifesto as a mandate to separate from the former union. On October 21, 1918, in the face of a dismembered empire, Renner and other German-Austrian delegates to the former Austrian Parliament met in the Lower Austrian *Landtag* to determine what would become of the territories of German-speaking peoples that remained. They called themselves a Provisional Assembly empowered with the right to draw up a new constitution that would plan for the future government of German-Austria (Deutsch-Oesterreich). Karl Renner was called upon to draft a constitution for the new state.[35]

Renner's dream of being the architect of his own state had been realized after all. Taking no chances that it would be frustrated again, he sought to please every possible element within German Austria. On October 30, when Renner addressed the Provisional Assembly with his proposed constitution, he was careful to point out that it did not contain the words "democracy," "republic," and "monarchy,"[36] Renner wished the support of the monarchists and socialists, for he did not intend a revolutionary regime, merely one that was stamped with his own character. The essential provisions of the first constitution of German Austria were that the Provisional Assembly was the only legislative body; the assembly elected from its members an executive body that possessed all rights previously exercised by the emperor; the three presidents of the State Council, the director of the chancery of the council, and the notary of the council were to constitute the executive directorate of the State Council; and the State Council appointed the ministers of state. Although some political commentators have called Renner's proposal "extremely democratic,"[37] one must realize that its immediate character was authoritarian; it took all action out of the hands of the people, robbing the proletariat in particular of the opportunity to establish a socialized state. While other Social Democratic lands established socialist, communist, or republican regimes in the wake of the lost war, Austria, under the guidance of men such as Renner, merely prolonged the centralized, essentially nondemocratic hierarchy of the past regime.[38] Renner had no intention of discarding the emperor unless the majority of the coalition so willed.[39] When Kaiser Wilhelm of Germany stepped down from his throne on November 9, 1918, so that a German republic could be proclaimed, Renner warned the Austrian Provisional Assembly that its existence was threatened.[40] He predicted that the Austrian proletariat would demand a republic, too, thus unleashing "a catastrophe" for the balanced coalition government of bourgeois, farmer, and worker that was Austria's only hope to avert "civil war."[41] Despite Renner's attempts to normalize conditions, the majority of the population demanded a republic, and on November 12, 1918, Austria became a republic. The Provisional Assembly, with Renner as chancellor of the State Council, completed the last stage of the Austrian "revolution" by executive decree and only barely averted a real social revolution.[42]

Karl Renner had helped to bring the ship of state into a safe harbor. He was the patriarch of the Austrian *Scholle*. The astounding sequence of events that elevated him to a position equivalent to that of emperor must have been difficult for even his imagination to grasp. The assumption of real power seemed to bring Renner to a more balanced, tolerant view of political realities. Although more conservative than those of the Social Democrats in that social change was not sought, his plans for the provisional government included representation by all parties of the political spectrum. When in power, Renner exercised a traditional Austrian view that all political voices had a legitimate role in the decisions of the state. This position is also evident in his ideas for the provisional government of Austria in 1945.[43] With his great respect for the law of his forefathers and the established norms of the society, perhaps Karl Renner was the best man to be the conservative buffer for any transition from the old to the new in a time of social chaos.

11

Otto Bauer: Success through Equivocation

The day after the German nation declared war upon Russia, Otto Bauer was called into service in the Austrian infantry regiment No. 75 in which he had served as a reserve lieutenant during peacetime.[1] His regiment was sent to the Russian front, so Bauer had at last the opportunity to confront his archenemy in physical conflict (for Bauer's antipathy to the Russians, see Chapter 5). Bauer's correspondence to intimates in the first few months of his war duty tells a great deal about his reaction to the war he had so long predicted and contrasts with his behavior after his return to Vienna in the fall of 1917, when he assumed leadership of the antiwar sentiment.

Bauer, like Renner, joined the Austrian cause enthusiastically and immediately sought to find a Marxist excuse for the spontaneity of his passions. In a letter to his wife in August 1914, Bauer developed a rationalization for his participation in the imperialist cause that followed the same path Renner took:

In the past three weeks I have learned quite a lot . . . I have come to know war in almost all its forms: advance and retreat, attack and defense, victory and defeat. The most worthwhile thing in the world to me . . . is the extension of my psychological insight, an improvement for which I have this campaign to thank. The war is the *most powerful of all mass actions*, and someone like myself would otherwise have no such chance to live so intimately with workers, artisans, and farmers, to learn to know them in the field where an officer eats, sleeps, and dies with his men. . . . It is much easier to bear the adverse circumstances when one realizes that millions of men are now in the same situation as myself and that all this mass suffering is *an instrument of historical progress*.[2]

This letter was reproduced in the *Arbeiter-Zeitung* and served Friedrich Austerlitz as an example of the way a Social Democrat should react to the war. The catharsis offered by the immediacy of life in the army and physical contact with the proletariat he had never known before was impressed into the service of his Marxism and his childhood identity. His decisions were listened to and obeyed. As a visible agent guiding the lives of others, he was able to see the consequences of his decisions. His dramatic propensity to manipulate meanings was transformed in the "theater" of war into actual strategy. Moreover, the dialectic of history became evidentially present. In a letter to Karl Kautsky in October 1914, Bauer, after reporting his military "successes," stated that he still had time in the day to reflect upon the big picture of the war.[3] He identified the war's progress with Kautsky's blueprint of social revolution as outlined in *Der Weg zur Macht* (The Way to Power), which predicted an expansion of capitalism that would necessitate conflict between nations and would generate an international socialism.[4] In Bauer's mind this seemed to create a Marxist justification for his support of the German imperialist cause, for in his defense of the homeland he was protecting an economy that would lead to socialism.

No matter what excuse Bauer found for his active involvement in hostilities with the Russians, however, his engagement brought him the sense "of being a whole man." It opened new vistas as a consequence of physical contact with his environment. Moreover, Bauer had assumed responsibilities that produced tangible effects; his successes as an officer in more than seven campaigns before his capture by the Russians earned him a promotion from reserve lieutenant to *Oberlieutenant* and eventually command of "four other officers and three times as many men as a captain commands during peacetime."[5] On November 13, 1914, when ordered to hold a position against the attacking Russians, all but four of Bauer's men deserted; although Bauer was forced to surrender, his battalion commander, Major Daubek, reported that Bauer had encountered the enemy with such "exceptional energy" that he was awarded the Gold Cross for his efforts.[6]

Bauer was sent to Siberia, first to Berezowka, east of the lake of Baikal, and then to Troizkosawsk on the border of Mongolia. Bauer's confinement was extremely difficult for him, particularly the mental suffering caused by his sudden lack of involvement with others. His letters to former Social Democratic associates clearly articulated the psychological stress of a man on the run suddenly left alone with himself: "I am further removed from the world of my wishes than ever before." And "I am healthy but I can hardly bear with my circumstances in other respects

. . . one must be imprisoned to understand what impatience and yearning are."[7]

To escape from his aloneness Bauer turned to mathematics, a pursuit he at first reported to those at home as "a useful and pleasant occupation"; but after a time this interest palled, and he began his Marxist history of philosophy, which also failed to fill the empty hours sufficiently: "It is a bitter pill to rely solely on my theoretical work so that I may bear with this complete isolation from the world."[8]

After the February revolution in Russia in 1917, Victor Adler obtained Bauer's release from Siberia through the intercession of the Scandinavian Committee of the Socialist International, which at that time was in close contact with the Russian soldiers, workers, and Farmers' Assembly preparing for the first international conference of socialists since the war began. Bauer, who was to be exchanged for a Russian captured by the Austrians, went to Saint Petersburg in July 1917 to await completion of the transaction. At the beginning of September 1917 he traveled with other exchanged prisoners to Galicia, where he was temporarily stationed awaiting further orders.[9] Although he spent only two months in Russia outside of Siberia and possessed a reading knowledge of Russian less than one year old, Bauer was considered an expert in Russian affairs.[10] He assumed a position in the Austrian Foreign Office after October 1917 as an adviser on Russian policy.[11] Bauer returned from Russia a convinced Menshevik-Internationalist, which he remained until after the Bolshevik revolution, when he temporarily became a Bolshevik.[12] Bauer's theoretical vacillations after his return from Russia led Karl Renner to compare his political personality to the moon in that his political opinions reflected whatever light happened to strike him at the time.[13] Bauer's changing opinions of Russia during the last year of the war did have some method to their turnings. He followed whatever wind he throught would carry him to the leadership of the Austrian Social Democratic party. The last illness of Victor Adler created a power vacuum that was first filled by Karl Renner; Bauer sought to challenge Renner's position.

During the war years before Bauer's release from Russia, Renner had constantly used him as an authority on social imperialism. Renner quoted passages from Bauer's *Die Nationalitaetenfrage und die Sozialdemokratie* to illustrate the necessity of an organic union of Danube states as well as the necessity of an imperialistic expansion through colonialism.[14] Renner's major apologia during the war, *Marxismus, Krieg, und Internationale*, had been dedicated to Bauer. Bauer was embarrassed by this attention, especially as Renner was at the zenith of his disrepute in September 1917, when Bauer arrived in Vienna from Galicia.[15] The star of Friedrich Adler and antiwar sentiment seemed to be on the ascension, and although Bauer had written all that Renner imputed to him and had supported the war until his capture, he found it necessary to repudiate his connection with Renner's ideas. Bauer, however, was a tactician concerning questions of power. In the months that followed his return to Vienna, he managed to play a double game, currying the favor of Victor Adler and the party oligarchy that shared Renner's views, while gradually assuming the leadership of the opposing left wing of the party created by Friedrich Adler, known formally as the Karl Marx Verein.[16]

Bauer's contact with the Karl Marx Verein, an organization whose adherents opposed the war from its inception, had resulted in his drafting a statement of principles called the Program of the Left, through which he attacked Karl Renner at the Parteitag in late October 1917.[17] The five major points of the program were (1) recognition of the Independent Socialist party of Germany (the fraction of German Social Democracy led by Karl Liebknecht and Rosa Luxembourg, who had voted against the war budget and consistently voiced their protest over participation in World War I), (2) priority of the class struggle over the fight against the foreign enemy, (3) condemnation of the "ministerialism" of Renner, (4) a call for the creation of independent national assemblies among the Austrian nations (though not necessarily outside the multinational framework), and (5) a call for an energetic fight against the chauvinistic socialism of Renner.[18] Bauer's military service prevented him from reading this statement at the Parteitag; this honor went to another member of the Karl Marx Verein, Gabriele Proft.[19] As a result, Bauer was able to maintain an illusion of not being connected with the radical tenor of his own statement. A curious deception was promoted wherein the party fathers and the radicals both claimed Bauer as their ally. This deception was furthered by Bauer's habit of self-contradiction, which enabled his political personality to hide until events allowed a more definite committal. After the Bolshevik revolution, when other moderate socialists complained of Bauer's growing radicalism, Victor Adler said that "one can rely on Otto not to commit excesses to the right or to the left for he is clever enough to be more of a politican behind the scenes in private conference than in his public statements."[20] Bauer thrived in this period as a diplomat and potential healer of "family" conflict. The skills he had acquired as an adolescent in reasoning with conflicting adults and with his sister were brought to bear on the social chaos of the party. Underlying the positive skills, however, was the "counterwill," which temporized and equivocated, postponing political actions that would heal the divisions between the opposing forces who looked to him as an ally.

Because the Program of the Left failed to be carried by the majority at the Parteitag in October 1917, the radicals wished to form a separate party within Austria based on the model of the Independent Socialist party of Germany. Bauer was urged to lead these radicals in open rebellion against the party fathers. Bauer pleaded with the radicals, in a curious argument, that no action should be taken that might divide the party. He held that such a division would be justified only if the majority of the party were in a position to make compromises with the bourgeois elements of the state. Given such a condition, an independent socialist body might exist to prevent reformism. Because this political condition prevailed in Germany, the Independent Socialist party of Germany was a valid movement; but political conditions in Austria allowed no possibility of compromise among political parties, so the left and right wings of Austrian Social Democracy must remain united. As if appalled by the enormity of such compromising casuistry, Bauer attacked the wishy-washy politics of many Austrian Social Democrats who had the habit of agreeing someone to death and then taking the opposite course: "In German Social Democracy principle stands openly against principle. It is otherwise in Austria. . . . We see the genuine Austrian trait of covering up contradictions rather than exposing them, hiding differences of will and attempting to decide them through 'smoothing over' [*Ausgleich*] rather than deciding them in battle."[21] Bauer's popularity and success with members of both left and right wings of Austrian Social Democracy lay in just such a quality of avoiding conclusive showdowns. His charisma seemed to flow from his ability to serve as an archetype of Austrian compromise and passivity to events.

Bauer's reaction to the Bolshevik revolution of 1917 in Russia typified his ability to use verbal and behavioral equivocation as an instrument for political success among his comrades. Bauer was genuinely impressed with the Bolsheviks' effectiveness in taking control of their country. In a letter to Kautsky on December 17, 1917, he expressed awe of Lenin and Trotsky, "who showed far more skill in carrying out their affairs" than he had expected. He admired their attempt to change the course of the war through their desire for peace as expressed in their conduct at the Brest-Litovsk negotiations with Germany. In regard to these peace efforts, Bauer stated that he was "in great suspense" and "especially curious about the results [of the peace talks] on the internal conditions of individual nations."[22] Here we see the emergence of his permanent concern with conflict, peace, and internal change in regard to his own person. The Bolsheviks assumed a role in his psychic drama, as had the Czechs, the Albanians, and other nations before the war. He credited them with forceful action that changed history and could bring peace. He brought a passionate conviction to his interchange with fellow Social Democrats in behalf of the Bolsheviks that stirred radicals in the party. Yet as Victor Adler knew, Bauer would never take similar action himself. Bauer was able to act out a revolutionary fervor in print, while consolidating his political influence with all dimensions of the socialist spectrum.

On January 4 Bauer wrote to Kautsky that he was pained by the attacks on the Bolsheviks by his fellow Austrian Social Democrats (presumably the majority of the party oligarchy); he defended their "dictatorship of the proletariat" in its nondemocratic manifestation as a form of control that was "temporary" and "necessary" to ensure the success of socialism in the Russian state; he objected strongly to the Russian Menshevik accusation that the Bolsheviks were the Jacobins of the Russian revolution. To be sure, he would have preferred that the revolution take a less violent form, that it be more democratic in its realization and continuation, but because of the reactionary directions followed by many compromising Russian socialists after the February revolution of 1917 the Bolshevik solution was the only one possible.[23] By March 1918 Bauer's support of the Bolshevik way was even stronger. In an article written for *Der Kampf* he stated that the Bolshevik understanding of a dictatorship of the proletariat, in its absolutist control of the state by a few trained revolutionaries, "is necessary in every state where the proletariat is still a minority of the population." Only by such methods could the "still unclear, not yet goal-conscious majority" be educated to the truths of socialism. Of course, by the end of this article he contradicted his justification of the Bolshevik method when he stated that "although we must support the Bolsheviks it does not follow that we share all their illusions or agree with their methods or must adopt their theories" such as government "by tour-de-force."[24]

Yet in facing the workers' strikes in Austria in January 1918, Bauer did an about-face, and one views it with more compassion than annoyance. Bauer was caught up in wonder at a nation (Russia) that had become socialistic even though a minority of the people were proletarian. Yet when the Austrian proletariat, also a minority, attempted to adopt the Bolshevik way and force their leaders to do the same, the Austrian Social Democratic oligarchy supported the existing government, and Otto Bauer, through a conspicuous silence, affirmed the suppression of the nascent revolution.[25]

In a study on the failure of the Austrian revolution of 1848 written before World War I, Bauer placed the blame for the collapse of the republican constitution on the liberal intellectuals' fear of arming the workers: "Above all the bourgeoisie feared the armed worker; in the debates over the national guard [the liberal intellectuals] did not allow that weapons should be possessed by the workers. The sweetest secret of bourgeois liberalism was expressed [by one of their number] when he said: 'Rather a return to absolutism than the danger of a complete freedom of property.'"[26] This "sweetest secret of bourgeois liberalism" of 1848 was extant in the recesses of Bauer's personality in 1918. Complete freedom of movement for the worker would endanger the role of his own personality in the world. If the worker was capable of determining the fate of his own person and property without awaiting the scientific directives of socialism, then Bauer and Austro-Marxism were beside the point. As Bauer phrased this feeling in the spring of 1918: "Marxism within the workers' movement has another task than to share all the errors and illusions expressed by the contemporary atmosphere of proletariat opinion. Against the particular interest of the worker in one land it holds the general interest of the proletariat of all lands. . . . Marxism seeks to interpret the direction of historical development and defend a political tactic against the seduction of [proletariat] illusion." With these words Bauer placed the guilt for the war enthusiasm in 1914 upon the workers and the passivity of some party oligarchs who followed the false path of this enthusiasm.[27]

In October and November 1918, Bauer again pointed out to the workers that their illusions countered the true path of history. When the Austrian Social Democratic members of Parliament, guided by Karl Renner, effected a coalition with the bourgeois parties of the state in the last weeks of October, Bauer quickly joined them. The true path of history for Bauer was to be where the most important politicians were, for it was the adults who were in charge who made history, not the unappeased will of those dependent upon the leaders. As a child, one advances only by moving one's parents, not by avoiding them. When militant workers and soldiers sought a leader from the Austrian Social Democratic hierarchy to give official recognition to their desire to overthrow the Provisional Assembly and provide them with direction, Bauer avoided assuming the Bolshevik mantle he had admired in print.[28] On November 1, 1918, Bauer read before the Provisional Assembly a statement he had composed entitled "Proclamation to the Germans in Austria" in which he urged the people to preserve order, abstain from violence, and respect the new government.[29] Apparently as a reward, Bauer was named foreign secretary of the German-Austrian republic on November 12, 1918.[30] As with Renner, fate had bestowed upon him the highest rank within the state that matched his dreams—for Renner it had been the "father" of the Austrian German hearth, for Bauer it was the diplomat who could heal all conflicts.

12

Max Adler:
Will and Idea in Wartime

Max Adler's olympian distance from the political arena of daily life did not prevent the chaos of the earthly polis from affecting his reason. The man who had struggled so hard to penetrate to the truth of the immediate reality in order to see clearly the general will of the times, and thus be in the forefront and in control of the general will, was carried in the stream of blind passion that supported the "Day of the German Nation."

For more than a year after the outbreak of the war, Adler struggled for an overview, a conceptual way to link the meaning of his present to the dogma of his past. A review of Adler's publications in *Der Kampf* during the world war provides a psychic autobiography of one who sought to save his will from submersion in the common stream. As long as the Austrian state had remained within the fixed banks of its century-old channel and Vienna had served as the immovable and unmoving center of all inactivity, Max Adler could neglect the torpid presence of the state in his concern with the will of the individual. When the state began to erupt and move in all directions, fed by the volcanic flow of Germany, Adler's dependence upon the state's presence, hitherto unconscious, became a powerful shadow that overwhelmed his previous distance from it. For the first time, Adler began to consider the state in his writings; in fact, in his first flush of recognition, Adler became a patriotic enthusiast of the state.

Before 1914 the state for Adler was a spontaneous generation of individual wills, a mirror image of living personalities. In the first article he published during the war, an essay on Ferdinand Lassalle, the state became a body divorced from the human personality. In a subtle shift of consciousness, Adler followed the pattern of Karl Renner, another lover of Lassalle, in finding the state to be an organism prior to the presence of the individual. The Promethean task of avoiding the abstract ideas relative to the state, which necessarily subordinated one's will to the impersonal "they," a task once vital to Max Adler, was forgotten in an instant. On the threshold of his entry to a mass hypnosis, Adler confessed in this article, "This is no time in which to review one's past and celebrate one's memory, even when such memory is the solidity of spirit that could strengthen the present and prepare the way for the future."[1] He was subsequently cursed with the burden of following a will beyond his person.

Characteristically, the force that he followed for the first time was invested with pedagogical authority; the state assumed the role of teacher with "the task of developing the germs of humanity into man." Seen in this light, what was formerly merely a negative presence of bourgeois power became a midwife of the spirit:

Today it is clear that what Lassalle designates as the essence and task of the state . . . stands in no way contradictory to a Marxist understanding. For the Marxist the state is the means whereby one is educated toward freedom, even though the historical state is also viewed by the Marxist as the compelling presence wherein the will of one class becomes the will of all. What may seem like a contradiction here ceases to be a contradiction when one regards the development in the historical structure of the state. For the historical structure of the state must pass through the various phases of class domination toward a form that allows increased freedom for the individual.[2]

Although at any given moment an individual might suffer from the seemingly arbitrary decisions that emanated from the impersonality of an unseen executive power, Adler held that with a proper understanding of the state as a historical structure that evolves toward a better organization for man's freedom, the individual might accept with appreciation his own role in history: "One cannot go astray in the fevered heat of the times if he preserves the Marxist-Lassallean manner of thought. One is lifted above the titanic storm and stress of events with the Marxist-Lassallean conceptual tool, and the chaotic nature of the times assumes its true aspect as regulated laws of historical becoming. One who is aware of this knows that what immediately may demand all of his personal freedom, yes, even may mean his surrender to annihilation [des Untergange preisgibt] is in terms of the whole only a winding that history must take.[3]

The surrender of one's personal vision to the exigencies of the time generated in Adler's twilight zone of consciousness a need to reformulate the principles upon which he had based his existence. In an article appropriately entitled "Das Prinzip des Sozialismus," Adler attempted to justify his support of the Austrian war effort with concrete economic and social arguments. The result, however, was merely a parroting of Karl Renner's principle of social imperialism:

Certainly, the way things were before the outbreak of the war allowed the people no choice between war and freedom . . . no state wished this war, but every one was compelled to join it, for all states today are driven *by the present system of economic organization.* . . . Because the war is a historical necessity, an even greater necessity exists for the proletariat to win theoretical clarity over the causes that have led to the present situation, and to see the consequences that must follow from the present situation. Appropriate historical goals for the future must be developed out of the historical necessity of the present.[4]

A careful reading of this statement exposes the still small voice of Adler's political conscience. Inevitably the question of human will rises to the surface of the stagnant water of Adler's passive pursuit of other war aims and theories. To be sure, Adler calls upon the proletariat to win a greater understanding of their actions and a future policy consequent to their actions, but it is apparent that the proletariat is here a catch-all for Adler's own guilt. Adler's growing unrest with the easy answers that cloaked his war enthusiasm led to an article in April 1915 entitled "Was ist Notwendigkeit der Entwicklung?" (What is necessity of development?), which brought the problematic of historical determinism and individual will into sharp focus. This article served as a bridge that led Adler toward socialists who had not been seduced by the passions of the majority:

Above all one must protect himself from being trapped by the abstraction that social life is a kind of law above our heads, a fate which carries men beyond their will, making them happy or destroying them as it wills, allowing them only to observe the consequences. Social development is not the fate of men, however, it is their work. Nothing occurs to man that he himself has not prepared, only many are not conscious of their role in what occurs, thus it seems to such men that a great deal happens to them beyond their will. Such men point to some mystical objietive force of social development which in its loss of real presence in their immediate lives becomes an inexorable force that directs "mankind" where it will.[5]

Adler, obviously guilty of this syndrome, then makes a distinction between two kinds of "necessity of development," one growing out of the decisions of "observers" and one out of the decisions of "actors." For the man who passively observes the facts of his environment, the actions to which he submits take on the cloak of necessity, but, Adler stresses, the real necessity in one's life can be found only within a conscious act initiated upon individual principle.[6] One must set his own goals, not wait for them to be thrust upon him. Then, by way of example, Adler loses himself to the abstraction of the proletariat once more:

The war imperialism can only be a preliminary stage of socialism *if the proletariat sets their own goals and forces the realization of these goals.* Therefore it is of overwhelming necessity that the proletariat keep itself from being seized [*anwandeln*][7] with the imperialistic spirit and maintain its class-conscious ideology with all its strength. In this effort, however, not much can be done at the present time. Because the proletariat of necessity must defend their homeland, socialism assumes the same goal as imperialism . . . here the old proverb "When two people do the same thing it is still not the same" assumes special meaning.[8]

In Adler's case the proverb underlined a "double-mindedness" that still could not differentiate his own goals from those inherited with the conundrums of his political party and its theory. The ideas of class and economic development still kept him paralyzed as an individual actor; he continued to observe the forces that existed around and outside of him. In June 1915, however, Adler removed one more veil between himself and responsibility for his own life. In an article entitled "J.G. Fichte ueber den wahrhaften Krieg," Adler stated: "Even yet the nightmare [*Alpdruck*] of the first days of the war burdens the deeper perceptions of sensitive people. And what contemporary philosophy proves impotent to explain, classical German philosophy, the source of all thought, makes possible. Above all the voice of Fichte makes itself heard as a leader of our time." Adler quoted Fichte as saying: "Only a war that proceeds from a state of reason, or lacking this state leads to its realization, can be called a true war . . . the justification of such a war does not lie in *what* we do . . . rather in *how* we do it, in what spirit. Only when a war is fought in a spirit that seeks to establish a realm of freedom for all is a war something other than a degradation of human culture."[9]

Fichte's philosophy of the isolated ego allowed Adler to regain the Olympus of intellect sacrificed a year before; Fichte's idealization of a German nation became an archetype that allowed Adler to retreat from the chaotic world formerly graced with that appellation, a world in which he had vainly sought to keep step. Adler developed in silence a personal arsenal of theory with which he might confront his fathers. Between June 1915 and November 1915 we hear nothing from him. Then in the November–December issue of *Der Kampf* Adler returned to the public world as a man with a vision. His article "Weltmacht oder Volksmacht?" (world power or people's power?), introduced the theme he would develop for the duration of the war. He returned to his major idea, the importance of the individual will in the face of group abstractions, but with an apparent self-consciousness of his former sins against this principle. He attempted in this article to awaken his fellow intellectuals to the unconsciousness with which they justified the war as a force of progress. He cried out against the "darkening of the intellect," the "infinite self-delusion," and the "admiration of all consequences without any critical attempt at understanding whatsoever" by members of Austrian Social Democracy. He continued that "history in the last years has not brought with it a genuine transformation or new ordering internally of social forces, it is in no way the result of a new creative unity of the people's will, rather only the product of extraordinary misery."[10]

The following month saw Adler's first attempts to provide his fellow intellectuals with a positive program of principle for relating to society within a nation at war. In an article entitled "Ueber Kriegsethik" (Over war Ethics) Adler examined the question, What is reality, and upon the ground of his answer suggested a concrete basis for an intellectual to turn against participation in the war effort.[11] In regard to the esoteric qualities of this article Karl Renner explained to Friedrich Adler, "Max Adler is very praiseworthy in his intentions, although I do not have any idea what the thing he discusses has to do with our people. Is it good to burden *Der Kampf* with such stuff?"[12] Max Adler's metaphorical path of argument provides the reason for Renner's difficulty in finding a foothold upon that ground:

In Grillparzer's profound fairy tale play Der Traum, Ein Leben,[13] there is a passage with a wonderfully gripping power. As Rustan sees that he is hopelessly entangled in the net of his dream crime, and as his physical and mental existence stands on the verge of collapse, suddenly reality breaks into the life of the dream. He hears a bell ringing in the night, and for a moment the dream picture disappears, as he says to himself: "Listen, it rings. Three o'clock. The day comes, the dream is soon over! . . . When the day comes, then I am no longer a criminal. No, things will be as they were before, as I was before." Since the outbreak of the world war there are many . . . who live within the nightmarish force of a horrible dream. . . . They stare into the world in which all that was formerly valuable to them now appears a valueless nonsense. . . . And no clock rings with its bright notes to release one from the torture of events in which he stands. . . . Philosophy could have been and should have been such a clock: for philosophy does not measure things in terms of the contemporary or historical, criteria that would involve one in the confusion [*Strudel*] of events, rather philosophy measures in terms of the pure laws of the human spirit. From the height of this tower of thought one may await with certainty the bell that will release him from the nightmare of events, from the compulsions and misery of the times, from the darkness of war in which all mankind has sunk.[14]

The timeless time, the bell removed from the ground of history, the bell of the human spirit above the confusion of the contemporary—such a bell was extolled as the salvation of the intellectual. The world of Vienna was relegated to the realm of dream life; Max Adler insisted that one live only in the daylight land of philosophy. One must dwell in the "ivory tower" above the masses until the healing light of day dispelled the crippling phantasms of the present. Adler's use of Grillparzer to develop this ethic of intellectual withdrawal from the nightmarish world of the present embraces a tremendous irony: Grillparzer adapted *Der Traum, Ein Leben* from the original by Calderon in such a way as to emphasize how a dream might expose the seeds of good and evil within a man, a revelation that might transform a man's consciousness of himself during the dream and, thereby, his later waking life.[15] Adler, however, seems only to wish an end to his dream and sees Grillparzer's play only as a paean to the reason of daylight, neglecting the self-revelation inherent in the nightmare. Instead of facing wartime Vienna and experiencing the hidden life that prompted his behavior in the first year of the war, Adler withdrew from the world and himself, awaiting an end to the painful pedagogy of the nightmare he sought to deny. Adler's bad dream was Karl Renner's new Europe.

The need for a conscious act founded upon individual principle within a society whose legal and informal norms jeopardize any individual action not within the ethos of the time, the state of a wartime nation, verges on martyrdom. Max Adler's resistance to cooperative action, his *puer aeternus* attraction to pure idea, and his natural inclination to introverted relations to events channeled his desire for a significant act into a verbal cul-de-sac. He identified with martyrs of the past who "died for ideas." His challenge would be to live for one. In an essay commemorating the five hundredth anniversary of Johannes Hus, he wrote: "To die for an idea which expresses the whole being and activity of he who is dedicated to death changes the character of death itself. It allows the most frightful death to appear as merely the highest completion of one's own life, as a victory of the spirit and the will not only over the ignorance and evil of an opponent, but also over one's own doubts and weakness." Adler qualified this statement by saying that one who died for his "fatherland" did not really embrace the proletariat, the real backbone of the state; thus, since the idea the patriot died for was false, his death could not be a noble one.[16] Friedrich Adler was taken by Max Adler's reflections on courage and publicly commended the notion a month before he himself lived its words.[17]

Max Adler, however, managed to avoid any action that might expose him to violation of Austria's war regulations. Although he had become a member of the radical Karl Marx Verein, Adler was among those members who discouraged any radicalism outside the closed circle of their discussion group.[18] As might be expected, when the streets of Vienna were filled with revolutionary workers in January 1918, Adler took no overt action, although in that month's *Der Kampf* an article by him appeared that would ironically highlight his schizoid separation between thought and deed: "Even if the political and labor union movement within socialism represents socialism's two *legs*, they are still *not the whole body*, above all not the head which provides the *intellect* that allows the feet to march and gives the feet direction. The political and labor union movement . . . may have a socialist meaning if they wholly subordinate themselves to socialism."[19]

Presumably, the article in which this statement appeared, an article commemorating the seventieth anniversary of the Communist Manifesto, was written before the strikes began in January.[20] Adler seems to be chiding the conservative nature of the political (Austrian Social Democracy) and union movements in Austria that monopolized the mantel of socialism; he was riding on the coattails of Friedrich Adler's revolutionary act and the recent Bolshevik revolution in Russia. Yet how macabre were Adler's medieval metaphors of the corporate body when this appeared in print, enabling the workers to read of their dependence upon party intellectuals at a time when they were betrayed by the mental paralysis of that intellectual.

In the last year of the war, in the months that preceded the Austrian "revolution" of October–November 1918, Adler manifested an increasing radicalism in all his utterances. He was a more overt supporter of the Bolshevik revolution than any of the other Austro-Marxists, yet his enthusiasm was phrased more as a celebration of the socialist idea over the philosophers of the bourgeois world than as a social upheaval of the Russian proletariat. He wrote on November 16, 1917, in the *Arbeiter-Zeitung*:

The old proverb "Ex oriente lux" [from the East comes enlightenment] has assumed a new, wonderful, magnificent truth in our day. In the dark night of madness and horror the Russian revolution has kindled a torch of reason. . . . The whole world now follows with breathless tension the fate of the revolution, especially the international proletariat. One must learn to see the conformity of this historical struggle between the forces of light which promise a beautiful future and the powers of darkness which offer a hopeless present with the passion of one's own reason and life interest [*Leidensschaftlichkeit des eigenen Vernunft und Lebensinteresse*]; moreover, one must stand with a clear understanding in the causes and goals of this historical event, and maintain an acute consciousness of one's task which grows from this event, and becomes a compelling need for everyone, especially, however, for the proletariat.[21]

Russia's every move after the Bolshevik revolution appeared to Adler as a realization of his dream—a state created by the general will. Adler stressed the consciousness and will of the Russian people and the selfless desire of the Bolshevik leaders to make way for the free development of the masses. As rumors of the violence in Russia came back to Austria and the Bolsheviks were pictured as barbarians by Social Democrats such as Renner, Max Adler excused the revolution's excesses in the name of historical necessity. He compared the Bolshevik mission with that of Jesus Christ and his promulgation of a new faith and a new law, writing: "Didn't Jesus Christ say when he sought to establish his teaching, that I come to you not to bring peace, but with a sword?"[22] And when in October 1918 German Social Democracy settled for a coalition with the bourgeois and Junker parties in a new parliamentary government, Adler disappointedly compared this compromise with the stormy renewal in ·Russia: "Any democracy which did not arrive at that state through revolution, that is, through the fire of a new transformation of nation impelled by the revolutionary will of people who wish to destroy all the old and repressive institutions, carries already the mark of impotence upon its brow."[23]

Adler's hopes for Russia were a vehicle for his own desires for personal renewal and for a social milieu that reflected his ideal conceptions. Personal and social change for Adler, however, would require positive social interaction that improved upon the social norms that had led to the general betrayal of the socialist principle he abhorred. A moment of decision came to him in October 1918 as it had to Otto Bauer. Would he cooperate with the more radical elements of the socialist party and seek to found the socialist state, following the model of the Bolsheviks, or would he withdraw into the compliant antagonism he had shared with his fellow party members before the war? On October 29, 1918, the day before Karl Renner made official the Austrian Social Democratic acceptance of a constitutional monarchy, Adler wrote:

We stand already in the middle of the revolution, even if one must admit that revolution is not that which the police and legal minds of the state see it as, namely, street battles, blood justice, and the dissolution of all order, concepts of revolution completely foreign to us Socialists. For as Lassalle said, revolution means the victory of the new principle: the rule of a new spirit in the people which in one fell stroke tears them away from their old life and fills them with new energy and new tasks and with a determined will. A will with which they will fight if necessary until death—that is revolution. And this revolution in full progress in central Europe.[24]

Again Adler turned to Lassalle and a subordination to the state of things and the disparity between violent words and nonaction. When radicals, especially Austrians who called themselves Bolsheviks, attempted to bring the fiery transformation of the state as experienced in Russia, Adler clung to the constitutional womb of Austrian Social Democracy. He attacked the Austrian Bolsheviks as a "party of confusion" and insisted that socialism had come to Austria without need of violence. After all, he reasoned, Austria had become a republic a few weeks after Austrian Social Democracy began to govern, and the bourgeois elements of the state had never desired a republic; when such progress was possible in a matter of weeks, the possibilities for the New Man and the New Society were unlimited.[25] Adler, never a politician, was able to rest in the delusion of the newness of the Austrian spirit throughout the crisis of decision and "revolution."

13

Friedrich Adler
Encounters His Fate

On the day that Austria began to mobilize for war against Serbia, July 27, 1914, Victor and Friedrich Adler traveled to Brussels, where the Second International had called an emergency meeting to decide upon a course of action. Victor Adler told the assembly that no resistance to the war was possible by Austrian Social Democracy; the mobilization and the war regulations precluded any action against the government. Friedrich Adler later said of this moment when he listened to his father describe the impotence of the Austrian Social Democratic party: "I had for the first time the strong sensation that I stood in contradiction to the conceptions of my father."[1]

The time had come for Friedrich Adler's overt challenge to his father's authority. His father, who was described as having aged ten years for every day of the crisis, at the end of July 1914, was on the brink of collapse.[2] Thus when Austrian Social Democracy made known through the "Day of the German Nation" editorial that it would physically and theoretically support the Austrian and German war goals, Friedrich resolved to begin his own war. Upon reading Austerlitz's editorial, Kathia Adler, realizing the betrayal by her father-in-law's party of every principle her husband believed in, proposed to Friedrich that they both commit suicide.[3] Friedrich, however, was ready for a new life. At first, he thought of waging an "underground" war against the Austro-German Social Democrats and the Habsburg regime: he considered resigning from all party functions that would bind him to the official channels of party obedience and of bringing out his own militant organ.[4] By the second week of August, however, he decided that it would be best to wage his war within the party structure.[5]

On October 8, 1914, the Austro-German Social Democratic oligarchy began a secret conference to debate the party's position on the war.[6] During these meetings Friedrich Adler challenged his fathers with force and conviction, showing more strength and self-confidence than ever before in his party life.[7] During the months of October, November, and December 1914 Friedrich's struggle with the party and especially with his father sharpened. His father hastened to assure others that the battle involved only principles, but the emotional pain he suffered evidenced the real ground of conflict. Victor Adler wrote of his son to Karl Kautsky:

You may imagine how happy I am to speak with you; you are so good to me and seek to strengthen my declining self-confidence—moreover, I'm so lonely! The political conflict with Fritz is *personally* not so bad, he is and remains my most intimate friend—but I suffer under the fact that I see him subjected to fanaticism, and thus fear that he cannot perform the services for the party that I expected from him—My hope is that in more quiet times his understanding of facts will return and the idolatry of the rectilinear which he calls "principles" will disappear—but it is not a "family tragedy," for that I have no talent; it only seems like one to people who look for touchy situations and who take everything *personally*.[8]

Friedrich Adler, too, sought to keep the attack on his father and his father's party devoid of personal connotations. Although mentioning other Social Democrats by name in his polemics in the fall and winter of 1914, he was conspicuous in his compunction to touch his father's person.[9] Only in allusion and allegory did he express the actual basis of his struggle with the party oligarchy. Upon this fratricidal ground Friedrich deployed two major theoretical forces: the specter of the Second International, which had collapsed when all the member European socialist parties chose social imperialism in its stead, and the Independent Socialist party of Germany, a revolutionary group whose members had separated from their parent body to incorporate the ideas of the Second International in their lives.

For the first year since the outbreak of the world war Friedrich Adler attempted to restore unity among the socialist parties in Europe through letters and articles.[10] Before the war these bodies had given Friedrich a platform of authority that aided him in his separation from the dominating presence of his father; their loss left him with no other choice than to find his unity in Vienna. The inexorable pull of Vienna and the necessity of approaching freedom through the hell and purgatory of his parent party are evidenced by the limits he set on his admiration of the Independent

Socialist party of Germany. His respect for this party, first manifested in an article published in January 1915,[11] grew from its members' courageous adherence to principle. It is noteworthy, however, that Friedrich did not follow their example and seek to establish a party outside the boundary of the majority expression. Rather, he followed a personal conception of unity that always won first place in his mind, sometimes complementing, sometimes contradicting the outer trappings of his Marxist creed. Thus when he was called into the Austrian army in February 1915,[12] he did not object on conscientious grounds, a logical step in the light of the antiwar principles he professed. Instead, he obeyed the call to duty, saving his martyrdom for an expression more personally meaningful than pacifism.[13]

Freed from the army because of his heart after only a few days' service, Friedrich reentered his conflict. His will somewhat weakened by his defeat at the hands of the majority in the fall and winter of 1914, Friedrich considered for a time leaving Austria to conduct a literary campaign against the war from Switzerland. He had been offered an editor's position on the *Volksrecht* in Zurich.[14] On the surface there seemed little reason to remain in Vienna; his wife and children had gone to Switzerland after the outbreak of the war, and there was little hope of success in the party, as evidenced by the outcome of the secret conferences a few months before. Nevertheless, Friedrich chose to remain in Vienna. In discussing this decision, he articulated the extraordinary emotional valence that linked him with the other Social Democrats in a love-hate bond of life and death: "I had . . . uncommonly intensive private talks with my party comrades in April of 1915. They all wished me to remain in Vienna; not only my father, but above all Seitz and Renner urged me to stay in Vienna, for they insisted it was important to the party that the Left wing be represented. Even Austerlitz wished me to remain, and in a meeting that took place [of the party oligarchy] only Pernerstorfer felt I should be allowed to go to Switzerland.[15]

Even though one might suspect some exaggeration of others' concern by Friedrich, who suddenly was in the limelight, it is not difficult to imagine that some such concern did exist among the party oligarchy. After all, Friedrich's presence gave their cause meaning; he understood and reacted to their language. Encouraged by these talks in April, Friedrich sought in the Reichkonferenz of Austro-German Social Democracy called for May 1915 to impress his antiwar policies upon the majority. This second attempt to take power within the party also met with defeat. He was disheartened, and his psychosomatic disease recurred, forcing him to take a five-week rest cure in the mountains. In April, shortly before his talks with the party oligarchy, Friedrich had purchased a revolver with the thought of committing a political assassination in order to awaken the proletariat and Social Democrats of Austria to the possibility of direct action. After his second failure within the party his thoughts again turned to a personal act of violence, a demonstration that would be evident to the eyes of the world. Friedrich later stated that he hesitated in carrying through is plan before October 1916 largely because he could not decide on the proper target—a man whose death would properly stir the Austrian public to action against the war.[16]

Friedrich had not yet given up the possibility of winning power through the party organization, as is evidenced by an article he contributed to *Der Kampf* in January 1916 entitled "Suenden der Minderheit oder Suenden der Mehrheit?" (Sins of the majority and sins of the minority?). The article stressed the importance of unity within Austrian Social Democracy in spite of tactical differences:

All party activity consists in common action toward the realization of the party program. Every individual act rests on the majority decision of a solidary community. *Two dangers* threaten the party, one from the side of the majority and one from the side of the minority. The majority is always in danger that its decision does not correspond to the party program, that it *contradicts the basic principles* of the whole movement which it represents, the principles that give the party meaning. The minority is in danger of *destroying the community of action*, of not complementing the majority, of going its own way and thereby disturbs the majority decision.[17]

The omnipotence of the written word, the torah of the spiritual fathers, continued to exert its magic over Friedrich's personality. Its abstract majesty absorbed his own will. His longing for solidarity, the union of his intellectual and emotional natures, was still projected onto the body of his fathers. Not until he realized his intellectual and emotional selves as being uniquely his own, freed from the metaphorical prison of his past, would Friedrich have the wholeness for which his being strived. In this article Friedrich used the word "solidarity" [*Solidaritaet*] no less than forty-two times in five pages. Friedrich's use of italics paralleled the allegorical use of image in providing a psychic text of his struggle for a whole personality. He italicized ten expressions within five pages, almost all of them reflecting states of division, states of wholeness, and types of consciousness relating to these states. When he was tired of the image of Austrian Social Democracy as an archetype of wholeness, Friedrich turned to the specter of the Second International, which he introduced as a body that before the war "lived with all its energy the solidarity of feeling and thought." Then he stated that although sins against the spirit of the Austrian workers' party were possible by both the majority and the minority, the majority was the bigger sinner because of its violation of the higher solidarity present in the Second International.[18]

Often the Austrian Social Democratic party and the Second International contended within his mind for the right to represent the potential unity of his person. A good example of this expressionistic syndrome that turned all principle into a mass of contradiction is provided by an article Friedrich wrote a few months before the act that would free him temporarily from such parasitic abstractions. The article was formally addressed to the Belgian Camille Huysmans, secretary of the Second International in the Hague, who was attempting to bring together the socialists of all European nations once more into a peaceful cooperation. Adler both attacked and supported Huysmans:

> You know from before the war how valuable not only the idea of the International is, but also the embodiment [*Verkoerperung*] as an organization. You also know how much meaning I gave to the functions of the International Bureau during the war, and remember that I attempted to counter the unjust attacks against the executive [of the International] by the German and Austrian party comrades. . . . Therefore I feel that I am not only authorized, but obliged, to express my opinion without reservation over your last proposal (the invitation to discuss international cooperation), and the theoretical basis from which this proposal emanates.[19]

Friedrich Adler thus began a curious argument wherein he blamed Huysmans for attempting to bring a peace between European socialists that hid insoluble contradictions which had necessitated the war: "You see . . . always only a *problem of diplomacy* and therefore have sought to hide the *essential problem of inner contradiction* withn the International instead of bringing it to consciousness. . . . No one can deny that we have learned in this war that the argument of defense of homeland is purely and simply *only a theoretical abstraction*, and that in the reality of the present, the struggle for the existence of nations is *inalienably bound up* with the struggle for the goals of an imperialist power politic."[20]

Adler identified the Social Democratic movement in all European countries as an inalienable part of each nation's economic organism; a future international brotherhood of socialists was not simply a problem that could be solved by the will to cooperate. Thus Adler's recognition of the "inner contradictions" between European peoples that must be brought to consciousness countered the admonitions he had directed to Austrian Social Democrats since the outbreak of the war, namely, that there was no excuse for Social Democratic participation in the war and that the Second Communist International must be maintained at all costs. To Huysmans he claimed: "The political content of the principle 'defense of homeland' is that *alone* which can build the *heart* of a socialist program for peace talks, thus also the program for a future international."[21]

In making what he called a "theoretical abstraction" on a previous page the "heart" of the socialist program for peace, Friedrich Adler manifested his enslavement to metaphor. "Defense of homeland" was a chauvinist abstraction in the mouths of those Austrian Social Democrats who opposed the unity inherent in the Second International, but it became an organ that gave life when challenged as a concept by the secretary of the Second International. Why? Perhaps because the higher unity of the Second International was real only as long as it was Friedrich's personal cause; as soon as it was promulgated by someone else and became possibility, Friedrich withdrew his energy from its "embodiment." Friedrich attached himself to any organizational image that had no possibility of success. This syndrome made sense in one who sought a personal union that could never be resolved simply in the formal coming together of bodies outside himself. As long as the metaphors of the Second International or the Austrian Social Democratic party could permit the picture of internal strife, he might dwell in their polemics. Should this strife be resolved, Friedrich must either seek a new abstract basis for his own conflict or become truly conscious of his state.

When Social Democrats such as Huysmans made more and more concrete efforts for an end to the war and a reunion of European socialists, Adler's mental state reached a critical tension. He was ready for a personal act that would prove his reality as an acting presence, an act divorced from any organization outside himself that might rob him of this realization of his person. In the month that preceded this act, Adler's theoretical writings exposed a man who knew that a former condition would come to an end. His attention was inevitably caught by expressions that voiced the apocalyptic possibility. As an example of this synchronistic syndrome, Adler reviewed a book by Paul Lensch in September 1916 entitled *Eine Sozialdemokraten Ende und Glueck* (The finish and fate of a Social Democrat). Lensch's position was similar to that of Karl Renner in that he saw the war bringing a new evolution of socialism. Friedrich Adler found the title of this book strangely provocative; he stated that only when Lensch was viewed as a man who had ceased to be a Social Democrat could one make sense of the title: "His end as a Social Democrat seems to be his fate (or happiness). At least this is the only way the mysterious title of his book . . . can be plausibly explained." Then, as if to show the error and mortality of Lensch and his view of socialism (yet really as an erection of a personal monument to the end of one state of existence and the pregnant vision of a new one), Adler punned the Nietzschean paean to self-overcoming, *Lenzchliches, Allzulenschliches* (human all too human).[22] This word play and selection of theme was the product of Adler's monomaniac intuition of what lay before him. Further evidence of his intuition appears in a second book review in the same issue of *Der Kampf* of Max Adler's *Zwei Jahre. . . .! Weltbetrachtungen Eines Sozialisten*, (Two years! reflections on the world war by a socialist), which discussed the death of martyrs. Friedrich Adler wrote: "In a beautiful chapter on the *death of martyrs* the special meaning of conscious dying for an idea is portrayed. Again and again appears the conviction that the class war *stands higher* than the war of nations. . . . Only the problem concerning the employment of force in the struggle of the classes remains to a certain extent open, and we hope that the author will find the opportunity to express himself on this problem at a future time."[23]

Of course, Max Adler was vague about the question of actual force, but Friedrich Adler did not wait for someone else to articulate his position. The will to action awaited only the release of a trigger taut from months of resolve. Adler's last publication before the assassination sounded as an ejaculation from the lips of a hunter who has sighted his target. On the eve of the second Reichkonferenz of Austro-German Social Democracy, Friedrich Adler announced to those who could read between his lines that he would no longer tolerate inaction:

The untiring and clearly conscious work of the opposition in the party has consisted and still exists in the awaking of the proletariat from their fatalism. One must bring them to an awareness of the necessity of their emancipation from the government by their creation of an independent politic. The essence of the great *struggle over the political standpoint* of the working class is debased with the expression "party conflict." An active politic of the proletariat is only possible again if the consciousness of their necessity in the party wins a dominance in their own thoughts, if the ideas of the opposition seize the masses. They must become the subject of this politic before they can exercise their presence as an object. And therefore all work of the opposition is aimed at winning fellow warriors, i.e., a struggle for the brains of the party comrades themselves.[24]

What had held back and was holding back his party comrades from decisive action? "The reason lies . . . in the *lacking necessity of autonomy* [*mangelnden Beduerfnis nach Selbstaendigkeit*] of the party comrades themselves, who are too accustomed to their life in the state so that in the party they are most comfortable with this state of affairs. They trust too readily in the wisdom of their leaders and conceive of independent thought as a waste of energy."[25]

On October 18 Friedrich Adler faced the party fathers for the last time. In a sitting of the Parteivorstand he engaged in an explosive exchange of opinions with Karl Renner and his father that led to his father's cry: "You are deliberately provocative, you obviously want someone to throw you out!"[26] He had, indeed, asked for this challenge. On October 21, 1916, Friedrich fired three bullets into the head of Count Stürgkh, prime minister of the Austrian war government. Count Stuergh was unfortunate enough to have perpetrated a particularly symbolic piece of authoritarianism two days after Friedrich's confrontation with the party fathers—he forbade the public meeting of a group of university professors who wished to debate various issues concerning the war, an act of paternalistic absolutism that marked him as the target for violent retaliation that had become inevitable.[27]

What of the act itself? How can we assert that this deed of violence liberated Friedrich Adler, if only temporarily, from the chains of the past? Of his state of mind immediately before the act Friedrich told his judges: "I thought in this moment only on the sacrifice of my own life . . . now my life is at an end! . . . Then came the thought: How would it be if I simply gave up my plan. No one would be any wiser." But he quickly discarded these seductive thoughts, reflecting: "There would be nothing but shame if now when you are so near to your goal you leave the thing undone and go away. . . . I had the distinct feeling that if I did not carry through the act that I felt to be a duty [*Pflicht*] an intolerable condition would result for my self-respect."[28] After perpetrating the deed, when he was assured that he had indeed been successful in the assassination, Friedrich experienced "a condition of complete spiritual peace and satisfaction,"[29] a condition that remained with him for months afterward in prison. Friedrich Adler, a man with a psychosomatic heart condition, was released from all anxiety and felt whole after an act that meant certain death for himself.

As we read of the moments of the act itself, we can see more clearly the link between the assassination and Friedrich's effort to encounter his personal father and party "fathers" in an expression of political independence: "I stepped up to Count Stürgkh and as far as I know fired three or four bullets in his head. I then cried loudly: 'Down with absolutism, we want peace!' I had decided on this slogan for my act as I sat at the table. I definitely cried out this slogan for I remember the physiological effect of its expression. This cry cost me a great deal of energy. Then I went to sleep and did not do anything more that was active."[30]

The killing of Count Stürgkh may be seen as a symbolic destruction of both the cultural fathers of his party and his personal father, for Friedrich did not remember the physiological process of pulling the trigger that resulted in the murder of Count Stürgkh, but rather the sensation that accompanied the slogan. "Down with absolutism, we want peace!" may be considered a genuine political articulation, but also a personal plea for freedom from the tyrants closest to him. It was in this outcry that Friedrich expressed his act of possessing all that his father had kept from him—the right to think and act as an autonomous person. Friedrich had described his passion for life as he sat in the restaurant preparing for that act of personal liberation in a phallic sense: "Side by side with the thought that it was my duty to execute the assassination was the full fury of my second soul, that entity which exists in all men, that in its lust for life holds to the world with clutching organs [*klammernden Organen*].[31]

When Victor Adler was told of what his son had done, he exclaimed as if in a dream, "Come on, that can't be," and laughed good-naturedly. Victor had been told within twenty minutes after the event. Having grasped the reality, about six o'clock that evening he went to the offices of the *Arbeiter-Zeitung*. On entering, he told the first person he met: "This is the time when fathers lose their sons." To Friedrich Austerlitz he said: "I believe Fritz's act will not hurt the party."[32]

In the long run, Victor was right, although for the next year the party's utterances turned toward the Left. Victor sought to counter the impact of Friedrich's act by proving it was the deed of a man who was mentally ill, an attempt ostensibly to save Friedrich from the death penalty when he came to trial but actually a conviction held by Victor from the time of the assassination. As Victor wrote to his brother-in-law two weeks after the act:

This is the first letter that I have been able to send through the censors to Germany, it is to you. Only a few words. The thing which we both do not wish to believe and still seems like a fairy tale [*Maerchen*] has hit us as you might imagine. For the time being only the news: Emma behaves like a heroine which is the most important thing to me, her sleep has not suffered; Fritz is so far unchangeably maintaining his ground, does not show the slightest depression, which seems to me to be a pathological euphoria. When he is not being questioned by the authorities, he occupies himself without a pause and with tremendous zeal in problems of epistemology and Ernst Mach. A decision in his case will not be reached for a long time because of the psychiatric investigation.[33]

Friedrich was reading not only Ernst Mach but also *Faust* and *Hamlet*.[34] Indeed, he was in the calm state of mind his father depicted, upset only by his parents' insistence on seeing his act as that of someone mentally ill. He wrote to his mother on November 11, 1916:

Yesterday when you visited me I had the impression again that you see my whole situation and everything that relates to me completely differently than it actually is. . . . You see me as being unhappy, which I am not nor ever in life was. Naturally my life might have taken another course than it did, but I am not in any aspect unsatisfied with the way it has turned out. The length of life never was important to me, only *the content* of life. And I am *completely* satisfied with the way in which I have lived my life. . . . You are always quick with your explanations of my behavior which are based upon pathology, and I see now that many of your assertions in my affair reflect such belief. . . . I hope the time comes when you are able to conceive of me as being a healthy man. I never have worried myself with a concern how my actions would affect those immediately around me, indeed such considerations I have always viewed as being immoral. *I also do not believe that my act was an attack on the life of those persons who care for me.* I, at any rate, do not have the slightest symptoms of remorse.[35]

In spite of this request, his parents, especially his father, continued to consider him mentally unbalanced. At the trial on May 17 and 18, 1917, father and son stood dramatically opposed. Friedrich gave a six-hour defense of his act and his historical person which portrayed his act and his life as the rational culmination of socialist principle,[36] and Victor undermined his son's oratory with insinuations and testimony regarding his son's insanity. The power of Friedrich's defense, however, had the day; he was sentenced to death[37]—a living death, unfortunately, for the abstract words he employed so well for self-justification at his trial blinded him permanently to the real goal of his struggle.

Of July 2, 1917, the Emperor Charles commuted Friedrich's death sentence to eighteen years imprisonment.[38] The emperor's words on this occasion were symbolic of the feelings within Austrian Social Democracy toward the painful meaning of Friedrich's act[39] and may also serve as the epitaph to his battle for personal clarity:

The politics of hate and retaliation, nourished by unclear condition, which unleashed the world war must after the war's end be replaced in every way and everywhere by a *politic of reconciliation*. This spirit must also dominate within the state. With this sign of reconciliation I exercise my duty as ruler under God's understanding, and will thereby be the first *who walks the way of charitable toleration*, spreading over the unfortunate political mistakes which occurred before and during the war that often lead to criminal acts the veil of forgetfulness [*den Schleier des Vergessens*].[40]

At the height of the Austrian "revolution" of November 1, 1918, Friedrich Adler was released from prison by the will of the emperor.[41] He met his father on November 2 and spent the duration of the war at his father's side.[42]

Conclusion

We are like sailors who must rebuild their ship on the open sea without benefit of a dock, or an opportunity to select the best replacement parts.

—*Otto Neurath*

The four Austro-Marxists stood naked in the essential limitations of their personalities and language during World War I. Wartime conditions put their characters and the principles they espoused over the years of their maturation to the crucial test of a society in chaos. Each man had sought to live within the aegis of socialist principle and the ideational and behavioral norms of the Austrian Social Democratic party. The conflicts between socialist principle and party norms emerged clearly after 1914. As long as the disjunctions between ideal and action that were normative for any Austrian Social Democrat could exist unchallenged, the Austro-Marxists functioned successfully within Austrian-German culture. But when these reinforcing social norms collapsed in the face of an emergency in the entire culture, a call to forms of action that were congruent with socialist principles went unheeded, and the language each man used to maintain his prewar sense of normalcy proved inadequate for steering him toward social effectiveness or personal health.

The attempt to find personal integrity within social chaos can bring the best elements of one's humanity to the service of everyday life. Each Austro-Marxist had moments during World War I when the healthiest strands of his character guided his action. Karl Renner's essential fairness and desire for a society that included all social points of view in a political solution each party could live with informed his political personality in the last weeks of World War I. Otto Bauer's ability to mediate between diverse interests and generations kept a divided party together in the same period. Max Adler found his ideological clarity in the middle years of the war, and his voice was one of the first to call socialists back toward their previously stated principles. Friedrich Adler had the courage to challenge the ersatz norms of his party fathers and follow a personal course of action.

The tragedy of the Austro-Marxists is that the healthier character traits they expressed in an isolated period during World War I were negated by accompanying traits that were bred in the unhealthy prewar and wartime milieus. Renner's German chauvinism and desire to be effective politically outstripped socialist principle. Otto Bauer's need for a cohesive party family turned his ability to mediate differences into a dissimulating ability to mask differences and compromise clear action. Max Adler's tocsin became, as it was before the war, a set of ideas that had no corresponding principles of action. Friedrich Adler distorted principled action with a political assassination whose overcompensatory nature must be seen as designed to end his political search for effective individuality.

The self-defeating and politically impotent actions of the Austro-Marxists have opened the question of cultural and personal health in the study of political history. Why is there a disjunction between one's articulated principles and one's attempts to live these principles in political or personal life? We have seen that a culture can educate its citizens in practices that allow the dissonance between thought and action to be denied. Norms of ideation can allow incomplete thought to be rewarded. Norms that isolate thinkers from each other on the basis of political affiliation or sterile competition enable theory to become infused with metaphors that serve the thinker's personality rather than an objective focus.

Each Austro-Marxist intuited at some point in his career the dangers that beset his theory and action. Renner's insight during World War I that an almost pathological striving for truth created imbalanced perspectives which were projected upon the working class typifies the sudden clarity the Austro-Marxists were capable of achieving in moments of their lives. Then, the individual and collective unconsciousness of social reinforcement closed their eyes to the essential problem of their political efficacy. Within the emotional bitterness of disappointed dreams, each Austro-Marxist was quick to blame his fellow for that man's failure of mind and language to grasp objective truth. Karl Renner wrote of Otto Bauer: "The things that were becoming, the people of the new generation, he did not see immediately, rather he took the easily effaced hallmark for the essence of the thing itself. [Bauer's] spirit did not live with the things, rather amidst the images of them."[1] Bauer, in turn, wrote of Max Adler: "Max Adler was never a politician in the *real* sense. Just as he remained trapped in the intellectual idealism of the Kantian school, so had his political thought never freed itself from the intellectual idealism, which could not be considered too meaningful to the needs and misery of the proletariat's class struggle, but only meaningful in the struggle and redemption of the socialistic ideal."[2]

Max Adler sought the real and scorned idealism as much as Bauer.

And Max Adler's statement on the theme of reality, perhaps the most sensible, was directed toward Friedrich Adler and his adherence to Ernst Mach: "Under the concept of social life a new conceptual realism has developed in recent times which leads almost every thinker right into a new metaphysic. Social life, society, appear only too often as essences-in-themselves, either as a secret connection between people, or more often a power over them, which includes them all as part of its elements. . . . In reality, however, it appears to me that we cannot seek social life other than the only place where it is really given, and that is only the case in the particular individual."[3]

Friedrich Adler's words about Karl Renner's relationship to the state give us a final picture of the abyss of metaphor that separates a man from his own life: "The 'idea of organization' of 1914 [Karl Renner's idea of the state permeating all levels of life] is a perspective in which only the forest and not the trees are seen. This metaphysical idea of organization will interest those individuals whose job it is to maintain the functioning of organizational mechanisms. The organization as an end in itself becomes an idea, upon which bureaucrats of all classes and all kinds unite."[4]

Each Austro-Marxist isolated a different aspect of the politics of metaphor, that language disorder that subordinated its adherents to an exclusive image that dissociated them from the very goals they sought, a full life, and effectiveness in the making of a just and creative society. Yet the position of the Austro-Marxists as above average intellects and thinkers who respected the continuity of an idea in the culture was evidenced in their theoretical production, which if incomplete in ideation and biased in judgments, deliberated issues with scope and counterpoint and frequently with new insight, thus providing its inheritors with a solid base of literature to approach the issues of their culture. Moreover, the Austro-Marxists dedicated their lives to a principled cause, and even if their political action was ineffective in achieving its goals, the men moved the idea of social democracy into the normative options of European culture, where it is practiced today.

The question that remains in the wake of the lives of the Austro-Marxists is how one may contribute effectively to change in a society. When cultural norms enforce certain blindnesses and problems that must be corrected, how can an individual rise above this milieu in his own social action? As Marx once said, "Someone must teach the teachers," for we tend to promulgate our own upbringing. The study of the Austro-Marxists has pointed to two directions by which an individual may improve his culture with a minimum of metaphorical distortion of his professed intent. The first and most important is self-awareness: one must clarify his own motives as he considers the general welfare. The second is careful inquiry, so that policies for social improvement are developed on the basis of scientific knowledge. Both these directions are ingrained in Austrian humanism, and we inherit these standards from Austrian culture in the work of men such as Sigmund Freud, Ludwig Wittgenstein, Rainer Maria Rilke, and other exceptional artists and scientists. Perhaps it is more difficult to pursue politics with such a twofold rigor, for in affecting the lives of a society directly one must face the immediate force of events as they occur. History does not allow the social activist time to test solutions in a laboratory. But a recognition of one of the most significant Social Democratic principles—human interdependence—may create a modesty in the social activist that will encourage him to use the scientific studies and humanistic insights of others whose life commitments enable them to test ideas. Perhaps we can rebuild society with better parts despite its constant crises and inherent blindnesses. Certainly, we must do better than the Austro-Marxists and Austrian Social Democracy in creating a norm of inquiry that can inform action, but we must feel a deep compassion for the Austro-Marxists and the Austrian culture when we see the scope of the cultural problem—change in history—that is our own to solve.

Notes

Introduction

1. For a history of Austrian Social Democracy between 1889 and 1914 see Vincent J. Knapp, *Austrian Social Democracy, 1889–1914* (Washington, D.C.: University Press of America, 1980). The best histories of the first generation of Austrian Social Democracy are Ludwig Bruegel, *Geschichte der oesterreicheschen Sozialdemokratie*, 5 vols. (Vienna: Wiener Volksbuchhandlung, 1922-25); Max Ermers, *Victor Adler: Aufstieg und Groesse einer Sozialistischen Partei* (Vienna: Verlag Dr. Hans Epstein, 1932); Clifton Gene Follis, "The Austrian Social Democratic Party, June 1914–November 1918" (Ph.D. dissertation, Stanford University, 1961); *Victor Adlers Briefwechsel mit August Bebel und Karl Kautsky* (Vienna: Wiener Volksbuchhandlung, 1954); and, *Victor Adlers Aufsaetze, Reden, und Briefe*, 11 vols. (Vienna: Wiener Volksbuchhandlung, 1922-29).

2. The Second International clarified its Marxist program in the Erfurt Program of 1891 in which it tied its goals and philosophy to Marx's *Communist Manifesto*. Before that there was a strong Lassallean movement in Social Democratic thought, which did not see class conflict as inevitable and approved of reform in cooperation with bourgeois parties. See Julius Braunthal, *History of the International, vol. 1, 1864-1914*, trans. Henry Collins and Kenneth Mitchell (London: Nelson and Sons, 1966). Between 1891 and 1914 controversies raged about the orthodx implications of Marx's social philosophy; see V.I. Lenin, *Materialism and Empirio-Criticism: Critical Comments on a Reactionary Philosophy*, vol. 13 of *Collected Works* (New York: International Publishers, 1927).

3. See Knapp, *Austrian Social Democracy*, esp. chapts. 2 and 3.

4. These student norms are described by two German-Austrian writers who grew up with them in Vienna: Stefan Zweig, *Die Welt von Gestern* (Frankfurt am Main: S. Fischer, 1955), translated as *The World of Yesterday* (Lincoln: University of Nebraska Press, 1964); and Arthur Schnitzler, *Jugend in Wien: Eine Autobiographie* (Vienna: S. Fischer, 1981), esp. Books 1-3.

5. See Carl E. Schorske, *Fin-de-Siecle Vienna: Politics and Culture* (New York, 1980), pp. 246–73.

6. Colin Murray Turbayne, *The Myth of Metaphor*, rev. ed. (Columbia: University of South Carolina Press, 1970), develops an understanding of metaphor taken from Gilbert Ryle, which holds that metaphor is the "presentation of the facts of one category in the

idioms appropriate to another" (Ryle, *The Concept of the Mind* [London: Hutchinson's University Library, 1949], p. 8).

7. Turbayne, *Myth of Metaphor*, pp. 21–26.

8. Freud calls such short- and long-term advantages *paranosic* and *epinosic* gains; see Freud, "Fragment of an Analysis of a Case of Hysteria," *Collected Papers*, 5 vols. (New York: Basic Books, 1959), 3:53-54 and n. 1. The creation of the metaphor and its abuse are seemingly unknown because they occur within an area of ideation which Freud terms the "preconscious," where the ego is also at work. This process is the same for normal as for neurotic individuals, and symptoms of a mental illness are equivalent in form and function to this syndrome of metaphorical abuse; see Freud, *Introductory Lectures on Psychoanalysis*, trans. and ed. James Strachey (New York: W.W. Norton, 1966), pp. 15-82, 257-72, 358-77, and 378-91.

9. My use of the term *instinct* combines the approaches of Sigmund Freud and Carl Gustav Jung. Freud defines an instinct as "denoting the mental representative of organic forces" and accepting "the popular distinction between egoistic instincts and sexual instinct; for such a distinction seems to agree with the biological conception that the individual had a double orientation, aiming on the one hand at self-preservation and on the other at the preservation of the species" ("A Case of Paranoia," *Collected Papers*, 3:461). Freud added a death instinct, or instinct for disintegration of organic life, in his later thought. Jung adds the instinct of personal self-development or individuation, which embraces religious, intellectual, and other aspects of the human spirit; see Jung, *The Basic Writings of C. G. Jung*, ed. Violet Staub De Laszlo (New York: Modern Library, 1959), pp. 50-54., 75-76, 405, and 534.

10. Anna Freud, daughter of Sigmund Freud, wrote a definitive study of ego defense in 1937, recognized by her father before his death. In regard to denial, see her *The Ego and the Mechanisms of Defense*, rev. ed. (New York: International Universities Press, 1966), pp. 83-92, 93-108.

11. See Sigmund Freud, *Civilization and Its Discontents*, trans. and ed. James Strachey (New York: W.W. Norton, 1961), pp. 88-91. Contemporary historian Hayden V. White explores the use of language by a particular society as it chooses to emphasize certain realities and exclude others in *Metahistory: The Historical Imagination in Nineteenth Century Europe* (Baltimore: Johns Hopkins University Press, 1973), and *Tropics of Discourse* (Baltimore: Johns Hopkins University Press, 1978). Although White does not infer psychological values to norms such as denial, his method of identifying the metaphorical patterns and their conceptual implications provides one basis for an evaluation of the mental health of a culture.

12. William M. Johnston, *The Austrian Mind: An Intellectual and Social History, 1848-1938* (Berkeley: University of California Press, 1972), pp. 2-3.

13. Among the modes of ego defense that will be explored in relation to Austro-Marxist thought and action are projection and introjection, as well as denial. As these concepts arise they will be defined in relation to the particular Austro-Marxist and his actions. Other psychodynamic operations that are pertinent in understanding the politics of metaphor will be explored at an appropriate point in the text. See Anna Freud, *Ego*, for a thorough review of Sigmund Freud's concepts of defense.

14. Peter Gay, *Style in History* (New York: Basic Books, 1974).

15. Carl Gustav Jung, *Psychological Types or The Psychology of Individuation*, trans. H. Godwin Baynes (London: Routledge & Kegan Paul, 1923). Sigmund Freud's theory of psychological types embraces the same distinctions in intellectual and behavior style but with differing conclusions as to their meaning; see Freud, "Libidinal Types," *Collected Papers*, 5:247-51.

16. Freud questions what standard should be used to determine whether a culture is healthy or neurotic in *Civilization and Its Discontents*, p. 81.

17. Austria in this study includes during the period considered the seventeen "crown lands" of Lower Austria, Upper Austria, Salzburg, Styria, Carinthia, Krain, Triest, Goerz and Gradiska, Istria, Tirol, Vorarlberg, Bohemia, Moravia, Silesia, Galicia, Bukowina, and Dalmatia. See Oscar Jaszi, *The Dissolution of the Habsburg Monarchy* (Chicago: University of Chicago Press, 1929), pp. 243-47, for a history of the system and the term "crown land."

18. Derived from a study of the Austrian censuses of 1890, 1900, and 1910; see Category D in "Ergebnisse der Volkszahlung," *Oesterreichisches statistischen Handbuches*, vols. 12, 22, and 32 (Vienna: K.K. statistischen Zentralkommission, 1893, 1903, 1913).

19. Zweig, *The World of Yesterday*, pp. 240, 55.

20. Hermann Bahr, *Bildung* (Berlin and Leipzig: Insel Verlag, 1900), p. 210.

21. *Statistisches Jahrbuch der Stadt Wien*, vol. 8, 1890 (Vienna, 1892), pp. 290-91; ibid., vol. 32, 1914 (Vienna, 1918), pp. 482-83. For an exhaustive bibliography of Vienna's press, see Kurt Paupie, *Handbuch der oesterreichischen Pressageschichte, 1848-1959* (Vienna: Wilhelm Brauemeuller Verlag, 1960), vol. 1.

22. The *Arbeiter-Zeitung*, organ of the Social Democratic party, for example, had a circulation of 9,000 in 1890 (as a biweekly), 15,000 in 1895 (as a daily), and 54,000 by 1914. These figures approximate the size of the party membership. See Sozialdemokratische Partei Oesterreich, *Protokoll der Verhandlungen des Parteitages der deutschen sozialdemokratischen Arbeiterpartei in Oesterreich, abgehalten in Wien vom 31. Oktober bis zum 4. November 1913* (Vienna: Wiener Volksbuchhandlung, 1913), p. 25 (hereafter cited as *Parteitag*, 1913).

23. See Schorske, *Fin-de-Siecle Vienna*, pp. 281-89, 292-95, 305, for a discussion of *Bildung* in Austrian-German culture.

24. See Johnson, *Austrian Mind*, pp. 66-73, for a succinct discussion of the Austrian educational system in the nineteenth and early twentieth centuries. For a critical history of the Austrian school system, see Ernst Papanek, *The Austrian School Reform* (New York: Friedrich Fell, 1962).

25. Karl Renner, *An der Wende Zweier Zeiten* (Vienna: Danubia, 1946), p. 281.

26. Ermers, *Victor Adler*, p. 193.

27. The *Volkpresse*, under the editorship of Rudolf Hanser and Adolf Heimann, called itself Social Democratic but opposed Victor Adler's tactical program. It had been a thorn in the side of Adler's orthodox Austrian Social Democracy since 1889. A showdown was inevitable, and finally in 1892 on the basis of party laws drafted in 1891, Hanser and the *Volkspresse* were expelled from the party. For a history of this affair, see *Victor Adlers Aufsaetze*, 6: 121ff., 126ff., 127ff., and 142ff.

28. Ermers, *Victor Adler*, p. 193.

29. At the Parteitag of 1894, the most contested issue was whether the staff of the *Arbeiter-Zeitung* was to be picked by the Austrian Social Democratic delegates as a whole or by the Viennese on the paper's editorial board. Victor Adler naturally supported the motion that the present editorial board alone should determine who should be hired. Adler won his motion by the narrow margin of 39 to 36, although most motions were carried unanimously. Apparently one reason for opposition was to leave open the possibility of non-Viennese intellectuals acquiring a post on the all-important paper. See the minutes of Sozialistiche Partei Oesterreich, *Verhandlungen des zweiten oesterreichischen sozialdemokratischen Parteitages, abgehalten zu Wien vom 25. bis einschliesslich 31. Maerz 1894 in Schwender's Kollosseum (Amorsaal)*, (Vienna: Wien Volksbuchhandlung, 1894) pp. 167-68, 176 (hereafter cited as *Parteitag*, 1894).

30. See Follis, "Austrian Social Democratic Party," pp. 11-12.

31. Approximately 33 percent of the membership of the party lived in Vienna. Most but not all the intellectuals in the party were in Vienna; see the statistics in *Parteitag*, 1913, p. 25.

32. The details of the Austrian Social Democratic party's organization can be found in the preface of each *Parteitag* report. For a general account of these changes see Julius Deutsch, *Geschichte der deutschoesterreichischen Arbeiterewegung: Eine Skizze von Julius Deutsch* (Vienna: R. Danneberg, 1919); and Follis, "Austrian Social Democratic Party," pp. 9–28.

33. *Victor Adlers Aufsaetze*, 6:121.

34. Blei, *Erzaehlung eines Lebens*, (Leipzig: Paul List, 1930), p. 143.

35. Sozialdemokratische Arbeiterpartei Oesterreich, *Verhandlungen der Parteitages der oesterreichischen Sozialdemokratie in Hainfield*, Vienna: Wiener Volksbuchhandlung, 1889, pp. 3–4 (hereafter cited as *Parteitag*, 1889).

36. Max Adler (A. Max), "Zu Frage der Organisation des Proletariats der Intelligenz," *Die Neue Zeit* 13, pt. 1, no. 21 (February 1895): 647.

37. Sigmund Freud, rooted in the individualism of his age, saw leadership within groups as a product of the members' desire for a leader who stood above them, who was more than their equal, and who was chosen because of his outstanding characteristics; see Freud, *Group Psychology and the Analysis of the Ego* (New York: 1960), pp. 67–68. Contemporary research, which focuses upon the interactional dynamics of the group, emphasizes that the effective group leader participates in and promotes the norms of his group; he is not an omnipotent individual beyond these norms; see W. R. Bion, *Experiences in Groups and Other Papers* (New York: Basic Books, 1961), pp. 121–22, and Morton A. Lieberman, Irvin D. Yalom, and Matthew B. Miles, *Encounter Groups: First Facts* (New York: Basic Books, 1973), pp. 433–35.

38. Immanuel Kant, *Religion within the Limits of Reason Alone*, trans. Theodore M. Greene and Hoyt H. Hudson (Chicago: Open Court Publishing Co., 1934), p. 176.

1. The Austro-Marxist Idea

1. See Tom Bottomore, and Patrick Goode, trans. and ed., *Austromarxism* (Oxford: Clarendon Press, 1978), pp. 2–3.

2. Some historians have included the German-Austrians Rufolf Hilferding, Gustav Eckstein, and Karl Kautsky among the Austro-Marxists. Between 1904 and 1918 Eckstein and Hilferding published within the series *Marx-Studien*, a joint effort of the Austro-Marxists. They spent most of their years after 1900 in Berlin working with Karl Kautsky, the founder of the *Neue Zeit*, the leading theoretical organ of German Social Democracy. Despite their shared political concepts, a distinction between Austrian and German Social Democracy must be maintained. Because my aim is to examine how the behavioral and ideational norms of Austria and the Austrian Social Democratic party served as a matrix for the Austro-Marxist political personality, I have excluded these men. Sharing my limitation of the Austro-Marxists to the four men I will deal with, for the same reasons, are Follis, "Austrian Social Democratic Party," and, though giving no criteria, Charles Adams Gulick, *Austria from Habsburg to Hitler*, 2 vols. (Berkeley: University of California Press, 1948), esp. 2: 1364–65. The term "Austro-Marxism" apparently was first employed before 1914 by an American socialist, Louis Boudin (Otto Bauer, "Max Adler, Ein Beitrag zur Geschichte des 'Austro-Marxismus,'" *Der Kampf* (Bruenn), 4, no. 8 [August 1937]: 300). I have been unable to locate this term in any of Boudin's writings.

3. Detlev Albers, Josef Hindels, and Lucio Lombardo Radice, *Otto Bauer und der "Dritte" Weg* (Frankfurt: Campus Verlag, 1979).

4. Peretz Merchav, "Otto Bauer und Max Adler," *Die Zukunft* 1 (January 1978): 35.

5. See Peter Heintel, *System und Ideologie: Der Austro-marxismus imn Spiegel der Philosophie Max Adlers* (Vienna: R. Oldenbourg, 1967).

6. Raimund Loew, "The Politics of Austro-Marxism," *New Left Review*, no. 118 (November–December 1979), pp. 17-20, 25-51; Knapp, *Austrian Social Democracy*, pp. 57-58.

7. Karl Marx, "Theses on Feuerbach," in *Basic Writings on Politics and Philosophy: Karl Marx and Friedrich Engels*, ed. Lewis S. Feuer, (New York: Doubleday Anchor, 1959), p. 245.

8. For a presentation of this argument, see Thomas Kuhn, *The Structure of Scientific Revolutions*, 2d ed. (Chicago: University of Chicago Press, 1979).

9. Leon Trotsky, *My Life* (New York: Scribner, 1930), pp. 208-9.

10. Jung, *Psychological Types*, pp. 480-89.

11. Ibid., pp. 428-45.

12. An excellent review of this controversy, bringing the arguments to the present need for an interpenetration of the two positions, is found in Derek Freeman, *Margaret Mead and Samoa: The Making and Unmaking of an Anthropological Myth* (Cambridge: Harvard University Press, 1983), pp. 3-64.

13. Max Weber's theoretical writings on the survey technique in 1908 create a model for research that combines behavioral observation, interview, and organizational analysis which is still fundamental to the study of the group process; see "A Research Strategy for the Study of Occupational Careers and Mobility Patterns," J.E.T. Eldridge, ed., *Max Weber: The Interpretation of Social Reality* (New York: Scribner, 1971), pp. 102-58.

14. The opening argument of Max Weber in his essay on the survey evidences the painful effort he had in demonstrating the validity of a "value-free" position in social science. Weber was not without a political position, and in it one may recognize the technocratic bias of his ethical neutrality; see his speech on socialism in 1918, which provides a rationale for a technical, bureaucratic social state, "Speech for the General Information of Austrian Officers in Vienna, 1918," ibid., pp. 191-222.

15. Alfred Adler's views on the psychological advantages one gains from mental illness and the roles of masculinity, aggression, and the inferiority complex in human action will be important in our consideration of Freidrich Adler. Sigmund Freud's review of Alfred Adler in 1914 is particularly lucid, even if biased; see Freud, *The History of the Psychoanalytic Movement*, ed. Philip Rieff (New York: Collier Books, 1963), pp. 83-91. Edmund Husserl sought the basis of human understanding in the logical operations of consciousness and a rigorous method of experiential description and analysis. For a discussion of Husserl's phenomenology, see Quentin Lauer, *Phenomenology: Its Genesis and Prospect* (New York: Harper & Row, 1965).

16. Max Adler, *Kausalitaet und Teleologie im Streite um die Wissenschaft*, vol. 1 of *Marx-Studien: Blätter zur Theorie und Politik des wissenschaftlichen Sozialismus*, 5 vols. (Vienna: Wiener Volksbuchhandlung, 1904-1923), pp. 202-3.

17. Max Adler, *Georg Simmels Bedeutung fuer die Geistesgeschichte* (Vienna: Anzergruber Verlag, 1919). For a review of the neo-Kantian movement in social criticism contemporary with Max Adler, see Karl Vorlaender, *Kant und der Sozialismus* (Berlin: Verlag von Reuther & Reichard, 1900), and Vorlaender, *Kant und Marx* (Tübingen: Verlag von J.C.B. Mohr [Paul Siebeck], 1911). A modern review of the several schools of neo-Kantian social criticism is found in Thomas E. Willey, *Back to Kant: The Revival of Kantianism in German Social and Historical Thought, 1860-1914* (Detroit: Wayne State University Press, 1978).

2. Karl Renner's Search for a Home

1. Karl Renner, "Karl Marx und die Arbeiter (Zu Marx's fuefundzwandzigsten Todestage)," *Der Kampf* 1 (March 1908): 241-42; emphasis added.

2. Quoted in Jacques Hannak, *Karl Renner und seine Zeit* (Vienna: Wiener Volksbuch-handlung, 1965), pp. 311-12.

3. See Freud, "Transference," *Introductory Lectures*, pp. 431-47; "The Dynamics of the Transference" (1912), *Collected Papers*, 2:312-22; and "Further Recommendations in the Technique of Psycho-Analysis, Observations on Transference-Love," (1915), ibid., pp. 377-91. Especially interesting in regard to transference and its appearance in nontherapeutic environments is Peter Loewenberg, "Emotional Problems in Graduate Education," *Journal of Higher Education* 40 (November 1969): 610-23; Loewenberg, who has studied the Austro-Marxists, describes the debilitating effect of unrecognized transference between graduate students and their advisers.

4. The healing potential of transference in life situations is described fully in Carl Gustav Jung, "The Psychology of the Transference," *The Practice of Psychotherapy*, trans. R.F.C. Hull, vol. 16, Bollingen Series 20 (Princeton: Princeton University Press, 1966), pp. 163-323.

5. Jacques Hannak, *Karl Renner und seine Zeit*, p. 56.

6. For sublimation, see Freud, *Ego*, especially the case study of altruism, pp. 122-34.

7. See Schorske, *Fin-de-Siecle Vienna*, pp. 181-207.

8. See Freud, *Civilization*, esp. pp. 81–92.

9. Renner, *An der Wende Zweier Zeiten*, p. 7.

10. Karl Renner, *Lyrisch-Soziale Dichtungen, eine Auswahl*, ed. Ernst K. Herlitzka, (Vienna: Ernst K. Herlitzka, 1950), pp. 11-12.

11. See Freud, pp. 52-53; Carl Frankenstein, *The Roots of the Ego: A Phenomenology of Dynamics and of Structure* (Baltimore: Williams & Wilkins, 1966), pp. 11-28, 60-65.

12. Frankenstein, *Roots of the Ego*, esp. p. 61; the implication of one's attitude type as a condition that can make actual experience more or less threatening is significant, for example, in Renner's case when we see how the external events that an introverted child might have disregarded as critical moments became crises for the extroverted Renner. Freud's libidinal types are similarly constitutive of certain significances in experience given their inclination. Renner would be called an "erotic-obsessional" type by Freud "dependent on persons who are *contemporary* objects and, at the same time, on the residues of *former* objects—parents, educators and ideal figures" ("Libidinal Types" [1931] *Collected Papers*, 5:249.

13. See Freud, *Three Essays on the Theory of Sexuality*, trans. and rev. James Strachey (New York, 1962), pp. 94-95, where Freud discusses the continuity of infantile object choice as one matures. Frankenstein's discussion of the persistence of infantile object influence in the person's later years is extensive and convincing; see *Roots of the Ego*, pp. 188-266.

14. Renner, *An der Wende Zweier Zeiten*, p. 11.

15. Renner points out that his sister Emilie who had "adopted" the infant Alnton was cool to him in the future because her child died (ibid., pp. 14-15). His continuing disquietude over his deceased brother is also evidenced by his interest in the play *Nathan der Weise* by G.E. Lessing, which has a dramatic recognition scene between two brothers separated over a lifetime (*Nathan der Weise* [Stuttgart: Reclam Verlag, n.d.], act 5, scene 8, pp. 128-34.

16. Renner, *An der Wende Zweier Zeiten*, p. 15.

17. Ibid., pp. 15-16, 22, 24.

18. Renner, "Karl Marx und die Arbeiter," p. 242.

19. Renner, *An der Wende Zweier Zeiten*, p. 8.

20. See Freud, *Ego*, pp. 109-21.

21. See Frankenstein, *Roots of the Ego*, pp. 158-62. If the father is absent, the child is forced to find meaning in external situations, and his ego will reflect such early demand for external relations (ibid., p. 234). Renner suffered this increased externalization in his ego

attitude. See Freud on the Oedipus complex, "The Development of the Libido and the Sexual Organizations" *Introductory Lectures*, pp. 329-38.

22. Renner, *An der Wende Zweier Zeiten*, p. 23.

23. Ibid., p. 7.

24. Oskar Helmer, *Aufbruch gegen das Unrecht* (Vienna: Wiener Volksbuchhandlung 1964), p. 74.

25. Renner, *An der Wende Zweier Zeiten,*, pp. 44, 47-48; final quote on p. 22.

26. Ibid., p. 151; emphasis added.

27. Ibid., pp. 107-8.

28. Ibid., pp. 109-10.

29. Ibid., p. 121.

30. See Freud, "The Ego and the Id" (1923b), *The Standard Edition of the Psychological Works of Sigmund Freud*, trans. James Strachey (London: Hogarth Press, 1953-1974), 19:28ff., and Anna Freud's extensive discussions of the superego's role in ego defense in *Ego*.

31. Freud, *Ego*, pp. 144-47.

32. Jean Piaget, *Six Psychological Studies*, trans. Anita Tenzer (New York: Vintage 1968), pp. 64-73.

33. Renner, *An der Wende Zweier Zeiten*, p. 175.

34. Ibid., pp. 158-60.

35. Ibid., p. 185.

36. Ibid., pp. 179, 186.

37. See Renner's loving description of the Viennese-German social order and his horror at the Czech nouveau riche who attempted to invade it, ibid., pp. 201-2.

38. Ibid., p. 199.

39. Ibid., pp. 199-200; emphasis added.

40. Ibid., p. 209.

41. Eugen Phillopovich was one of the founders of the Austrian Fabian society, a conscious imitation of the English model that sought to bring socialism through parliamentary participation. Phillopovich never involved himself in the Austrian Social Democratic party, presumably because it was too radical in its concept. See Hannak, *Renner*, pp. 57-59.

42. Jaszi, *Dissolution of the Habsburg Monarchy*, p. 180. Although Jaszi states that Renner's plans were "an enlargement of the principles of the Kremsier constitution," he gives the impression that Renner's enlargement was original in spirit and feasible in its projection.

43. Renner prepared an edition of Lassalle's writings after World War I; see Hannak, p. 313. As we shall see, such a move after Renner's behavior during the war was in the spirit of a sacrifice to one's patron god.

44. Renner, *An der Wende Zweier Zeiten*, pp. 217-18.

45. Ibid., pp. 245-46, 278; see also Hannak, *Renner*, pp. 48-49.

46. The "common-sense" characteristics of English pragmatism may seem to jar with the portrait I draw of Renner; but his English interest always retained a Germanic abstraction. Renner's topographical manipulation of administrative organizations found a source of inspiration in the model of English local self-government. England became for Renner, at least before its treachery in World War I, a utopia, a prime specimen for many of his abstractions on territorial nationals and the ground of language. See his article "Ein Zerrbild der Autonomie," *Der Kampf* 5 (February 1912): 200-205, wherein Renner not only holds up English self-government as the only alternative for Austria but gives lessons in English pronunciation at the bottom of each page.

47. Renner, *An der Wende Zweier Zeiten*, p. 251. The German text reads: "Ich fand es mit Reucksicht auf den Sozialismus beklagenswert, dass Karl Marx, dessen ganze Lehre eine einzige gewaltige Induktion aus den Wirtschaftstatsachen ist . . . dass bis heute keiner seiner

Interpreten das Werk aus dem Hegelschen in den John-Stuart-Millschen Stil, aus der abstrakt-destruktiven in die konkret-induktive Methode uebertragen hat."

48. Ibid., p. 226.

49. Ibid., p. 272.

50. Adolf Schaerf, "Karl Renner," *Neue Österreichische Biographie Ab 1815*, 9 (Vienna: Amalthea, 1956): 10.

51. See Norbert Leser, *Zwischen Reformismus und Bolschewismus* (Vienna: Europa, 1968), p. 351.

52. See Immanuel Kant, "What Is Enlightenment?" in *On History, Immanuel Kant*, ed. Lewis White Beck (New York: Library of the Liberal Arts, 1963), pp. 3-10. Kant's view of mental health presages Freud's recognition that marriage can be a regression to dependent, infantile forms of relations that one had with one's parents; see Freud, "Female Sexuality" (1931), *Collected Papers*, 5:258-59.

53. Renner, *An der Wende Zweier Zeiten*, pp. 212-13, 219.

54. Ibid., pp. 203-4.

55. In the introduction to *An der Wende Zweier Zeiten*, p. 5, Renner outlines four epochs of his life. Only the first was published; the second was to extend from his entry to the parliamentary library in 1897 until his entry into Parliament itself in 1907; the third was to extend from 1907 until 1919, when Renner became chancellor of the new Austrian state; and the fourth was to cover from 1920 until the outbreak of World War II. Losing sight for a moment that he is projecting his autobiography, Renner states in the Introduction that the second epoch will be called *Reichskrise* (Crisis of the state), the third, *Untergang der Donaumonarchie* (Decline of the Danube monarchy), and the fourth, *Zusammenbruch der ersten Republik* (Breakdown of the first republic); nothing can be more apropos of my thesis that Renner stifled a full development of his life by submerging his identity with that of the State than this confusion of the major stages of his own life with the political metaphors of Austria.

56. Renner, *An der Wende Zweier Zeiten*, p. 291.

57. Ibid., p. 298.

58. Ibid., p. 228; emphasis added.

59. Hannak, *Renner*, p. 66; Renner quoted in ibid., p. 597.

60. See Renner's tribute to Victor Adler, "Viktor Adler sechzigster Geburtstag," *Der Kampf* 5 (July 1912): 442-47, and to Pernerstorfer, *An der Wende Zweier Zeiten*, p. 281.

61. See Hannak, for activities and significant dates of Renner's life; also, Schaerf, "Karl Renner," pp. 9ff.

62. Hannak, *Renner*, p. 622.

63. Concurring with this opinion of Renner's relationship to Marxism, Hans Mommsen, a historian of nationality conflict and theory in the Austrian state, writes: "Renner was a lawyer; he was interested primarily in the constitutional-legal side of issues. In his earlier studies he took a positivistic legal standpoint, the normal one for Austrian constitutional law, and only later approached the question of nationality from a Marxian analysis. He conceived only dimly the political social structure of the nationality conflicts, continuously directing all problems of nationality back to the considerations of legal life, the rights that were denied to the 'children of nature' [*Naturburschen*] by Austrian law" (*Die Sozialdemokratie und die Nationalitaetenfrage im Habsburgischen Vielvoelkerstaat*, vol. 1, *Das Ringen un die supranationale Integration der Zisleithanischen Arbeiterbewegung (1887-1907)* [Vienna: Europa, 1963], p. 328).

3. Renner and the Interpretation of the State

1. Freud, *Civilization and Its Discontents*, p. 12.

2. Karl Renner, *Staat und Nation* (Vienna: Josef Dietel, 1899), pp. 10-11.

3. See Jaszi, *Dissolution of the Habsburg Monarchy*, pp. 243ff., for a history of the system and the term *Cisleithanian*; also Karl Renner, "Was sind unsere Kroenlaender?" *Der Kampf* 1 (June 1908): 400-409, for a legal analysis of the crown land.

4. Otto Bauer, "Der Boehmische Ausleich," *Der Kampf* 5 (August 1912): 481-88.

5. See Schorske, *Fin-de-Siecle Vienna*, pp. 116-80, for a discussion of Georg von Schoenerer, leader of the Austrian Pan-German sentiment in the last decades of the nineteenth century.

6. Karl Renner (pseudo. Rudolf Springer), "Die Frage der Kreis und Kroenlaender Verfassung," Part III, *Deutsche Worte* 19 (1900): 71.

7. Renner's reference to his creation of districts (*Kreisen* as "middle places" (*Mittelstelle*) ("Was sind unsere Kroenlaender?" p. 403), is evidence of his unconscious adherence to the Habsburg brand of state hierarchy and his wish to preserve its essential form. The centralized, imperative authority over diverse nations and multifarious peoples inherent in the Habsburg hierarchy, if not actually effective during its death throes, remained a necessity for Renner. As we shall see, this clinging to the necessity of centralized authority in matters of civil law often led him into legal antinomies when Renner attempted to define more exactly what might be decided by the "national corporations" he spoke of, or to what specific areas the civil powers of the districts might extend as agencies independent of Habsburg initiation.

8. Karl Renner (pseudo. Rudolf Springer), "Die Theorien zur Loesung der Nationaliaetenfrage," *Akademie: Revue Socialisticka* 9 (1899): 496. See also idem, "Territorialoder Personalhoheit?" ibid., 8 (1899): 344ff.; Renner, *Staat und Nation*, pp. 10-12.

9. Renner, *Staat und Nation*, p. 13-17.

10. As quoted in Hannak, *Renner*, p. 240.

11. See discussion of Social Democratic reaction to Renner's theory in Mommsen, *Die Sozialdemokratie*, 1: 330. Renner mentions the accusations quoted in the text in his article in *Deutsche Worte* of 1899; see Karl Renner (pseudo. Rudolf Springer), "Die innere Gebietspolitik mit besonderen Ruecksicht auf Oesterreich," *Deutsche Worte* 18 (1899): 437, n. 5.

12. Renner, "Die innere Gebietspolitik," pp. 433, 437ff.

13. Karl Renner, "Das Klasseninteresse des Proletariats an der Amtsprache," *Der Kampf* 1 (January 1908): 164.

14. Ibid., pp. 169-71.

15. See esp. Otto Bauer, "Nationale Minderheitschulen," *Der Kampf* (October 1909): 13ff.; Franz Tomascheck, "Nationale Minderheitschulen als sociale Erscheinung," *Der Kampf* 3 (December 1909): 63ff.; and Jakob Pistiner, "Minderheitschule und Assimilation," ibid., pp. 115ff.

16. Karl Renner, "Die nationalen Minderheitschulen, ein Schlusswort," *Der Kampf* 3 (March 1910): 253-55.

17. Karl Renner, *Das Selbstbestimmungsrecht der Nationen in besonderer Anwendung auf Oesterreich* (Vienna: Dauticke, 1918), pp. 14-15.

18. Renner, *Staat und Nation*, p. 1.

19. Ludwig Gumplowicz, *Rasse und Staat* (Vienna: Manz, 1875).

20. Renner, *Staat und Nation*, pp. 4-5, 7.

21. Quoted in ibid., p. 9.

22. Ibid., pp. 13-15.

23. See Mommsen, *Die Sozialdemokratie*, 2: 318-30.

24. Oscar Jaszi writes of Kremsier and Renner: "This plan of Dr. Renner . . . may be regarded as an enlargement of the principles of the Kremsier constitution (with the difference, however, that he would abolish the antiquated crownlands and substitute for them a fourfold division: Inner Austria, the country of the Sudets, the Littoral, and the Carpathian provinces)" (*Dissolution of the Habsburg Monarchy*, p. 179). Also see Mommsen, *Die Sozialdemokratie*, p. 318.

25. Eoetvoes conceived of nations as "historical-political individualities" and opposed the "crown land" system as an artificial barrier to the natural life of nations. Although not going as far as Renner did with the idea of national corporations with their own land, he did support ideas that lent themselves to recognition of increased autonomy for nations within the Austrian state. His chief writings on the subject were *Ueber die Gleichberechtigung der Nationalitaeten in Oesterreich* (Pest: C.A. Hartleben, 1850) and *Die Garantien der Macht und Einheit Oesterreichs* (Leipzig: F.A. Brockhaus, 1859). See Jaszi, *Dissolution of the Habsburg Monarchy*, pp. 244-45, 315-17, for a discussion of the ideas of Eoetvoes.

26. Fischhof (who was also important to Otto Bauer) participated in the revolution of 1848 as a liberal. Like Renner later, Fischhof conceived of a supranational state that granted its nations great autonomy in the handling of their cultural affairs. His system was dualistic yet part of one state. It was general enough in conception not to become a problem in any specific detail. Fischhof's major work on these ideas is *Oesterreich und die Buergschaften seines Bestandes* (Vienna: Wallis Hauser, 1869. For a discussion of Fischhof, see Jaszi, *Dissolution of the Habsburg Monarchy*, pp. 110-11, and Mommsen, *Die Sozialdemokratie*, 1: 318.

27. Otto Lang in 1897 proposed national parliaments based upon historical-geographic lines that recall Eoetvoes's concept of "historical-political individualities" with parallel national and state administration. His major writings on this theme was *Die Verfassung als Quelle des Nationalitaetenhaders in Oesterreich. Studie eines Patrioten* (Vienna and Leipzig: M. Breitenstein, 1897), and *Grundzuege feur eine endgueltige Loesung der Nationalitaetenfrage in Oesterreich, Ideen und Betrachtungen eines Patrioten* (Vienna and Leipzig: M. Breitenstein, 1897). F.R. von Herrnritt, a professor of law at the University of Vienna, wished to improve the legal status of nationalities within the Austrian state. His book, *Nationalitaet Rechtsbegriff* (Vienna: Manz, 1899), discussed a constitutional change that would protect the cultural needs of Austrian nations. Alfred von Offermann was a follower of Adolf Fischhof and author of *Die verfassungsrechtliche Vervollkommnung Oesterreichs* (Vienna: W. Braumúller, 1899). Offermann conceived a supranational state that divided national and state functions, in what Mommsen has termed a two-level system in contradistinction to Renner's attempt at an integration of national and state authority by creation of *Mittelstelle* (*Kreisen*). Etbin Kristan was a Social Democratic contemporary of Renner who during the Bruenn meeting of Austrian Social Democracy in 1899 that discussed the nationality question attacked Renner's ideas as unrealizable within the real context of politics. See Sozialdemokratische Arbeiterpartei Oesterreichs, *Verhandlungen des Gesamtparteitages der Sozialdemokratie in Gesterreich, abgehalten zu Bruenn vom 24 bis 29. September 1899 im "Arbeiterheim"* (Vienna: Wiener Volksbuchhandlung, 1899), p. 85 (hereafter cited as *Parteitag*, 1899). On all four men, see Mommsen, *Die Sozialdemokratie*, 2:318-19, 328.

28. August Bebel's *Die Frau und der Sozialismus* was first published in 1879, but because of the laws in Berlin against socialists and socialist publications, the first edition was hidden from the public. The book became so popular that by 1895 the twenty-fifth edition was published (Stuttgart: J.H.W. Dietz). Renner reviewed the book in 1909 in *Der Kampf* in honor of the fiftieth edition. See Karl Renner, "Bebel's 'Frau,' Zur fuenfzigsten Auflage des Buches," *Der Kampf* 3 (December 1909): 98ff. Renner speaks of this book as his first contact with socialist thought in *An der Wende Zweier Zeiten*, p. 196.

29. Renner, "Bebel's 'Frau,'" pp. 98-99.

30. Karl Renner, "Die Freiheit ueber alles," *Der Kampf* 1 (April 1908): 296, 292-93.

31. Karl Renner (pseud. Rudolf Springer), *Staat und Parlament, Kritische Studie ueber die oesterreichische Frage und das System der Interessenvertretung* (Vienna: Wiener Volksbuchhandlung, 1901), p. 5.

32. See Jean-Jacques Rousseau, "Whether the General Will Can Err," *The Social Contract* (Middlesex, England: Penguin Books, 1968), pp. 72-73.

33. Hannak, *Renner*, pp. 58-59.

34. Renner mentions this incident in a 1903 article on electoral reform (pseud. Rudolf Springer), "Die intellektuellen und industriellen Klassen und die Wahlreform: Mehrheits— oder Verhaeltniswahl?" *Deutsche Worte* 22 (1903): 308.

35. Karl Renner, "Unser Parteitage," *Der Kampf* 3 (October 1909): 3.

36. Karl Renner, "Das nationale Problem in der Verwaltung," *Der Kampf* 1 (October 1907): 26-27.

37. Renner experienced a social-psychological estrangement from bourgeois society as a consequence of his father's loss of property that was never overcome and gave impetus to his socialistic thought and practice. Karl Marx writes of such a condition prompted by one's investment of selfhood in property ("Economic and Philosophic Manuscripts," in *Karl Marx, Friedrich Engels: Collected Works*, 12 vols. (New York: International Publishers, 1976), 3:270-82).

Renner uses the term "alienation" (*Entfremdung* strictly in the sense of one's physical property being estranged. The psychological implications of the term, well known to Marx when writing in 1844, were foreign to Renner's vocabulary. See *The Institutions of Private Law and Their Social Functions*, trans. Agnes Schwarzwald, ed. Otto Kahn-Freund (London: Routledge and Kegan Paul, 1949), p. 88.

38. Renner, *Institutions of Private Law*, p. 251. Renner establishes the law as integral to human development even more strongly earlier in the text when he states that law functions to preserve the species: "The most ancient form of family constitution is an application of the natural law for every social order, then every economic and consequently every legal institution must fulfill a function therein. Marx and Engels have called this preservation of the species the production and reproduction of the material conditions of life on an expanding scale. It is the production and reproduction of human individuals as well as as of their conditions of existence. Thus, all legal institutions taken as a whole fulfill one function which comprises all others, that of the preservation of the species" (ibid., pp. 69-70). Obviously, to Marx "every economic and . . . every legal institution" did not serve the law of natural selection and heredity or he would never have become the father of communist economic revolt. Breaking into Renner's logic is the force of his own German bias that would preserve the authority of the state and the German hearth.

39. Preface to Marx's *Critique of Political Economy*, as quoted in ibid., p. 55, n. 2.

40. Friedrich Engels, preface to Marx's *Der Achtzehnte Brumaire*, 3d ed. (Hamburg, 1885), as quoted in ibid., p. 55, n. 2.

41. Ibid., pp. 252-53.

42. Revisionism was a movement in Social-Democratic thought in the 1890s and first decade of the twentieth century that believed economic change could be realized by compromise and cooperation with the existing bourgeois state rather than by political revolution. Revisionists did not see an inevitable dialectic in history which moved economics towards socialism; people made changes, and the power to change was in their reasoned problem-solving. See Gulick, *Austria from Habsburg To Hitler* 2: 1366-67. The major voice of Revisionism was the German Social Democrat Eduard Bernstein; see his *Die Voraussetzungen des Sozialismus und die Aufgaben der Sozialdemokratie* (Stuttgart: J.H.W. Dietz, 1899). For an exhaustive history of Revisionism and its effects on German and Austrian Social Democracy, see Erika

Rikkli, *Revisionismus, Ein Revisionversuch der deutschen marxistischen Theorie (1890-1914)*, Zuercher Volkswirtschaftliche Forschungen, vol. 25 (Zurich: R. Girsberger, 1936).

43. Renner, *Institutions of Private Law*, p. 46.

44. Karl Marx, "Economic-Philosophic Manuscripts of 1844," in *Karl Marx, Friedrich Engels: Collected works*, 3:313.

45. Ibid., p. 326.

46. Renner, *Institutions of Private Law*, pp. 46-47.

47. Ibid., p. 91.

48. Ibid., p. 53.

49. Ibid., pp. 268-69.

50. Ibid., p. 259.

51. Ibid., p. 88.

52. Ibid., p. 49.

53. Ibid., pp. 63, n. 13, 71, 78, n. 40.

54. Ibid., pp. 2-3. This recognition by Kahn-Freund puts into focus Renner's tendency to refer to the "cultural fathers" of his superego when deciding the justness of an issue. Renner was reinforced in such a tendency by the cultural norms of European law. The Anglo-Saxon tradition, it seems, resists superego dominance in cultural institutions such as the law.

55. Ibid., p. 8.

56. See especially Kahn-Freund's discussion in the "Introduction" ibid., pp. 9, 12-16.

57. Ibid., pp. 3-4.

58. See Knapp, *Austrian Social Democracy*, pp. 177-200.

59. Karl Renner, "Die 'Unfruchtbarkeit' des Volkshauses," *Der Kampf* (November 1909): 54-59.

60. Karl Renner, "Die Entwaffnung der Obstruktion," *Der Kampf* 3 (January 1910): 146.

61. Karl Renner, "Politische Windstille," *Der Kampf* 4 (February 1911): 193-200.

62. See Otto Bauer, "Gefahren des Reformismus," *Der Kampf* 3 (March 1910): 243-44.

63. Karl Renner, "Soziale Demonstrationen," *Der Kampf* 5 (October 1911): 1-4.

64. Karl Renner, "Steuerkaempfe und Steuerreform," *Der Kampf* 7 (February 1914): 193.

4. The Party as Family for Otto Bauer

1. *Otto Bauer, Eine Auswahl aus seinem Lebenswerk*, ed. Julius Braunthal (Vienna: Wiener Volksbuchhandlung 1961), pp. 14, 16. Except when otherwise noted, the biographical facts of Bauer are derived from this source.

2. See Sigmund Freud, "Fragment of an Analysis of a Case of Hysteria," *Collected Papers*, 3:13-146. The identification of "Dora" was kept a secret by Freud and his closest associates for reasons of medical ethics and the political sensitivity of Otto Bauer's position. A letter by Kurt Eissler to Hannah Fenichel, dated July 8, 1952, in the possession of the Sigmund Freud Archives, Library of Congress, establishes the identity of "Dora" as Ida Bauer; an unpublished manuscript by Peter Loewenberg, "Austro-marxism and Revolution: Otto Bauer, Freud's "Dora" Case, and the Crises of the First Austrian Republic," Department of History, University of California at Los Angeles, contains this information. Loewenberg cites the inference of this relationship in my dissertation (Blum, "The 'Austro-Marxists' Karl Renner, Otto Bauer, Max Adler, and Friedrich Adler and "Austro-Marxism" in Austria, 1890 to 1918: A Study in the Politics of Metaphor" [University of Pennsylvania,

1970], p. 208, n. 23) as the first scholarly identification of the relationship between Otto Bauer and "Dora." For an analysis of the relationship of brother and sister, see Arnold Rogow, "A Further Footnote to Freud's 'Fragment of a Case of Hysteria,'" *Journal of the American Psychoanalytic Association* 26 (1978): 331-56.

3. Philip Rieff argues that Freud should have paid more attention to the social dynamics of the family, which made mental defense to the point of illness inevitable in a child; Freud treated Ida Bauer as if with his help she could simply return to normal in such a setting. ("Introduction," in Sigmund Freud, *Dora: An Analysis of a Case of Hysteria* [New York: Collier, 1971], p. 10). Ida and Otto probably inherited the disposition to the disease; their father contracted syphilis before his marriage and exhibited symptoms of paralysis and mental disturbances associated with that venereal infection in the lifetime of his children. For a discussion of the etiology of hysteria see Freud, "A Reply to Criticisms on Anxiety-Neurosis" (1895), *Collected Papers* 1:107-27. Reference to the syphilis of Philip Bauer, the father, is in Freud, "Fragment of an Analysis of a Case of Hysteria," *Collected Papers*, 3:26-27, 28 (n. 1). Otto and Ida's mother was an obsessive compulsive; a description of her behavior, which matches Freud's symptomatology of the obsessional, defensive neuropsychosis, may be seen in *Otto Bauer, Eine Auswahl aus seinem Lebenswerk*, pp. 5-10. Freud called the mother's condition a "housewife psychosis," stating that she lacked the insight needed to justify the form of defense being an obsessional neurosis; see Freud, "Fragment of an Analysis of a Case of Hysteria," p. 28.

4. Arnold Rogow makes a similar diagnosis; see "Dora's Brother," *International Review of Psychoanalysis* 6 (1979): 239–59. Bauer's writings in both neurotic and normal times show the pervasiveness of a certain style of equivocation and level of abstraction. His peers reinforced his habits of thought for they found justification in the bold language that never was specific enough to promote action. If as Freud posits, there can be a neurotic culture, then the norms of that culture will support neurotic character types; Bauer was typical of the neurotic edge of Austrian-German culture.

5. The physical symptoms replace the symptomatic idea that could lead to the cause of the condition for the hysterical individual. The hysteric has a psychic gap in consciousness, a gap in the time the illness was first established neurologically. The hysterical personality cannot think through to the root of the original crises; rather, a disabling physical symptom emerges that takes one's concentration away from the disturbing event that caused the psychic trauma. The hysterical person creates the headaches, nervous coughing, even paralysis, to divert any thought that might lead to the psychic gap of the telling event(s). The displacement of attention may be through mental evasion, too; there are hysterics, and Otto and Ida are included, who use rational strategies to evade coming to grips with the times that cannot be faced; see Sigmund Freud, *The Origins of Psychoanalysis: Letters to Wilhelm Fliess, Drafts and Notes: 1887-1902*, ed. Marie Bonaparte, Anna Freud, and Ernst Kris (New York: Basic Books, 1954), esp. Letter 39 on Hysteria, pp. 154-55, and on the mental evasions of hysteria, Freud, "The Defense Neuro-Psychoses" (1894), *Collected Papers*, 1:65-66

6. See Freud, "A Case of Successful Treatment by Hypnotism, with Some Remarks on the Origin of Hysterical Symptoms through 'Counter-Will,'" (1893), *Collected Papers*, 5:33-46, esp. pp. 38-40. In his analysis of the expectational state of mind, Freud describes the "counter-will" and "antithetic idea" in the hysteric that cripple his action. One can be resolved on an action and have it suspended by the "counter-will"; this syndrome of behavior is most significant in understanding Bauer's equivocation.

7. The hysteric creates a pseudo-history of events that surrounds the psychic gap which he cannot and will not penetrate. Some historical accounts may be accurate if they do not touch the area of the psychic gap; see Freud, "Fragment of an Analysis of a Case of Hysteria," p. 41, for this appreciation. Otto Bauer's pseudo-histories are evident throughout

his historical writings. Freud states that obsessive-compulsive neurotics are most prone to such rational strategies, and hysteria can move toward obsessive-compulsion as the neurotic individual grows more ill. For the variety of rational strategies of evasion in obsessive thinking, see Freud, "Notes upon a Case of Obsessional Neurosis," (1909), *Three Case Histories* (New York: Collier, 1963), pp. 77-78.

8. See Philip Rieff, *Freud: The Mind of the Moralist* (New York: Doubleday Anchor Books, 1959), pp. 90-91, for a review of Freud's analysis of Ida Bauer's hyperintellectualism, which resisted dealing with the causes of her neurosis. Ida's style is echoed by Otto in his Social Democratic polemics. Treating reality as a dramatic event is related to making pseudo-histories in that one seeks to manage life by manipulating its outcomes and meanings. The neo-Freudian, Eric Berne, has studied how individuals develop "life scripts" which they use to shape the interactions they have with others over a lifetime. The ego-defense of theatrical reality is an attempt, in part, to give oneself information about one's problem. See Eric Berne, *Beyond Games and Scripts: Selections from His Major Writings*, ed. Claude M. Steiner and Carmen Kerr (New York: Ballantine, 1976), esp. pp. 135-312.

9. See *Otto Bauer, Eine Auswahl aus seinem Lebenswerk*, pp. 10-11, Rogow, "A Further Footnote to Freud's 'Fragment of a Case of Hysteria,'" pp. 346-47.

10. It is reported in Freud's study of Ida Bauer that Otto would seek to avoid taking sides in disputes between his parents but gradually was moved to support his mother. Nevertheless, in late adolescence he could say to Ida that their father should not be criticized for his affairs with other women because it gave him some happiness. His fairness, even when Freud says an Oedipal fixation would have been the natural tie that sided him with his mother, shows his strong superego impulse to find equity in conflicts. See Freud, "Fragment of an Analysis of a Case of Hysteria," pp. 29, 33-77.

11. Renner's identification with the aggressor combined attributes of his personal father and an impersonal public world whose representatives entered and disrupted his home. Bauer's identification involved his father and the public world, too; only in Bauer's case his father manipulated the public world rather than being a victim of it, thus Bauer took on a style of world controller. See Freud, *Ego*, pp. 109-21.

12. *Otto Bauer, Eine Auswahl aus seinem Lebenswerk*, p. 10.

13. Ibid.

14. See Leser, *Zwischen Reformismus und Bolschewismsus*, p. 415; Joseph Buttinger, *In the Twilight of Socialism: A History of the Revolutionary Socialists of Austria* (New York: Frederick A. Praeger, 1953), pp. 42-43.

15. Napoleon's tendency to reveal plans that it was in his own interest to keep secret is seen as a hysterical trait by Jung. See Stendahl, *A Life of Napoleon* (London: Rodale Press, 1956), p. 20; for Jung's thoughts on hysterical extraversion, *Psychological Types*, p. 421.

16. Bauer's equilibrium theory was not formally so named until after World War I; see Otto Bauer, "Das Gleichgewicht der Klassenkraefte," *Der Kampf* 17 (January 1924): 57-65. The theory was developing earlier in his attempt to justify the decision not to use the general strike or other assertive means to further social legislation in the face of an obstructive Parliament. He formulated the notion of a pause in history when the classes were in balance; see Bauer, "Ruhepausen der Geschichte," *Der Kampf* 3 (September 1910): 529-36, and "Volksvermehrung und social Entwicklung," *Der Kampf* 7 (April 1914): 322-29.

17. Robert Musil, *The Man without Qualities* (New York: Secker and Warburg, 1965), p. 59.

18. Julius Braunthal, *Victor und Friedrich Adler, Zwei Generationen Arbeiterbewegung* (Vienna: Wiener Volksbuchhandlung, 1965), p. 28-29.

19. See Victor Adler to Karl Kautsky, *Victor Adlers Briefwechsel mit August Bebel und Karl Kautsky*, A 129, July 9, 1918, p. 660: "One can rely on Otto not to commit excesses to the

right or to the left for he is clever enough to be more of a politician behind the scenes in private conferences than in his public statements."

20. Otto Bauer, editorial message, *Der Kampf* 1 (October 1907): 1.

21. *Otto Bauer, Eine Auswahl aus seinem Lebenswerk*, p. 19.

22. Otto Leichter, "Otto Bauer, 'der Mensch,'" *Die Zukunft* 8/9 (August, September 1951): 217.

23. Ibid., p. 218.

24. *Otto Bauer, Eine Auswahl aus seinem Lebenswerk*, p. 12.

25. Sigmund Freud, "The Aetiology of Hysteria" (1896), *Collected Papers*, 1:207.

26. *Otto Bauer, Eine Auswahl aus seinem Lebenswerk*, pp. 11-12.

27. See Freud, *Origins of Psychoanalysis*, pp. 109 (n.1), 111-12, 114-15, 152-53; also, Freud "Inhibitions, Symptoms, and Anxiety" (1926), *The Standard Edition of the Complete Psychological Works of Sigmund Freud*, trans. James Strachey, (London, 1959), 20:126, 128. Finally, Anna Freud places the operation of projection in a readable case study in *Ego*, pp. 122-23, 126-27. Bauer's projection of his own disturbing needs and traits is especially evident in his occasional studies of individual personality. See his studies of Victor Adler, August Bebel, Sigmund Kunfi, Max Adler, Ignaz Seipel, and Julius Martow in *Otto Bauer, Eine Auswahl aus seinem Lebenswerk*, pp. 205-44. For example, in discussing how Victor Adler was a "physician" to the Marxist attitudes of party members, keeping them in touch with concrete realities, he unwittingly exposed his own chief problem never conquered (p. 209); in his surprising paean to Ignaz Seipel, on the occasion of his death, he evidenced how Seipel was his mirror image, perhaps even the image of his father, as he manifested "unusual self-control . . . and an impenetrable mask which gave him the appearance that he was a cold, passionless man" (239).

28. *Otto Bauer, Eine Auswahl aus seinem Lebenswerk*, p. 12.

29. Otto Bauer, "Das Finanzkapital," *Der Kampf* 3 (June 1910): 391-97.

30. Otto Bauer to Karl Kautsky, 1904, Karl Kautsky Archive, item K.D. II, 463, Instituut voor Sociale Geschiedenis, Amsterdam.

31. Otto Bauer, "Buecherschau," *Der Kampf* 1 (November 1907): 94.

32. Otto Bauer, "Die Arbeiterbibliothek," *Der Kampf* 1 (October 1907): 48.

33. Otto Bauer, "Eine Parteischule fuer Deutschoesterreich," *Der Kampf* 10 (January 1910): 173-75.

34. Ibid., p. 174.

35. Oskar Helmer, "Die Parteischule in Klagenfurt," *Der Kampf* 5 (October 1911): 39.

36. Heinrich Wissiak, "Die Parteischule in Bodenbach," *Der Kampf* 4 (October 1910): 16.

37. Helmer, "Die Parteischule in Klagenfurt," p. 39.

38. Inflation is a Jungian concept that is associated with the process of projection. When one sees others in the environment as having the attributes that are really his own, he tends unconsciously to equate the public world with his own person. Thus the impulsion of his needs as they are projected onto others seems to carry a historical-social significance for everyone who is in the shared public world. The projecting individual gains a heightened self-importance because he sees what is happening and important (in others). "In other words, if the individual identifies himself with the contents awaiting integration, a positive or negative inflation results. Positive inflation comes very near to a more or less conscious megalomania; negative inflation is felt as annihilation of the ego. The two conditions may alternate" (Jung, "The Psychology of the Transference," *Practice of Psychotherapy*, 16:263-64.

39. Leo Por, *Kautsky und Otto Bauer in der Beleuchtung der Psycho-analyses* (Budapest: Verlag Emmerich Faust, n.d.).

40. See his description of his condition in a letter to Karl Kautsky, March 30, 1910, Kark Kautsky Archive, item K.D. II, 480.
41. Otto Bauer to Karl Kautsky, September 25, 1913, ibid., item K.D. II, 498.
42. *Otto Bauer, Eine Auswahl aus seinem Lebenswerk*, p. 10; see also the letter to Kautsky, (September 25, 1913).
43. *Otto Bauer, Eine Auswahl aus seinem Lebenswerk*, pp. 21-22.
44. Otto Bauer, "Victor Adler," ibid., p. 208.

5. Bauer's Cultural Dialectics

1. Por, *Kautsky und Bauer*, p. 1.
2. Bauer to Kautsky, January 26, 1906, Karl Kautsky Archive, item K.D. II, 472.
3. Bauer to Kautsky, March 13, 1906, ibid., item K.D. II, 474.
4. Bauer to Kautsky, February 4, 1906, ibid., item K.D. II, 473.
5. Kautsky to Adler, September 26, 1909, *Victor Adlers Briefwechsel mit August Bebel und Karl Kautsky* p. 502.
6. Otto Bauer, *Die Nationalitaetenfrage und die Sozialdemokratie* (Vienna: Wiener Volks-buchhandlung, 1907), pp. 122-23.
7. Ibid., p. 21.
8. Ibid., p. 114.
9. Ibid., p. 1.
10. Ibid., p. 26.
11. Ibid., pp. 30, 112-13.
12. Ibid., p. 111.
13. Ibid., p. 139.
14. Ibid., p. 373.
15. Ibid., pp. 371-72.
16. Ibid., p. 164.
17. Otto Bauer, *Deutschtum und Sozialdemokratie* (Vienna: Wiener Volksbuchhandlung, 1907), pp. 13-14.
18. Ibid., p. 210.
19. Ludo Hartmann, "Zur Nationaler Debatte," *Der Kampf* 5, (January 1912): 152ff.
20. Otto Bauer, "Die Bedingungen der Nationalen Assimilation," *Der Kampf* 5 (March 1912): 247-59.
21. Ibid., pp. 262-63.
22. Ibid., pp. 263, 249.
23. Otto Bauer, "Gesamtparteitage und Gewerkschaftfrage," *Der Kampf* 4 (September 1911): 557.
24. See Pavel Eisner, *Franz Kafka and Prague* (New York: Golden Griffin Books, 1950), for the argument that the Czechs served the same function for Franz Kafka—as a metaphorical vehicle for his neglected self.
25. Bauer, "Gesamtparteitage und Gewerkschaftfrage," p. 564.
26. Otto Bauer, "Zu neuen Formen," *Der Kampf* 4 (July 1911): 445-51.
27. Bauer to Kautsky, March 11, 1911, Karl Kautsky Archive, item K.D. II, 485.
28. See Mommsen, *Die Sozialdemokratie*, 1:438, 447; Bauer to Kautsky, July 8, 1911, Karl Kautsky Archive, item K.D. II, 491.
29. Bauer, "Zu neuen Formen," p. 451.
30. Otto Bauer, "Die Gesamtpartei," *Der Kampf* 6 (October 1912): 8, 13.

31. Otto Bauer, (pseud. Karl Mann), "Bourgeoisie und Militarismus," *Der Kampf* 5 (July 1912): 451.

32. Otto Bauer, "Oesterreich auswaertige Politik und die Sozialdemokratie," *Der Kampf* 1 (January 1908): 148.

33. Otto Bauer (pseud. Heinrich Weber), "Elemente unserer auswaertigen Politik," *Der Kampf* 2 (November 1908): 87.

34. Jaszi, *Dissolution of the Habsburg Monarchy*, p. 418. Carl Schorske, *German Social Democracy, 1905-1917* (Cambridge: Harvard Univ. Press, 1955), p. 87.

35. Otto Bauer, "Die starke Regierung oder die starke Democratic," *Der Kampf* 3 (December 1909): 105.

36. Otto Bauer (pseud. Heinrich Weber), "Nationale und Internationale Gesichtspunkte in der awswaertigen Politik," *Der Kampf* 2 (September 1909): 540, 537.

37. Otto Bauer, "Der Kampf um Albanien," *Der Kampf* 6 (December 1912): 107-10.

38. See Otto Bauer, "Nach dem Balkankrieg," *Der Kampf* 6 (August 1913): 344-45.

39. Ibid.

40. Otto Bauer, "Der zweite Balkankrieg," *Der Kampf* 6 (August 1913): 488.

41. Otto Bauer, "Parlamentarismus und Arbeiterschaft," *Der Kampf* 1 (August 1908): 486.

42. Ibid., pp. 487–88.

43. Otto Bauer, "Die Lehren des Zusammenbruchs," *Der Kampf* 2 (August 1909): 484.

44. Otto Bauer, "Buecherschau," *Der Kampf* 4 (January 1911): 191.

45. Ibid., p. 191. See also Mommsen, *Die Sozialdemokratie und die Nationalitaetenfrage in habsburgischen Vielvoelkerstaat*, vol. 1, p. 316.

46. Otto Bauer, "Buecherschau," p. 192.

47. Ibid., pp. 191, 192.

6. Max Adler, the Eternal Youth

1. See *Neue deutsche Biographie* (Berlin: Duncker and Humblot, 1952), s.v. "Max Adler."

2. Max Adler (pseud. A. Max), "Zur Frage der Organisation des Proletariats der Intelligenz," *Die Neue Zeit* 13, no. 21 (February 1895): 647.

3. Ibid., p. 690.

4. Adler's concept of the "new person" (*Neue Menschen*) was articulated as early as 1904 in his address commemorating the hundredth anniversary of Kant's death; see *Immanuel Kant zum Gedaechtnis!* (Vienna: Franz Deuticke, 1904). A reprint of the address with new notes was published in *Wegseiser. Studien zur Geistesgeschichte des Sozialismus* (Stuttgart: J.H.W. Dietz, 1914), pp. 47-77. In 1924 he published a work called *Neue Menschen* (Berlin: E. Laube). The concept is grounded in a new education into social reality wherein the individual is taught to see the possibility of change in the present so that one is not "corrupted" (*verderbt*) by accommodating to present reality; see "Immanuel Kant," *Wegweiser*, pp. 76-77.

5. Adler, *Wegweiser*, p. 195.

6. The polarities encompassed by *Brand* and *Peer Gynt* are seen by many critics to encompass the dilemma of man, modern man in particular. The twentieth-century search for solid values with which to base a self-identification usually finds its focus through the ethical imperative of *Brand* or the existential gropings of *Peer Gynt*. See Henrik Ibsen, *Peer Gynt* (New York: New American Library, 1964), pp. xxxiii-xxix.

7. Max Adler, "Fichte's Idee der Nationalerziehung," *Der Kampf* 7 (February 1914): 207. Fichte, according to Adler, had postulated a "transition age of man" when instinct and

reason would battle for ascendancy, i.e., the Peer Gynt–Brand struggle. Adler clearly saw that the twentieth century was such an age. Freud, who sought to awaken man to the truth of instinct and Peer Gynt, would have answered Adler that only by dwelling in the facts of the self, in its everyday manifestations, could ideas be really valid and not merely "paralogisms" of self-evasion.

8. Max Adler, "Allerlei Kriegsmetaphysik," *Der Kampf* 9 (December 1916): 442-43.

9. Adler, "Fichte's Idee der Nationalerziehung," pp. 206-7.

10. The first work of Adler, *Kausalitaet und Teleologie im Streite um die Wissenschaft*, is the best source of his thought linking Kant and Marx. A good short survey is in his essay "Das Formalpsychische im historischen Materialismus," *Marxistische Probleme. Beitraege zur Theorie der materialistischen Geschichtsauffassung und Dialektik* (Stuttgart: J.H.W. Dietz, 1914), pp. 1-17.

11. This idea will be more fully explored in chapter 7. Kant introduced the category of community in his discussion of the pure concepts of understanding (*Critique of Pure Reason*, trans. Norman Kemp Smith (London: MacMillan, [1968]), B 108-B 111, pp. 114-16).

12. The study of groups as interdependent communities in which individuals achieve opportunity and identity did not begin until the 1930s in Europe or the United States. Before that, groups were seen primarily as a negative force acting upon individuals; see "Groups: The Study of Groups" and "Group Behavior" in the *International Encyclopedia of the Social Sciences* (New York: Macmillan, 1968), 6:259-64, 265-75.

13. Adler, *Immanuel Kant*, p. 52.

14. Friedrich Abendroth-Weigend, "Max Adlers transzendentale Grundlegung des Sozialismus: als Beitrag zur Methodenfrage des Marxismus verstanden" (Ph.D. dissertation, University of Vienna, 1959), p. 114.

15. Max Adler's curriculum vitae, item Ad 16216, Staatsamt feur Unterricht, Vienna. This document and others completed by Adler for the University of Vienna in 1919 may be examined only with the permission of the minister of education for Austria. There is a fifty-year moratorium on all documents at the Staatsamt feur Unterricht, where copies of the university files are kept (the original copies of Adler's curriculum vitae and other papers housed at the University of Vienna were destroyed in an air raid during World War II). Adler's papers are under the item number 16216; included among the documents is a description by Adler of the courses he will teach for the fall semester of 1919 (item 16216 19).

16. See s.v. "Max Adler" in the following: *Neue deutsche Biographie*; *Oesterreichisches Biographisches Lexikon, 1815-1950* (Graz-Cologue: Hermann Boehlhaus, 1957); *Philosophen-Lexikon* (Berlin: Walter de Gruyter, 1949). Articles on Adler generally deal with aspects of his ideas rather than describing or reporting any aspect of his personal life.

17. Renner, *An der Wende Zweier Zeiten*, pp. 278-79.

18. Abendroth-Weigand, "Max Adlers transzendentale Grundlegung," p. 114.

19. See *Neue deutsche Biographie*. s.v. "Max Adler."

20. See Carl Gustav Jung, *Symbols of Transformation: An Analysis of the Prelude to a Case of Schizophrenia*, 2d ed. trans. R.F.C. Hull, Bollingen Series 20 (Princeton: Princeton University Press, 1967), 5:258-59; the condition is more fully analyzed by M.L. von Franz in *Puer Aeternus*, (Santa Monica: Sigo Press, 1981).

21. According to Jung, one is healthy if, when confronted with the force of an idea that has collective validity, one integrates the idea into the existing forms of culture that correspond to it and does not identify oneself too closely with the origin of the idea or its magnitude. A neurosis develops when the individual uses the energy of the idea as a defense against developing the other aspects of his psychobiological life. The defense strategy uses the same psychodynamic processes of thought and behavior as in Freud's understanding of the psychoneuroses, i.e., metaphorical abuse of the idea, hyperintellectualism, and a tendency to project the idea onto the environment as a symbol for the unrealized aspects and conflicts of

one's life. The thought suffers, and the idea is never properly developed. See Jung's discussion of compulsion by a collective idea (i.e., an archetypal idea), in Jung, *Archetypes and the Collective Unconscious*, 2d ed. trans by R.F.C. Hull, Bollingen Series 20 (Princeton: Princeton University Press, 1969), 9, pt. 1: 8, 47-48.

22. I mention this controversial analogy to highlight the force of the idea Adler struggled with. One can read Kafka's *The Castle* as a tale of the inescapable rootedness of the individual in the social world (*vergesellschaftung*) whose invisible but omnipresent structures must be discovered. Adler's *Das Raetsel der Gesellschaft* (Riddle of Society), written at the end of his life, reflects such a theoretical position. Adler was attracted to Nietzsche and may have seen a similar position to his in sections of the *Gay Science*, for instance, in which Nietzsche refers to Kant's insight that truth is with the common man, but at a level that cannot be popularly seen (Aphorism 193).

23. Abendroth-Weigand concurs: "The basic premises of Max Adler's work and theory were unchanging over his lifetime. Everything there is to know about him as a thinker and a socialist can be found in his first two publications "Max Adlers transzendentale Grundlegung," p. 1). Adler's second work, on Kant, was also published in 1904.

24. Jung, pp. 3-41.

25. Max Adler, *Das Raetsel der Gesellschaft zur Erkenntnis-Kristischen Grundlegung der Sozialwissenschaft* (Vienna: Saturn Verlag, 1936), pp. 118-19.

26. Jung, *Archetypes*, pp. 20-21. See also M.L. von Franz, "The Process of Individuation," in *Man and His Symbols*, ed. C.G. Jung, (New York: 1979), pp. 171-85.

27. Max Adler, "Der Schatten. Drama von M.E. Della Grazie. Erstauffuehrung im Wiener Burgtheater," *Deutsche Worte* 20 (1901): 342-44, 348.

28. Such study could be made of human interaction with persons, objects in the environment, cultural artifacts, or any experience; see Lauer, *Phenomenology*, p. 94: "The ideal of philosophy would be to grasp acts so perfectly that their objects would be grasped perfectly. Even where the ideal is not attained, however, Husserl claims that objects can be adequately distinguished in this way. . . . He intends the principle to be applicable to all objects, whether they be events, logical categories, social structures, or abstract qualities, even though the ultimate nuances of the objects may not be successfully determined."

29. Adler, *Das Raetsel der Gesellschaft*, pp. 288-89 and note.

30. Adler, "Immanuel Kant," *Wegweiser*, p. 67.

31. Georg Simmel, "Dantes Psychologie," *Zeitschrift fuer Voelkerpsychologie und Sprachwissenschaft* (1884), 15:18-69, 239-76; Simmel, *On Individuality and Social Forms*, ed. Donald N. Levine, (Chicago: University of Chicago Press, 1971), pp. 141-214.

32. Adler, *Georg Simmels Bedeutung fuer die Geistesgeschichte*, p. 42.

33. The schemata in Kantian terms are the transcendental structures of imagination that guide comprehension of perceived experience. They are a combination of a category of the understanding, such as community, with a form of intuition, that is, sensible elements of space and time, so as to provide a regulative vision that produces each particular moment of perceived experience; see Kant, *Critique of Pure Reason*, B 177-B187, pp. 180-87.

34. Max Adler, *Die Staatsauffassung des Marxismus, Ein Beitrag zur Unterscheidung von Soziologischer und Juristischer Methode* (Darmstadt: Wissenschafliche Buchgesellschaft, 1964); the work was first published in 1922 in the *Marx-Studien*, vol. 4, pt. 2.

35. The schemata that guide individual judgment in moments of perception and decision are laws of consciousness, thus rules of our organism. Kant's sense of the human species gradually achieving a healthy civilization by recognition of the rules of its own makeup is similar to Marx's idea that the human species in culture moves inevitably to the communist state simply by recognition of its own needs in more rational forms of political and social organization. Max Adler draws this parallel in "Immanuel Kant," *Wegweiser*, p. 64. The

implication is that if one could identify and define the schemata of the social a priori, a standard of health would be created for human interaction against which the variances of given cultures could be measured.

36. In an extended debate with the neo-Kantian Rudolf Stammler over a period of years, Adler's chief objection was to Stammler's failure to ground his studies of legal norms in a thorough relation to Kant's categories of consciousness; see, for example, *Marxistische Probleme*, p. 181. Stammler's understanding of Kant's ethics and practical reason allowed him to omit such an explicit grounding; see chapter 7 on Stammler and his study of the regulating norms of culture. Adler criticized Simmel for lacking a theoretical basis for his thought.

37. Adler, *Marxistische Probleme*, pp. 166-67.

38. See ibid., p. 227, n. 8.

39. Adler, *Kausalitaet und Teleologie*, p. 156.

40. Bauer wrote of Adler's concern with death: "Max Adler struggled his whole life with the problem of death. The thought was unbearable to him that a rich and creative spirit could suddenly be destroyed by some chance of fate that destroyed the body. That was certainly the personal root of his devotion to the philosophy of Kant: if space and time are nothing but forms of our intuition, to which nothing must of necessity correspond in the unknown realm of the *Ding an Sich*, may we not then, in order to satisfy the needs of our mind, postulate a realm beyond our experience that is timeless and spaceless, where the spirit lives eternally? I was in my youth a pupil of his philosophy; I became mistrustful of his Kantianism and Kant for the first time when in a friendly conversation I realized that for him epistemology satisfied a metaphysical need" (Bauer, "Max Adler, Ein Beitrag," p. 301).

41. Adler, *Kausalitaet und Teleologie*, p. 156 n.

42. See Plato, *Phaedo* (63b-65a). One could read this passage as an affirmation of Max Adler's resistance to a historical ego, but when one considers how Socrates freed himself *through* experience and reflection on that experience, we realize that his words are not a life-denial; see also Plato, *Symposium* (209c-210c) as Diotima describes how to embrace life in a knowing manner.

43. Otto Bauer, "Deutsche Parteiliteratur," *Der Kampf* 3 (July 1910): 479.

7. Max Adler, the Incomplete Theoretician

1. The words "lazy," "lax," and "thought lacking the power to create unity" appear throughout Adler's criticism of other thinkers. For example, the "laziness" of thinkers [*Denk-faulheit*] who do not interpret Kant correctly, in "Immanuel Kant," *Wegweiser*, p. 52; the "lax" thought of Stammler in defining social science in *Marxistische Probleme*, p. 158; and the lack of strength to create unity in Simmel, who allowed so much of life to lie beside him as accidental and unexplained matter, in *Georg Simmels Bedeutung*, p. 42.

2. Adler, *Immanuel Kant*, p. 20. The poetry is from Goethe's *Faust* (lines 661-63). I have used the translation of Randall Jarrell, *Goethe's Faust*, pt. 1 (New York: Farrar, Straus, and Giroux, 1976), p. 34.

3. Faust is a character in the tradition of Promethean heroes in European, especially German, culture. The individual who through intellect brings a new vision of life and im-provement to civilization is an honored archetype; see Oskar Walzel, *Das Prometheussymbol von Shaftesbury zu Goethe* (Leipzig: Teubner, 1910). Faust is also a positive symbol of the *puer aeternus*. At a certain stage of development, the culture-bringer becomes a child so that he can see the world more openly. See Jung, "Answer to Job," *Psychology and Religion: West and East*, 2d ed. trans. R.F.C. Hull, Bollingen Series 20 (Princeton: Princeton University Press, 1969), 11:457. For Adler this would have meant relaxation of the reified Marxist concepts

and a return to open, phenomenological introspection of social experience, even if evidence eventually reinstated these concepts.

4. Adler, *Kausalitaet und Teleologie*, p. 222.

5. Adler, *Das Raetsel der Gesellschaft*, pp. 32-33.

6. Ibid., p. 289.

7. Ibid., pp. 91-92, n.

8. See Edmund Husserl, *Logische Untersuchungen, Prolegomena zur reinen Logik*, 2 vols. (Halle: Max Niemeyer, 1900-1901); *Ideen zu einer reinen Phaenomenologie und phaenomenologische Philosophie* (Halle: Max Niemeyer, 1913).

9. Ernst Cassirer developed an understanding of Kant that paralleled Max Adler's search for the "psychic forms" that condition individual judgment. His major work in this area was the *Philosophy of Symbolic Forms*, 3 vols. (New Haven: Yale University Press, 1955, 1957). Cassirer's *Kant's Life and Thought* (New Haven: Yale University Press, 1981), pp. 271-360, offered a thorough discussion of the problematic of teleology and causal understanding central to Adler's search for the social a priori. Cassirer's *Freiheit und Form* (Berlin: Cassirer, 1916) offered a history of the problem of individuality within the laws of understanding and spirit in German culture from Luther through the early nineteenth century.

10. Adler's criticism of Rudolf Stammler began with Stammler's publication of *Wirtschaft und Recht nach der materialistischen Geschichtsauffassung* in 1896. Adler's articles were not published, however, until their inclusion in *Marxistische Probleme* in 1914. He did not publish them at first because he had not made a "sufficient analysis of the social concept" and the "epistemological foundation of social life," which he accomplished in *Kausalitaet und Teleologies*. See Adler's reflection on Stammler in *Marxistische Probleme*, p. 150, n. 1; and the articles on Stammler in ibid., pp. 150-83, 214-54. Stammler consumed an inordinate proportion of Max Adler's thought; his significance will be developed below. It is interesting that Adler's earliest Marxist thinking was an attempt to show the failure of will in Stammler to insist on a definite epistemological basis for social norms, yet he rejected cultural evidence that could have helped his own research.

11. Immanuel Kant, *Idea for a Universal History from a Cosmopolitan Point of View*, in *On History*, trans. Beck, Anchor, and Fackenheim, p. 15. *Sich mehr als Mensch* is translated as "more than a man." The sense of Kant's thesis that one finds his capacities as a person in social dialogue, which is strengthened by Adler's interpretation, makes such a translation nonsensical. A literal translation is "more as [*als*] a person"; see Adler, "Immanuel Kant," *Wegweiser*, p. 55.

12. Kant, "Idea for a Universal History," p. 16.

13. Adler, "Immanuel Kant," *Wegweiser*, pp. 60-61.

14. Kant, "Idea for a Universal History," p. 15; Adler, "Immanuel Kant," *Wegweiser*, p. 56.

15. Adler, "Immanuel Kant," *Wegweiser*, p. 64.

16. Ibid., pp. 60-61; also Adler, *Marxistische Probleme*, pp. 1-17, 35-59. Adler attacked historical materialists, who saw the dialectic as a mystic force in history apart from the decisions of individuals. The forward movement of the historical dialectic was a result of a positive view of human thought; Adler, as Kant and Marx, expected the majority of people to realize the best solution for themselves given the existing dilemmas.

17. Max Adler, "Dialektik des Werdens," *Der Kampf* 4 (December 1911): 125-26.

18. See Sigmund Freud, *Introductory Lectures*, pp. 448-63.

19. Most of Marx's writings that reflected his careful analysis of the role of consciousness in social experience were not published until 1932. *The German Ideology* and the "Economic and Philosophic Manuscripts of 1844," which contain the most discursive analyses of consciousness, appeared in the *Marx-Engels Gesamtausgabe* in 1932, published in Berlin; see

"Chronology: Marx's Chief Works" in *The Portable Karl Marx*, ed. Eugene Kamenka (New York: Penguin Books, 1983), pp. ci-cxii. Max Adler had access only to a bowdlerized version of *The German Ideology* published by Franz Mehring in 1902; see *Gesammelte Schriften von Karl Marx und Friedrich Engels, 1841-1850*, 3 vols. (Stuttgart: J.H.W. Dietz, 1902). Mehring deliberately excluded epistemological writings such as the *Economic and Philosophic Manuscripts of 1844* from the edition so as to stress the social revolutionary materialism of Marx. Max Adler squeezed blood from a stone; see his comments on Marx's few published statements on consciousness in *Kausalitaet und Teleologie*, pp. 5-6, and "Das Formalpsychische im historischen Materialismus," in *Marxistische Probleme*, pp. 4-5 and n. 2.

20. Adler developed the processes and implications of a social therapy gradually. His last work, *Das Raetsel der Gesellschaft*, contains the added checks on true judgments that include the opinions of others and a phenomenological psychology that offers a systematic etiology of experience; see pp. 90-91, 288-89. The notions are in his first two works, especially the discussion of the antagonistic nature of social intercourse as a necessary dimension of involvement. Freudian psychology relies on a dialogue between the individual and the analyst; without the necessary presence of the analyst, the individual would not be able to listen to his own words as a social fact or have the intervention that could cause a heightened sense of reflection; see Freud, *New Introductory Lectures on Psychoanalysis* (1932), in *Standard Edition*, 22: 12-14. The systematic etiology is likewise critical in helping the individual arrive at an understanding of the true judgment; see ibid., p. 13.

21. Adler, *Kausalitaet und Teleologie*, p. 202.

22. Ibid., pp. 202-5.

23. Ibid., p. 241.

24. Adler stressed the necessity of goodwill among individuals who serve as tests for a true judgment (*Das Raetsel der Gesellschaft*, p. 91). For Kant goodwill is the highest state of human action, for any skill or disposition without it can lead to harmful ends (*Fundamental Principles of the Metaphysics of Morals* [Indianpolis: Bobbs-Merrill, 1949], pp. 14-15). The existentialist philosopher and Marxist Jean-Paul Sartre made good faith the fundamental attitude for any approach to an authentic, that is, true, transaction between individuals (*Being and Nothingness*, trans. Hazel Barnes [New York: Washington Square Press, 1966], pp. 86-118). The analytic experience requires the same goodwill between patient and doctor to clarify distorted aspects of situations.

25. Concentration on word selection and the sequence of verbal associations was Freud's earliest approach to interpretation of unconscious forces that shaped experience. See his *Psychopathology of Everyday Life* in *Standard Edition*, vol. 6. Carl Gustav Jung began his relationship to Freud with studies in word association; see Jung, *Experimental Researches*, trans. Leopold Stein in collaboration with Diane Riviere, Bollingen Series 20. (Princeton: Princeton University Press, 1973).

26. Adler, *Kausalitaet und Teleologie*, p. 204.

27. Faust's search into the nether world of experience in Part II might be said to symbolize the search for the inner structures of the mind that shape experience. Jung points out the relationship between Faust's experience with the Cabiri in Part II and the thinking function which Faust has repressed in his desire for action; see "A Psychological Approach to the Trinity," *Psychology and Religion*, pp. 164-67.

28. Immanuel Kant, "Dialectic of Teleological Judgement," *The Critique of Judgement* (London: Oxford University Press, 1952), pp. 72-74.

29. Adler, *Marxistische Probleme*, p. 204 and n. An earlier, more extensive discussion of Kant's understanding of the casual root of the teleological judgment is found in *Kausalitaet und Teleologie*, pp. 157-69.

30. Freud discusses "perfect logic" under the concept of rationalization. A logical rea-

son is always found to connect disparate realities in order to allow the conscious mind a sense of concord; see Freud, "A Case of Obessional Neurosis," *Collected Papers* 3:330 and n. 3.

31. Adler, *Kausalitaet und Teleologie*, p. 199 and n. 1.

32. Kant, "Introduction," *Critique of Judgement*, pp. 16-17, n.1.

33. There is a surprising shallowness in Freud's treatment of Kant. His ironic aspersions on Kant's "unrealistic" view of moral judgment neglect passages in Kant that must have been brought to his attention. See *New Introductory Lectures on Psycho-Analysis* (1932), pp. 61, 74, and 163, n. 1. Carl Jung, when Freud's disciple, wrote to Freud in 1910 of the claims by some that Kant had discovered the basic principles of psychoanalysis; see *The Freud/Jung Letters, The Correspondence between Sigmund Freud and C.G. Jung*, ed. William McGuire, trans. Ralph Manheim and R.F.C. Hull, Bollingen Series 94, (Princeton: Princeton University Press, 1974), Letter 206J, p. 346.

34. Karl Marx, "Comments on James Mill, Elemens d'economie politique (1844)," in *Marx, Engels, Collected Works*, 3:218.

35. Marx wrote extensively on the concept of alienation in 1843-44; see *Marx, Engels, Collected Works*, 3:217-18, 275-80, 306-26.

36. See Cassirer, *Kant's Life and Thought*, pp. 331-60.

37. Adler, "Der Schatten," p. 338.

38. Ibid., pp. 337, 348.

39. Adler, *Marxistische Probleme*, p. 267.

40. Max Adler, "Zur Revision des Parteiprogramms," Part I, *Arbeiter-Zeitung* 22 (October 1901): 8.

41. See Sozialdemokratische Arbeiterpartei Oesterreichs, *Protokoll ueber die Verhandlungen des Gesamtparteitages der sozialdemokratischen Arbeiterpartei in Oesterreich, abgehalten zu Wien vom 2. bis 6, November 1901* (Vienna: 1901), hereafter cited as *Parteitag, 1901*.

42. Adler, "Zur Revision des Parteiprogramms," p. 7.

43. *Parteitag, 1889*, p. 1.

44. *Parteitag, 1901*, p. 1.

45. Adler, "Zur Revision des Parteiprogramms," p. 7.

46. Victor Adler to Karl Kautsky, October 22, 1901, in *Viktor Adlers Briefwechsel mit August Bebel und Karl Kautsky*, A 67, p. 374. Kautsky to Adler, October 25, 1918, ibid., K 100, p. 375.

47. Victor Adler to Karl Kautsky, April 12, 1918, ibid., A 128, p. 654.

48. Karl Vorlaender was an intellectual historian of neo-Kantian thought sympathetic to Max Adler's writings and socialism; see Vorlaender, *Kant und Marx, Ein Beitrag zur Philosophie des Sozialismus*, (Tübingen: J.C.B. Mohr [Paul Siebeck], 1911). Paul Natorp was interested in social pedagogy and the problem of individuality within an interdependent society; see ibid., pp. 132-41. Franz Staudinger sought to link Marx's method of social analysis with the Kantian critical philosophy; see ibid., pp. 141-52. Rudolf Stammler could have been most helpful to Max Adler as a stimulus for cultural research; see his *Theory of Justice*, trans. Isaac Husik, (South Hackensack, N.J.: Augustus M. Kelley [Rothman Reprints], 1969).

49. In this essay in which Kant discusses the socializing nature of man, he sets forth various theses, which in part are based upon the study of civic constitutions. He infers a progressive development of the idea of human autonomy and thereby a gradual enlightenment of man concerning his own nature; see "Idea for a Universal History," p. 11. Stammler carries out his investigation in *Theory of Justice*.

50. Immanuel Kant, *Fundamental Principles of the Metaphysics of Morals*, trans. Thomas K. Abbott (Indianapolis: Bobbs-Merrill, 1949), pars. 56-57, pp. 45-46.

51. Immanuel Kant, *Critique of Practical Reason*, trans. Lewis White Beck (New York: Bobbs-Merrill, 1956), par. 20, p. 18; par. 26, p. 25.

8. The Party as Father for Friedrich Adler

1. Braunthal, *Victor und Friedrich Adler*, pp. 28, 29, 32, 90-91.

2. Bahr dedicated some of his own work to Emma Adler (*La Marquise d'Amaequil*) in which he describes her as a beautiful autumn night (*pale comme un beau soir d'automne*) (Ermers, *Victor Adler*, p. 221). On Sunday afternoons at their house on Berggasse the leading artists of Vienna would gather (ibid., p. 221; Braunthal, *Victor und Friedrich Adler*, pp. 35-36.) Emma wrote fiction and historical novels and did translations (ibid., p. 30) and corresponded at length with with Karl Kautsky. The correspondence in the Kautsky Archive includes forty-eight letters written between 1895 and 1934, numbered as items D. I. 53-100; they had a great deal to do with her literary endeavors.

3. Braunthal, *Victor und Friedrich Adler*, pp. 30-31.

4. Victor gave no quarter to the subjective, "irrational" realm of human understanding which Emma represented. His biographer, Max Ermers, stated that "neither for himself, nor for others, did he allow the dark symbolism, the double meanings or dreamings of the mind" (*Victor Adler*, p. 224). Women's judgment was identified generally by Adler with subjective excess. He opposed their right to vote, early in his career, and later when he allowed it, he still withheld their right to appear as witnesses before juries (ibid., p. 239).

5. Friedrich's sister Marie, born in 1881, had her first attack of mental illness in 1897 and by 1900 it had become a permanent condition (Braunthal, *Victor und Friedrich Adler*, pp. 91, 99, 276).

6. All Victor's children and his wife exhibited extremes of character, which in all cases but the younger son Karl I may venture to call hysterical. Karl Adler (born in 1885) was said to be a caricature of Victor Adler's faults (*Laster*), while Friedrich was a caricature of his virtues (*Tugenden*) (Ermers, *Victor Adler*, p. 243).

7. Victor Adler to Karl Kautsky, *Victor Adlers Briefwechsel mit August Bebel und Karl Kautsky*, A 92a.

8. As quoted in Braunthal, *Victor und Friedrich Adler*, p. 187.

9. Ibid., pp. 179-82.

10. Ibid., pp. 181-82.

11. Ibid., pp. 178-79.

12. Ibid., pp. 182-84.

13. Ibid., pp. 184, 190.

14. Bebel wrote to the elder Alder on September 10, 1901: "I advise you again to keep your Fritz under control. The young man has lost again the little [reason] he managed to realize during the vacation" (*Victor Adlers Briefweschl mit August Bebel und Karl Kautsky*, B 70, p. 371).

15. Braunthal, *Victor und Friedrich Adler*, pp. 184-85.

16. Ibid., p. 186.

17. Ibid.

18. Ibid., pp. 192, 194.

19. Ibid., pp. 189-94.

20. Friedrich Adler to Karl Kautsky, December 18, 1905, Karl Kautsky Archive, item K.D. I, 102a.

21. Braunthal, *Victor und Friedrich Adler*, pp. 195-97. The position was given instead to Albert Einstein.

22. Ibid., pp. 196-97.

23. Ibid., pp. 199-200.

24. Ibid., p. 200.

25. Ibid., pp. 200-201.

26. Victor Adler to August Bebel, July 11, 1911, *Victor Adlers Briefwechsel mit August Bebel und Karl Kautsky*, A 101, p. 536.

27. Julius Braunthal says of Friedrich Adler's change of heart about his post on the *Volksrecht*: "Either his position had been challenged, or great tasks awaited him" (*Victor und Friedrich Adler*, p. 200).

28. Ibid.

29. See Adler to Bebel, July 11, 1911.

30. Braunthal, *Victor und Friedrich Adler*, p. 178 n.

31. Friedrich Adler's doctor from 1911 until December 1915, Ludwig Braun, told him in 1915 that his condition was psychologically initiated. Adler mentioned this at his trial in 1917, when he was labeled a "hereditary psychopathic personality" by the Austrian state psychiatrists (Friedrich Adler, *Vor Dem Ausnahmegericht* [Jena: Thueringer Verlagaustalt, 1923], pp. 151-54). Julius Braunthal maintains that his condition was myocarditis, "a heart disease which affects the nervous system, manifesting itself with periodically returning states of exhaustion which make one incapable of work" (*Victor und Friedrich Adler*, p. 178 n.).

32. Braunthal, *Victor und Friedrich Adler*, p. 178 n.; see also Friedrich Adler's description of this time in his *Vor Dem Ausnahmegericht*, p. 151.

33. Friedrich Adler, "Der Wert des Parlamentarismus," *Der Kampf* 4 (June 1911): 415.

34. Alfred Adler, "Ueber Verebung von Krankheiten," *Der Kampf* 1 (June 1908): 425-30. Adler calls this the "inherited ecology of illness." Certainly, the heart was a likely organ to be affected, for it symbolized the courage Friedrich would need in the life-and-death struggle with his father as well as the warmth and life of emotions so little recognized by his father.

35. An article published by Friedrich Adler in *Der Kampf* a month before his heart attack indicates that he knew of Alfred Adler: "Minderwertig in Internationalismus," *Der Kampf* 4 (August 1911): 495-99.

36. The reality of this relation is open to question. Internationalism became popular among many Austro-German Social Democrats when the Second International voted against the Czech separatists (for example, Karl Renner's enthusiasm about the Second International as the Roman Empire during the period between 1911 and 1914). When the war came, however, only Friedrich Adler continued to believe in the reality of the Second International as a body with supreme authority. Adler's support of the Second International and internationalism follows the syndrome set forth by Alfred Adler: a man who is *minderwertig* in one organ will overcompensate by clinging to an idea (an abstraction) that can make his weakness seem a strength. This behavior does not bring about a cure of the condition; it is a subterfuge that permits the sufferer to gain self-esteem and power and prevents a head-on meeting with what ails him.

37. Friedrich Adler, "Wissenschaft und Partei," *Der Kampf* 6 (November 1912): 85-87.

38. Braunthal, *Victor und Friedrich Adler*, p. 207.

39. See the documents presented in Rudolf Neck, *Arbeiterschaft und Staat in ersten Welt-krieg 1914-1918 (A. Quellen*, Volume 1 *Vom Kriegsbeginn bis zum Prozess Friedrich Adlers, August 1914-Mai 1917* (Vienna: Europa Verlag, 1964). The party hierarchy's change of tone in response to the popularity of Friedrich Adler's act can be seen, for instance, in the demand a month after Friedrich Adler's trial that Karl Renner resign his post in the Austrian war government, on the grounds that Austrian Social-Democrats do not participate in a government that has war as its aim. Renner had been serving in the Ministry of Food since October 1916. See the statements of Parteivorstand concerning Renner's recall in Hannak, *Renner*, pp. 279-80.

40. Braunthal, *Victor und Friedrich Adler*, pp. 249-50.

41. See Julius Braunthal's discussion of Friedrich Adler's relation to the question of the Third Communist International in ibid., pp. 288-91.

42. Braunthal, *Victor und Friedrich Adler*, pp. 298-99. For a more detailed account of the 2 ½ International see Julius Braunthal, *History of the International*, vol. 2, *1914-1943*, trans. John Clark (London: Nelson and Sons, 1967), pp. 264-70, 468-92. For a merciless account of the personal activity of Friedrich Adler in the 2 ½ International, see Jacques Hannak, "Fritz Adler zum 70sten Geburtstag," *Die Zukunft* (July 1949): 195-97.

43. Hannak, "Fritz Adler zum 70sten Geburtstag," p. 196.

44. Adler uses the expression *a priori*, the Kantian term for the organizing schemata in consciousness that regulate our vision of the world. The Jungian idea of the archetype is roughly equivalent, except it includes a spiritual dimension that it represents. Any contact with the eternal images of archetypes brings with it a religious feeling. The danger in relating to an archetype, as described in Max Adler's influence by the archetype of the *puer aeternus*, is to succumb to a behavior pattern that allows the archetypal energy to usurp one's personality. Archetypes are collective, or species, forces, carrying an idea that is greater than any individual. The Oedipus complex, in Friedrich's case, seems a better etiology for his struggle with socialism; his highly personal relationship to the party, because of his father's influence, had the all-embracing feelings of a religious mission.

45. Braunthal, *Victor und Friedrich Adler*, pp. 324-25.

46. Ibid.

9. Friedrich Adler: From Physics to Marxism

1. Friedrich Adler, "Wozu brauchen wir Theorien?" *Der Kampf* 2 (March 1909): 256.

2. Ibid., p. 260.

3. See Braunthal, *Victor und Friedrich Adler*, pp. 197-98.

4. Ibid., p. 178.

5. On the role of mathematics in the neurotic personality, Henri Michaux writes: "Mathematics, most often, goes hand in hand with a psychological, even a neurotic attitude. . . . A character disposition impels some to use this faculty to the maximum (a faculty almost everyone possesses) in which they gratify an escape tendency, without attracting attention to themselves" (*Light through Darkness* [New York: Orion Press, 1963], p. 41).

6. Friedrich Adler writes of the significance of historical materialim in his education: "At sixteen years of age I read the work of Friedrich Engels *Herrn Eugen Duehrings Umwael- zung der Wissenschaft*. . . . it forced me for the first time to look at the problem: HOW DOES THE MECHANICAL MATERIALISM OF SCIENCE RELATE TO THE HISTORI- CAL MATERIALISM OF MARX AND ENGELS? I was at that time an enthusiastic follower of both teachings. For the next decade I could not turn away from this question, yet I did not find a solution either" (Friedrich Adler, *Ernst Machs Ueberwindung des mechani- schen Materialismus* [Vienna: Wiener Volksbuchhandlung, 1918], pp. 5-6).

7. See Braunthal, *Victor und Friedrich Adler*, p. 191.

8. See Friedrich Adler, "Die Entdeckung der Weltelemente (zu Ernst Machs 70. Ge- burtstag)," *Der Kampf* 1 (February 1908): 231-32.

9. Adler, *Ernst Machs Ueberwindung*, pp. 15-16, 21.

10. Friedrich Adler, "Die Entdeckung der Weltelemente," pp. 233-34.

11. Friedrich Adler, *Ernst Machs Ueberwindung*, p. 7.

12. There were Marxist and non-Marxist Machians. The Marxist Machians are ex-

plored in V.I. Lenin, *Materialism and Empiro-Criticism*. Mach's thought has encouraged the study of the history of science as paradigms representative of particular ages, with the objectives, methods, and standards of proof developing and changing in relation to the basic assumptions of that scientific generation. Thomas Kuhn's *The Structure of Scientific Revolutions* is indebted to Mach.

13. Adler, *Ernst Machs Ueberwindung*, pp. 30, 32-33, 19.

14. Ibid., p. 23.

15. Ibid., pp. 56-62.

16. See Robert Musil's discussion of Mach's theory of observation and description of phenomena in *Beitrag zur Beurteilung der Lehren Machs* (Reinbek bei Hamburg: Rowoklt, 1980), pp. 15-42.

17. For a critique of mathematical language that demonstrates its "subjective" base, see Ernst Cassirer, *Substance and Function*, trans. William Curtis Swabey and Marie Collins Swabey (New York: Dover, 1953), pp. 3-67.

18. Adler, *Ernst Machs Ueberwindung*, pp. 77-82. The same idea appears in Adler's article "Die Entdeckung der Weltelemente," pp. 233-34.

19. Adler, *Ernst Machs Ueberwindung*, pp. 32-33.

20. Toward the end of his life Mach referred to this type of experience as "nirvana" (ibid., p. 29). The Indian concept was the closest he could come to expressing that the state might be glimpsed but was impossible to maintain in this life.

21. Adler, *Ernst Machs Ueberwindung*, p. 78.

22. See Ernst Mach, "Sinnliche Elemente und naturwissenschaftliche Begriffe," *Archiv für die gesamte Psychologie* 136 (Bonn, 1910), pp. 263-74. Friedrich Adler discusses this idea in *Ernst Machs Ueberwindung*, pp. 73-77, 102.

23. Ibid., pp. 76-77.

24. See Robert Musil's critique of Mach's language, in *Beitrag zur Beurteilung der Lehren Machs*, pp. 79-124. Musil, who was to become one of the great Austrian writers of the century, saw the license that the relativist Mach took with science when employing succinct aphorisms. An aphoristic language has the advantage of allowing a reader to use the images of everyday life; meanings tend to have multiple possibilities, however, with everyday images. Law is more often asserted than demonstrated. The Austrian philosopher Ludwig Wittgenstein sought through aphorism to demonstrate lawful structure in human experience. By writing thoroughly of particular experiences, he sought to engage the reader in a common language that would expose the structure of one's thought and feelings within the rules of the situation. See *Philosophical Investigations*, trans. G.E.M. Anscombe (New York: MacMillan, 1953). Such a command of image was reputed to Socrates in the *Symposium* when Alcibiades said that he was a Silenos, whose rude images, if followed and gotten into, led one into a direct confrontation with the gods.

25. Mach was sympathetic with socialism and the German and Austrian Social Democratic parties. He even left the Austrian Social Democratic press (*Arbeiter Zeitung*) and educational association (Volksbildungsverein in Wien) a donation in the will he drew up in 1899. But his physical activity was always limited to his research. See Adler, *Ernst Machs Ueberwindung*, p. 27-29.

26. Ibid., pp. 35-36. See also Adler, "Die Entdeckung der Weltelement," p. 231. In the *Kampf* article, which appeared ten years before the book on Mach, this quotation appears under the heading "Die absolut unveraenderlichen Koerper" (the absolute unchangeable body). In the book, it appears under the heading "Mechanische Materialismus" (mechanical materialism). The more metaphorical title of the earlier printing corresponds, it seems, to the crises of Friedrich Adler's existence in the years before 1918.

27. Adler, *Ernst Machs Ueberwindung*, pp. 73-74.

28. Ibid., pp. 74-75.

29. Friedrich Adler, *Vor dem Ausnahmegericht*, (Jena, 1923), p. 61.

30. Adler, *Ernst Machs Ueberwindung*, pp. 84-85.

31. Adler to Kautsky, April 29, 1903, Karl Kautsky Archive, item K.D. I, 107.

32. See Adler, "Wissenschaft und Partei," p. 85.

33. Friedrich Adler's articles in *Der Kampf* were "Die Entdeckung der Weltelemente" and "Wozu brauchen wir Theorien?" His articles in *Die Neue Zeit* were "Materialistische Geschichtsauffassung und Mathematik," vol. 24, pt. 2 (1906): 223ff pseud. Fritz Tischler); "Friedrich Engels und die Naturwissenschaft," vol. 25, pt. 1 (1907): 620-38; and "Der Machismus und die Materialistische Geschichtsauffassung," vol. 27, pt. 1 (1909): 671-87.

34. These concepts are discussed in *Ernst Machs Ueberwindung*, pp. 168-77. They were first discussed in the articles in *Der Kampf* and *Die Neue Zeit* (see n. 33), to which Adler referred in this synthesis in the book.

35. Adler, *Ernst Machs Ueberwindung*, p. 171.

36. See Lenin, *Materialism and Emperio-Criticism*, in *Collected Works*, vol. 13. See esp. the foreword to the English edition by A. Deborin, pp. ix-xxiv.

37. Adler, *Ernst Machs Ueberwindung*, pp. 171-76.

38. Adler, "Wozu brauchen wir Theorien?" p. 260.

10. Karl Renner as German Chauvinist

1. Karl Renner, "Sympathien und Antipathien," *Der Kampf* 2 (January 1909): 165-69.

2. Karl Renner, "Ueber Innsbruck hinaus!" *Der Kampf* 5 (January 1912): 149.

3. The "Day of the German Nation" was the headline of the editorial written by Friedrich Austerlitz in the *Arbeiter-Zeitung*, the Austrian Social Democratic daily newspaper, on August 5, 1914. The editorial approved of German Social Democracy's voting of war credits for the German government and supported the coming war by stating that the Western allies were mounting an attack "on the German essence." The article became the archetypal instance of the betrayal of international socialism in the heat of the first days of the war. For a discussion of the effects of the article, see Julius Braunthal, "Introduction," *Austerlitz Spricht* (Vienna: Wiener Volksbuchhandlung, 1931), and *Victor Adlers, Aufsaetze*, 9: 112.

4. Karl Renner (pseud. Josef Hammer), "Was ist Imperialismus?" *Der Kampf* 8 (January 1915): 24-33.

5. Karl Bruel, *Heath's New German and English Dictionary*, rev. and enlarged by J. Heron Lepper and Rudolf Kottenhahn (New York: Funk & Wagnall 1939), p. 270.

6. Renner had become a co-leader, with Franz Domes, of the Austrian cooperative societies in 1911. The Hammerbrotwerke was in deep financial trouble, and Renner found a way to transfer funds from the cooperatives into the industry to keep it alive. During World War I, with Renner's financial entrepreneurship, the Hammerbrotwerke thrived. See Gulick, *Austria from Habsburg to Hitler* 1:317-19, 325-28.

7. Rudolf Hilferding, *Das Finanzkapital, Eine Studie ueber die juengste Entwicklung des Kapitalismus* (Vienna: Wiener Volksbuchhandlung, 1910). This work was included as part of the Austro-Marxist body of theory, appearing as the third volume of *Marx-Studien*.

8. Renner, "Was ist Imperialismus?" pp. 28-33.

9. Renner subordinated the individual to the imperative beyond him, emanating from the inexorable demands of "history." Man obeyed the law; he did not make laws himself. For

Hilferding's critique of Renner's position, see Rudolf Hilferding, "Historische Notwendigkeit und notwendige Politik," *Der Kampf* 8 (May 1915): 206-15. Although Renner is not mentioned, his interpretation is opposed. Also see Rudolf Hilferding, "Europaer, nicht Mitteleuroparer!" *Der Kampf* 8 (November–December 1915): 257-65, opposing the idea of a "middle-European" community as elaborated by Friedrich Naumann, a political theorist used by Renner to develop further his arguments of supporting the war. Finally, Hilferding took on Renner personally in "Phantasie oder Gelehrsamkeit?" *Der Kampf* 9 (February 1916): 54-58, calling him a man lost in a fantasy (p. 55) that poses a danger to Social Democracy and the future of socialism (p. 56).

10. Karl Renner, "Der Krieg und die Internationale," *Der Kampf* 8 (February 1915): 50.

11. Ibid., pp. 60-62.

12. Karl Renner, "Was Siegt im Kriege?" in Renner, *Oesterreichs Erneuerung, Politischprogrammatische Aufsaetze*, 3 vols. (Vienna: Viener Volksbuchhandlung, 1961), 1:12-14. (The article first appeared in the *Arbeiter-Zeitung* on June 18, 1915. Hereafter I will cite both the collection of the *Arbeiter-Zeitung* articles in *Oesterreichs Erneuerung* and the date the article first appeared in the *Arbeiter-Zeitung*.)

13. "Mitteleuropa" was a descriptive term introduced by the social theoretician Friedrich Naumann for the European capitalist community of German-speaking lands; for men such as Renner it included the Balkans and Hungary. Renner knew Naumann as early as 1901-03 when Renner contributed articles to Naumann's publication *Die Hilfe* (See Hannak Renner, p. 291).

14. Renner, "Was Siegt im Kriege?" p. 14.

15. Ibid.

16. See Karl Renner, "Der Uebernationale Staat," *Oesterreichs Erneuerung*, 1:38-43 (*Arbeiter-Zeitung*, October 21, 1915). See also Karl Renner, "Zollvereine und Weltwirtschaft," *Oesterreichs Erneuerung*, 1:124 (*Arbeiter-Zeitung*, May 16, 1915). He speaks of the future superstate of Germany-Austria-Hungary, which will extend from Holland-Belgium to Turkey and Persia.

17. Karl Renner, Friedrich Naumman's "Mittel-Europa," *Oesterreichs Erneuerung*, 1:38 ((*Arbeiter-Zeitung*, October 20, 1915).

18. Ibid.

19. Renner, "Der Uebernationale Staat," p. 39.

20. Renner, "Der Uebernationale Staat," p. 43. Renner derived his information from a letter sent by Hermann Hesse (the Nobel Prize-winning German writer of *Steppenwolf*, *Das Glasperlenspiel*, and others) to the *Frankfurter Zeitung*, October 13, 1915. The letter, a masterpiece of chauvinism, is reproduced; it is quite an interesting document for American readers who knew Hermann Hesse solely as a man removed from the concerns and passions of the political world. The fever of the war can be measured by such facts as this letter by Hesse. It appears on pp. 42-43 of the aforementioned article.

21. Karl Renner, "Der Anteil der Nationen am Staate," *Oesterreichs Erneuerung*, 1:58. (*Arbeiter-Zeitung*, November 3, 1915).

22. Renner was considered a "red" by the ruling circle of the Habsburgs. Thus, although his ideas might be borrowed, he never was directly praised or called in for conference in affairs of state. See Hannak, *Renner*, p. 183.

23. Karl Renner, "Männer-Massregeln-Einrichtungen," *Oesterreichs Erneuerung*, 1: 76-77 (*Arbeiter-Zeitung*, September 8, 1915).

24. See Max Adler, "Proletarische oder buergerliche Staatsideologie," *Der Kampf* 9 (April 1916): 129-39; Friedrich Adler, "Mutwilliger Streit oder politischer Gegensatz," *Der Kampf* 9 (April 1916): 148-52. Almost the entire April 1916 issue of *Der Kampf* was directed

against Renner. In 1915 these men had written against Renner's political position, but the articles cited are the first that publicly denounced him.

25. Renner, *Oesterreichs Erneuerung*, 1:v.

26. Hannak, *Renner*, p. 597.

27. Gulick, *Austria from Habsburg to Hitler*, 1:318-19.

28. Hannak, *Renner*, pp. 279-80.

29. Sozialdemokratische Arbeiterpartei Oesterreichs, *Protokoll der Verhandlungen des Parteitages der deutschen sozialdemokratische arbeiterpartei in Oesterreichs, abgehalten in Wien vom 19. bis 24. Oktober 1917*, (Vienna: Wiener Volksbuchhandlung, 1917), pp. 121-22 (hereafter cited as *Parteitag, 1917*).

30. See Hannak, pp. 288-96; Follis, "Austrian Social Democratic Party," pp. 323-24; and *Parteitag 1917*, pp. 84-85.

31. Follis, "Austrian Social Democratic Party," pp. 339-41; Otto Bauer mentions this animus against the Bolsheviks in a letter to Karl Kautsky dated January 4, 1917, Kautsky Archive, item K.D. II, 503. Bauer was in sympathy with the Bolsheviks and their methods, though he soon changed his mind.

32. The so-called "Left" which crystallized around the image of Friedrich Adler and the ideas of Zimmerwald spoke out for the self-determination of Austrian nations during the final months of the war. These men included Otto Bauer, Max Adler, and, of course, Friedrich Adler. All, however, spoke against the Bolshevik violence during 1918. And when the violence of revolution began in the streets of Vienna, all sought to quell it, supporting the parliamentary way.

33. See Ludo M. Hartmann, "Deutschland und wir," *Der Kampf* (April 1918): 215-19; Friedrich Austerlitz, "Nationale Politik in Oesterreich," *Der Kampf* 11 (August 1918): 521-30; Friedrich Austerlitz, "Der deutschoesterreichische Staat," *Der Kampf* 11 (November 1918): 713-18.

34. Karl Renner, "Was hat ein Internationales Programm zu leisten?" *Der Kampf* 11 (June 1918): 384-89.

35. See Hannak, pp. 331-35. For details of this constitutional draft see Gulick, *Austria from Habsburg to Hitler*, 1:56-57, and *Die Verfassungsgesetze der Republik Deutschoesterreich*, (Vienna and Leipzig: Hans Kelsen, 1919), pt. 1, pp. 11-16.

36. Follis, "Austrian Social Democratic Party," p. 423.

37. Gulick, *Austria from Habsburg to Hitler*, 1:57.

38. See Renner's description of the Provisional Assembly's powers in his speech before the Provisional Assembly on October 30, 1918 (Hannak, *Renner*, p. 341).

39. The State Council had the authority to demand the resignation of Emperor Charles but did not do so even after the Austrian Social Democratic party on November 1, 1918, stated its position that Austria should in the future be a democratic republic (Hannak, *Renner*, pp. 343-44).

40. See Hannak, *Renner*, p. 348. A full account of this speech is found in Bruegel, *Geschichte der oesterreichischen Sozialdemokratie*, 5:393-96.

41. Bruegel, *Geschichte der oesterreichischen Sozialdemokratie*, 5:393.

42. Renner promised the Provisional Assembly in his speech on November 11, 1918, that even if a republic were declared, "the normal life of the state will continue, and political changes will not be distributed by social eruptions, which we all feel to be intolerable at this time. We will maintain order even at the risk of violently affecting the social life" (ibid., p. 393). At the exact moment the Republic of Austria was declared to the populace by the president of the State Council, the Social Democrat Seitz, on November 12, 1918, shots rang out, and the Communist Red Guard attempted a coup d'etat which was rapidly put down by the government. See Gulick, *Austria from Habsburg to Hitler*, 1:61. Constant dili-

gence was required by Austrian Social Democrats and the new government to maintain order and prevent real revolution (ibid., pp. 69-83).

43. See Adolf Schaerf, *Zwischen Demokratie und Voksdemokratie, Oesterreichs Wiederaufrichtung im Jahre 1945* (Vienna: Wiener Volksbuchhandlung 1950), pp. 12-13.

11. Otto Bauer: Success through Equivocation

1. *Otto Bauer, Eine Auswahl aus seinem Lebenswerk*, ed. Julius Braunthal (Vienna: Vierner Volksbuchhandlung, 1961), p. 24.

2. As quoted in "Ein Instrument der Geschichte," *Arbeiter-Zeitung*, October 18, 1914, p. 4. The article is anonymous, but proof of Bauer's authorship is in a letter from Friedrich Adler to Karl Kautsky. October 19, 1914, Kautsky Archive, item K.D. I, 113.

3. See Bauer to Kautsky, October 19, 1914, Kautsky Archive, item D.D. II, 490.

4. See Otto Bauer's review of Kautsky's *Der Weg zur Macht*, *Der Kampf* 2 (May 1909): 337-44.

5. *Otto Bauer, Eine Auswahl aus seinem Lebenswerk*, p. 24.

6. Ibid., pp. 25-26.

7. Ibid., p. 26.

8. Ibid., pp. 26; the history is "Das Weltbild des Kapitalismus" ibid., pp. 102-39.

9. Ibid., p. 27.

10. Bauer spent July and August 1917 in Petersburg as a guest of Theodor and Lydia Dan, who were Mensheviks. He caught up on political events and in an effort to read Russian newspapers had to learn Russian. While in Petersburg he made acquaintance with the various factions of Russian Social Democracy (ibid., pp. 27-28).

11. See Jacques Hannak, *Maenner und Taten* (Vienna: Wiener Volksbuchhandlung 1963), p. 28, for a discussion of Bauer's assignment and the reaction of the Western press to its significance.

12. Bauer to Kautsky, September 28, 1917, Kautsky Archive, item K.D. II, 500, in which he says he supports the position of Martow and his followers (i.e., Menshevik-Internationalists).

13. Renner's statement of Bauer's vacillating mind appears in "Der Taktische Streit," *Der Kampf* 11 (January 1918): 30 n. "When our Heinrich Weber came back from Russia, he confessed that he was a Menshevik of the Internationalist direction, that means in practical terms—he was mistaken. When he left Russia [the Menshevik International] direction still had meaning. Today he feels himself a Bolshevik, probably, but not only a Bolshevik for Russia, rather a Bolshevik for Austria, too. And that is again a mistake." The moon analogy appears on pages 25-26 of the same article.

14. See Bauer, *Die Nationalitaetenfrage und die Sozialdemokratie*, p. 485, for his conclusion that colonialism is unavoidable as culture progresses toward socialism and that as long as the worker benefits, colonialism is beneficial. See ibid., pp. 440-61, for his outline of a multi-national state of the future, which would be assured by the capitalistic expansion into the Danube basin.

15. For Bauer's movements in September 1917 while on leave from the army, see Victor Adler to Karl Kautsky, *Victor Adlers Briefwechsel mit August Bebel und Karl Kautsky* September 4, 1917, A 124, p. 639, and Kautsky to Adler, ibid., October 4, 1917, K 157, p. 640. Also see Follis, "Austrian Social Democratic Party," p. 308; and Julius Deutsch, *Geschichte der oesterreichischen Gewerkschaftsbewegung* (Vienna: Wiener Volksbuchhandlung, 1929-1932), 2: 36.

16. The Karl Marx Verein was established formally in March 1916. It opposed the war

and socialist participation in the war. A complete list of its members (including Max Adler) and their addresses in Vienna can be found in Neck, *Arbeiterschaft und Staat im ersten Welktrieg 1914-1918*, pp. 140-41.

17. See Follis, "Austrian Social Democratic Party," p. 308; *Victor Adler Briefwechsel mit August Bebel und Karl Kautsky*, p. 638 n.; Deutsch, *Geschichte der oesterreichischen Gewerkschafts-bewegung*, 2:36.

18. See Follis, "Austrian Social Democratic Party," pp. 308-13; Hannak, *Renner*, pp. 288-89.

19. *Victor Adlers Briefwechsel mit August Bebel und Karl Kautsky*, p. 638 n.; Hannak, pp. 288-89.

20. Victor Adler to Karl Kautsky, *Victor Adlers Briefwechsel mit August Bebel und Karl Kautsky*, July 9, 1918, A 129, p. 660.

21. Otto Bauer, "Wuerzburg und Wien," *Der Kampf* 10 (November–December 1917): 328.

22. Bauer to Kautsky, December 17, 1917, Kautsky Archive, item K.D. II, 502.

23. Bauer to Kautsky, January 4, 1918, Kautsky Archive, item K.D. II, 503.

24. Otto Bauer (pseud. Heinrich Weber), "Die Bolschewiki und wir," *Der Kampf* 11 (March 1918): 143-44, 147.

25. Bauer made no public statements about the January strikes. His letter to Karl Kautsky, dated January 4, 1918, was written immediately before the strikes began. The letter was pro-Bolshevik. We do not hear from Bauer again until his article, "Die Bolschewiki, und wir," in *Der Kampf* in March presumably written in February 1918). He may have been silent because a process had been started against him by the Army General Staff during the January strikes on the suspicion that he was connected with the Bolsheviks. The process against him continued until May 24, 1918, when the Army General Staff cleared him because of the tone of such articles as "Die Bolschewiki und wir" (Hannak, *Maenner und Taten*, pp. 29-32).

26. Otto Bauer, "Geschichte," review of Dr. Alfred Fischel's *Die Protokelle de Verfassung-sausuhusses ueber die Grundrechts* (Vienna, 1912), *Der Kampf* 2 (January 1912): 191.

27. Bauer, "Die Bolschewiki und wir," pp. 148-49. Bauer wrote, of course, as though he had not gone to battle patriotically as an officer and had not written "Ein Instrument der Geschichte."

28. See Braunthal, *Victor und Friedrich Adler*, p. 280.

29. Gulick, *Austria from Habsburg to Hitler*, 1:58.

30. Braunthal, pp. 31-32.

12. Max Adler: Will and Idea in Wartime

1. Max Adler, "Ferdinand Lassalles Fuenfzigster Todestag," *Der Kampf* 7 (December 1914): 482.

2. Ibid., pp. 484-85.

3. Ibid., p. 486.

4. Max Adler, "Das Prinzip des Sozialismus," *Der Kampf* 8 (January 1915): 5.

5. Max Adler, "Was ist Notwendigkeit der Entwicklung?" *Der Kampf* 8 (April 1915): 174.

6. Ibid., pp. 175-76.

7. Adler's choice of the word *anwandeln* in this context is indicative of his condition. The word *anwandeln* connotes as a verb "befall, come over, come upon, attack, seize (of illness, etc.); was wandelte dich an? what has come over you" (Cassell's *German and English Dictionary* (London: Cassell & Company Ltd., 1950).

8. Adler, "Was ist Notwendigkeit der Entwicklung!" p. 177.

9. Max Adler, "J.G. Fichte ueber den wahrhaften Krieg," *Der Kampf* 8 (June 1915): 233, 238-39.

10. Max Adler, "Weltmacht oder Volksmacht?" *Der Kampf* 8 (November–December, 1915): 365-66.

11. Max Adler, "Ueber Kriegsethik," *Der Kampf* 9 (January 1916): 33-42.

12. As quoted in Hannak, *Renner*, p. 241.

13. *Der Traum, Ein Leben*, in *Grillparzer's Werke*, vol. 5 (Leipzig and Vienna: Bibliographisches Institut, 1903).

14. Adler, "Ueber Kriegsethik," p. 33.

15. See a discussion of the play, originally by the Spanish dramatist Calderon, *Der Traum, Ein Leben, Grillparzer's Werke*, 5:9.

16. Max Adler, *Zwei Jahre . . . ! Weltkriegsbetrachtungen eines Sozialisten* (Nuremberg: Fraenkische Verlags Austalt, 1918), p. 31.

17. See Friedrich Adler's review of Max Adler's *Zwei Jahre . . . !*, *Der Kampf* (September 1918): 344.

18. See Neck, *Arbeiterschaft und Staat im ersten Weltkrieg 1914-1918*, p. 141.

19. Max Adler, "Die Bedeutung des Sozialismus," *Der Kampf* 11 (January 1918): 47.

20. The strikes began the third week of January 1918. As a rule the articles written for a particular month were finished by the last week of the preceding month. The proofs for the finished issue were completed by the first week of the month, sent to press, and distributed. Evidence of such a process is given in Karl Renner's letter to Friedrich Adler, January 3, 1916, in Hannak, *Renner*, p. 241.

21. Max Adler, "Die Mahnung der Russischen Revolution," *Arbeiter-Zeitung*, November 16, 1917, p. 1.

22. Max Adler, "Der russische Buergerkrieg und der Sozialismus," *Arbeiter-Zeitung*, September 10, 1918, pp. 1-2.

23. Max Adler, "Die Verantwortung der Demokratie," *Arbeiter-Zeitung*, October 17, 1918, pp. 2-3.

24. Max Adler, "Die Zeit wird gross!" *Arbeiter-Zeitung*, October 29, 1917, p. 2.

25. Max Adler, "Eine Partei der Verwirrung," *Arbeiter-Zeitung*, November 19, 1918, pp. 1-2.

13. Friedrich Adler Encounters His Fate

1. Braunthal, *Victor und Friedrich Adler*, pp. 211-12.

2. Ibid., p. 211.

3. Friedrich Adler, *Vor dem Ausnahmegericht* p. 200.

4. Braunthal, *Victor und Friedrich Adler*, p. 218.

5. See Friedrich Adler's letter of resignation from the party, August 8, 1914, in *Vor dem Ausnahmegericht*, pp. 13-15; and his letter of August 13, 1914, in which he decided to stay within the party and fight for his viewpoint, ibid., pp. 15-19. A discussion of this episode is in Braunthal, *Victor und Friedrich Adler*, pp. 218-19.

6. See *Victor Adlers Aufsaetze, Reden und Briefe* 9:104-21. The meetings were held between the *Vertrauensmaenner* of the party, and admission was by invitation only. The minutes were presumably taken stenographically, and then typed, by Otto Gloeckel and Gustav Pollatschek and deposited in the *Parteiarchiv*.

7. A letter of Friedrich Adler's mother Emma to Karl Kautsky on October 27, 1914, gives a magnificent picture of Friedrich Adler's posture before the party and the others'

reception of him (October 27, 1914, Kautsky Archiv, item K.D. I, 62). Emma Adler says of her son, "Too bad that you weren't at the meeting two weeks ago . . . Friedrich spoke like a god! He has grown unimaginably in the last two years. Even his [heart] gives him no trouble. It was painful for me—nine-tenths of those present were enemies [to his person and position], and it was especially painful for me that one misunderstands such a selfless and pure person. These people are always so foolish—they will not forget whose son Friedrich is, and they made comparison—as if there could not be two different men who can be virtuous, but in different ways. On the same evening [Ellenbogen] answered him in a way that treated him, a 35 year old man, like a little child who needed his nose wiped."

8. Victor Adler to Karl Kautsky, November 26, 1914, *Victor Adlers Briefwechsel mit August Bebel and Karl Kautsky*, A 113, p. 602.

9. See Braunthal, *Victor und Friedrich Adler*, p. 223 and n. 24. The hidden hostility manifested itself more openly by the time of Friedrich's trial in 1917. The love-hate relationship that underlay the politics of Victor and Friedrich Adler is barely touched on by Braunthal, who politely masks the drama between father and son.

10. See Friedrich Adler's autobiographical sketch of his war years activities given to the Austrian police upon his arrest for the assassination of Count Stuergh in his *Vor dem Ausnahmegericht*, pp. 202-6; and Braunthal, *Victor und Friedrich Adler*, pp. 218-27.

11. Friedrich Adler, "Die Sozialdemokratie im Deutschland und der Krieg's," *Der Kampf* 8 (January 1915): 33-42.

12. See Ermers, *Victor Adler*, p. 326. Friedrich was to be sent to join the Landwehrinfanterieregiment No. 1. He had a heart attack (myocarditis) and was excused from the service on medical grounds.

13. One may assume that his psychosomatic attack a few days after his call to the military was an ingenious gambit of his self to save the real showdown between himself and his father for a better ground. By not refusing the draft he matched Otto Bauer's gesture of military courage; the heart attack then removed him to the real arena—Vienna and the life of the party.

14. Braunthal, *Victor und Friedrich Adler*, p. 225.

15. Friedrich Adler, *Vor dem Ausnahmegericht*, p. 204.

16. Ibid., pp. 205, 221-22.

17. Friedrich Adler, "Suenden der Minderheit oder Suenden der Mehrheit?" *Der Kampf* 11 (January 1916): 9.

18. Ibid., pp. 5-10.

19. Friedrich Adler, "Offener Brief an Camille Huysmans," *Der Kampf* 9 (May–June 1916): 193.

20. Ibid., p. 194.

21. Ibid., p. 195.

22. Friedrich Adler, "Eines Sozialdemokraten Ende und Glueck," *Der Kampf,* 9 (September 1916): 341-42.

23. Friedrich Adler, "Welkriegsbetrachtungen eines Sozialisten," *Der Kampf* 9 (September 1916): 344.

24. Friedrich Adler, "Die Reichskonferenz der Sozialdemokratie Deutschlands," *Der Kampf* 9 (October 1916): 345.

25. Ibid., pp. 346-47.

26. Braunthal, *Victor und Friedrich Adler*, p. 227.

27. Ibid., p. 225.

28. Ibid., p. 230.

29. Ibid., p. 230.

30. Friedrich Adler, *Vor dem Ausnahmegericht*, p. 230.

31. Friedrich Adler, *Vor dem Ausnahmegericht*, p. 229.

32. Braunthal, *Victor und Friedrich Adler*, pp. 230-32.

33. Victor Adler to Adolf Braun, November 12, 1916, *Victor Adlers Briefwechsel mit August Bebel und Karl Kautsky*, A 121, p. 632. See Braunthal, *Victor und Friedrich Adler*, pp. 232-33 and the footnotes on those pages for a discussion of Victor Adler's preparation of psychiatric information with which to plead a case of insanity for his son.

34. Braunthal, *Victor und Friedrich Adler*, p. 234.

35. Friedrich Adler, *Vor dem Ausnahmegericht*, pp. 140-42.

36. The complete text of this defense is in ibid., pp. 44-116.

37. See Friedrich Adler, *Vor dem Ausnahmegericht*, pp. 180-81.

38. *Arbeiter-Zeitung*, September 7, 1917, p. 1.

39. The reaction of the Austrian Social Democratic party hierarchy to Friedrich Adler's assassination of Count Stuergh was one basically of forgive and forget. There was a party moratorium, it seems, on public utterances before Friedrich Adler's trial in May 1917. After the trial Friedrich Austerlitz wrote an article in *Der Kampf* entitled "Friedrich Adler und die Partei" (10 [May–June 1917]: 132-41), which attempted to bury Adler's ghost forever. The article treated Friedrich Adler as a misguided child; its tone was backbiting and vicious but condescendingly forgave Friedrich for his "political naivete." Friedrich's ghost refused to remain quiet, however; he had his past articles published in book form through Karl Kautsky in February 1918 (Adler, *Die Erneuerung der Internationale, Aufsaetze aus der Kriegszeit*). In response to this reminder that he still lived, Wilhelm Ellenbogen served as a voice of the party fathers to put him down again; Ellenbogen wrote an article in the March 1918 issue *Der Kampf* entitled "Friedrich Adler und sein Buch" (pp. 156-59), which again treated him as an irresponsible though well-meaning fanatic.

40. *Arbeiter-Zeitung*, September 7, 1917, p. 1.

41. Braunthal, *Victor und Friedrich Adler*, p. 280.

42. Friedrich refused to lead the Austrian Communist party that had arisen; he was offered its leadership immediately upon his release from prison. See Braunthal, *Victor und Friedrich Adler*, pp. 280-81.

Conclusion

1. Hannak, *Renner*, pp. 316-17.

2. Bauer, "Max Adler," pp. 300-301.

3. Toch, "Max Adlers Weg von Kant zu Marx," p. 256.

4. Friedrich Adler, "Die Ideen von 1789 und die Ideen von 1914," *Der Kampf* 9 (July 1916): 246.

Index

Adler, Alfred, 29, 149, 215 n. 15; on inferiority complex, 235 nn. 35, 36; on inherited ecology of illness, 235 n. 34;

Adler, Emma (Friedrich's mother), 140-41, 204-05, 243-44 n. 7; creativity of, 234 n. 2

Adler, Emma Frida (Friedrich's daughter), 145

Adler, Friedrich, 1, 45, 49, 78, 82, 175, 182–83, 191, 192, 193, 208, 209
—assassination of Count Stürgkh, 203-04
—attitudes of: on Bolsheviks, 236 n. 41, 240 n. 32, 245 n. 42; on imperialism, 175, 239-40 n. 24; on Independent Socialist Party of Germany, 197; on international socialism, 197, 199, 200-201, 235 n. 36
—as editor of socialist periodicals, 146-47
—education of, 143-45, 155
—ego defenses: denial, 134-35, 197, 205-07, 244 n. 9; hyperrationality 153, 154-55, 161, 165; identification with the aggressor, 148, 151-52; inferiority complex, 149; projection, 150-51, 197, 199-201, 202, 203-04, 208, 235 n. 36, 237 n. 26, 244 n. 10; psychosomatic illness, 148-49, 198, 235 n. 31, 244 n. 12, 244 n. 13; reification of concept, 148-50, 157, 159-60, 162, 163, 164, 165, 209; sublimation, 141-42, 155
—family of, 140-42, 234 n. 6, 235 n. 34
—father's relationship with, 142-51
—as introverted thinker, 24, 25
—and Labor and Socialist International

(2½ International), 151, 236 nn. 41, 42
—and Machian existentialism, 159, 162
—and Machian Marxism, 236-37 n. 12
—neurosis, 7, 30, 144, 148-49, 151, 235 n. 31, 236 n. 44
—Oedipus complex, 30, 148, 150, 152, 197, 201-02, 203-04, 236 n. 44, 244 n. 9
—party as "cultural fathers", 149-50, 155, 160, 161, 163, 165
—philosophical orientation of, 20, 24, 25, 26, 28, 29, 30
—physics and historical materialism, 144, 146, 154-55, 159-64, 236 n. 6
—professional experience of, to 1911, 145-47, 235 n. 27
—resistance to World War I, 196-98, 241 n. 2
—and "shadow," 151-52
—socialism as a religious experience, 142, 152
—will to challenge "fathers", 146, 148, 197, 202, 203-04, 207, 243 nn. 5, 7

Adler, Johanna Alice (Friedrich's daughter), 145

Adler, Karl (Friedrich's brother), 234 n. 6

Adler, Kathia (Katherina Jakoblewna Germanishkaja) (Friedrich's wife), 145, 196

Adler, Marie (Friedrich's sister), 234 n. 5

Adler, Max, 1, 14, 19, 21, 22, 44, 45, 140, 154, 175, 202, 208, 209
—and art as idea, 134-35
—attitudes of: on Bolsheviks, 193-94, 240